FINDING THE CENTER

ALSO BY DENNIS TEDLOCK

Teachings from the American Earth: Indian Religion and
    Philosophy *(with Barbara Tedlock)*

The Spoken Word and the Work of Interpretation

Popol Vuh: The Mayan Book of the Dawn of Life

Days from a Dream Almanac

Breath on the Mirror: Mythic Voices and Visions of the Living
    Maya

The Dialogic Emergence of Culture *(with Bruce Mannheim)*

FINDING THE CENTER
THE ART OF THE ZUNI STORYTELLER
TRANSLATED BY DENNIS TEDLOCK

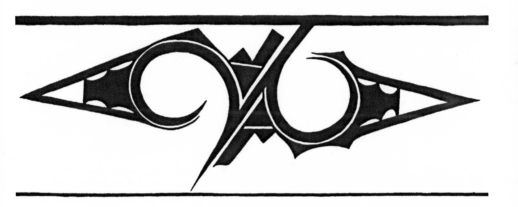

FROM LIVE PERFORMANCES IN ZUNI BY
ANDREW PEYNETSA & WALTER SANCHEZ

SECOND EDITION

UNIVERSITY OF NEBRASKA PRESS   LINCOLN AND LONDON

This book was published with assistance from the McNulty Endowment
at the State University of New York at Buffalo

The illustrations on the title page and pages 29, 65, 165, 243, and 295 are
adapted from *The Rain Bird,* by H. P. Mera. Those on pages 1, 75, and 285
are adapted from *The Pueblo Potter,* by Ruth L. Bunzel. Those on pages 57,
125, 215, and 319 are adapted from *The Excavation of Hawikuh,* by
Watson Smith, Richard B. Woodbury, and Nathalie F. S. Woodbury.

Library of Congress Cataloging-in-Publication Data
Tedlock, Dennis, 1939–
    Finding the center : the art of the Zuni storyteller / translated
by Dennis Tedlock from live performances in Zuni by Andrew Peynetsa
and Walter Sanchez. — 2nd ed.
        p.   cm.
    Includes bibliographical references.
    ISBN 0-8032-4439-8 (cl. : alk. paper). —
    ISBN 0-8032-9440-9 (pa. : alk. paper)
    1. Zuni poetry—Translations into English.   2. Zuni Indians—
Folklore.   3. Folklore—Performance.   4. Tales—New Mexico.
I. Title.
PM2711.Z95T43   1999
897'.4—dc21   99-27307
                                                        CIP

Hom aaky'asse
lilh to'naawan ts'inaawe.

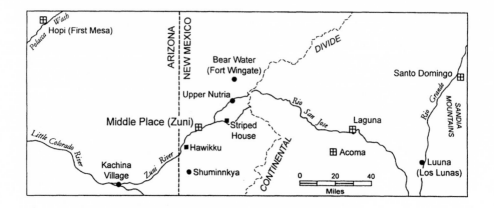

THE ZUNI REGION
Places Mentioned by the Storytellers

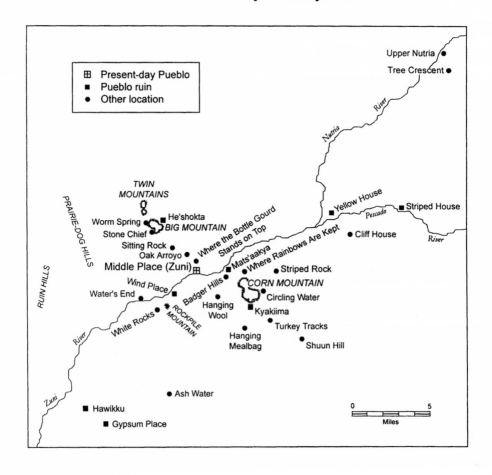

Contents

Designs from Zuni Pottery

Maps

Photographs

Selections from the original Zuni performances
and oral renditions of the translations may be heard
at the Electronic Poetry Center website
of the State University of New York at Buffalo

http://epc.buffalo.edu/authors/tedlock

Preface

Storytelling is a performing art. At Zuni and elsewhere, storytellers have at least as much in common with dramatists, actors, orators, and poets as they do with writers of prose fiction. The sounds they produce have often been transcribed and translated as prose, but there is much more to storytelling than assembling vowels and consonants into gray masses of words and sentences. It is not only words that give shape and movement to a story's characters and their actions, but the ways in which those words are voiced.

At some moments storytellers speak at just the right level to let everyone present hear their words clearly, but at other moments they may give a particular passage extra force by speaking loudly, or they may demand a more delicate kind of attention by speaking softly. Sometimes they produce the wavelike rises and falls of pitch that mark the beginnings and ends of ordinary sentences, but there are other times when they separate pitches into the terraced levels of a chanting voice. There may even be passages where they break into song.

The language of storytelling does not emerge in long paragraphs, but in lines like those of plays or free verse. This is where timing comes into play, as performers vary the pace of a story by producing longer and shorter periods of sound and silence. They may pause neatly between sentences, or let an unfinished sentence dangle for a moment, or run two sentences together, or give a single word a line all to itself—all this in ways that express ongoing changes in the shapes of the story's action. A well-placed silence is as audible as anything else in a performance, so real the listeners can almost touch it.

One of the main kinds of action that takes place in Zuni stories, as in many other traditions around the world, is dialogue among the characters. At Zuni as elsewhere, performers nearly always quote dialogues directly rather than paraphrasing them. Sometimes they add a description of the manner or tone in which a character speaks, much as prose writers do, but more often they simply enact it, sounding deliberate or hesitant, harsh or gentle, pained or pleased. In passages without dialogue they often use the equivalent of a fiction writer's free indirect style, producing a third-person narrative while at the same time sounding as though they were thinking a character's thoughts or sharing a character's experiences.

So it is that a story is composed of a multiplicity of voices, not only because the characters speak differently from one another (and on different occasions), but because the narrative itself is carried by more than one voice. In fact it is this multivocality, more than anything else, that makes stories sound different from prayers, speeches, or poems. The sounds of contrasting voices can be heard quite clearly even in a language unknown to the listener, making it easy to guess that the speaker must be telling a story.

All the Zuni stories translated in this book, one of them with a facing-page Zuni text, are presented in the form of scripts. The words are scored for changes of loudness and for shifts between speaking and chanting, and they are divided into lines rather than paragraphs, with each change of line representing a pause. Tones of voice and gestures are noted as well—and so, too, occasionally, are the performer's sighs, laughs, facial expressions, and interactions with listeners. The stories can be read silently, of course, which leaves their sounds to the voices inside the reader's head. But a proper study, like the study of any other script or poem, demands the use of the vocal organs. That is what "studying" a text originally meant in English: to read it aloud.

The original performances were tape-recorded in the field, all but one during a period of ethnographic and linguistic research that kept me in the field from November 1964 until January 1966. I carried out this work with the permission of two successive heads of the Zuni tribal government, Fred Bowannie and Robert Lewis. I was a graduate student at the time, working on my dissertation in anthropology under the direction of John L. Fischer of Tulane University. But it was while I was an undergraduate that I got my first taste of *Shiwi'ma* (as Zunis call their language), in a linguistic field methods course taught by Stanley Newman at the University of New Mexico. I made my first visit to Zuni in 1958, attending the famous Sha'lako ceremony with a group of anthropology students led by R. Gwinn Vivian, now at the Arizona State Museum.

At the beginning of my fieldwork I found it easiest to talk to Zunis of my own generation, all of whom were bilingual. All could remember stories and summarize them, but none had the skills necessary for an actual performance. Even in the past the storytelling role had fallen largely to people who were old enough to be grandparents, and not all grandparents had chosen to become storytellers. It was no small problem for me to find performers who were willing to let themselves be recorded by an outsider, and then solve the further problem of finding someone with the time and patience to help with the desk work of transcribing and translating the recordings.

The end of my difficulties began when I met Joseph Peynetsa, a young man who held a clerical job at a Bureau of Indian Affairs boarding school on the edge of the Zuni Reservation. He suggested that Andrew Peynetsa, his father's brother, might be willing to tell stories, and he drew a map showing the location of Andrew's house. It turned out to be in the oldest and highest part of the town of Zuni, no more than fifty yards from the spot Zunis reckon as the middle of the earth.

When I met Andrew for the first time, he pretended shock at my suggestion that he might know some stories. He did this for the delectation of the large and merry audience around his family's dinner table, but then he shifted to a more proper stance, modestly claiming to know three stories and then, maybe, a few more than that. When he began describing what he knew his family joined in, recalling one story after another. Then a visitor arrived, a man named Walter Sanchez. Andrew immediately proposed to Walter that the two of them should work together, telling stories back and forth while I recorded them. Walter agreed to this arrangement and so, with delight, did I. It meant that even on occasions when I was the only other person present, whoever was telling a story at the moment could address himself to a fluent speaker of Zuni. We held our first recording session the very next evening.

Andrew Peynetsa and Walter Sanchez were both born at home, outside the world of hospitals and calendar dates. The year of birth they shared, 1904, had been assigned to them by federal bureaucrats who needed to fill out forms. Walter was a monolingual speaker of Zuni, but Andrew, who had gone through the ninth grade at Albuquerque Indian School, knew a good deal of English. He also spoke a little Navajo and Spanish, together with some Dutch he had picked up from homesteaders in the area. The two men and their wives spent part of each year farming and gardening in Upper Nutria, a hamlet in the northeastern part of the reservation. When I first met them both men did their heavy farm work with teams of horses, but Andrew switched to a tractor in 1967. Walter died in 1972, followed by Andrew in 1976. Andrew's wife Catherine, well known for her beadwork, still lives in the same house where I first went looking for Andrew. Joseph Peynetsa is presently a counselor for the Zuni Housing Authority.

With one exception, the stories in this book were recorded on January, February, and March evenings in 1965. Andrew was quite willing to talk about the stories he and Walter were telling, but when I raised the problem of making detailed transcriptions and translations of the tapes, he suggested that Joseph would be the right person to help me. Joseph was working full time, but he set aside as many evenings as he could for working on the tapes. He repeated what he heard in Zuni, suggested literal English glosses, and answered my questions; meanwhile I wrote everything down in longhand. For him, our work became an unconventional way to learn how to tell stories. By the time I left the field in 1966, he had performed for his family.

My dissertation, which I defended in New Orleans on Bastille Day in 1967, was focused not on Zuni stories as such but on the contexts of their telling and their place among other Zuni genres of verbal performance. It was, in fact, the earliest dissertation written as a contribution to a new area of research Dell Hymes had called the "ethnography of speaking," devoted to the study of speech as an activity in its own right. I wanted to go on to put together a book devoted to the stories themselves, but I felt that the problems caused by the traditional prose format were just as great as the ones that arose from translating Zuni sentences into English ones. I was not pleased at the prospect of joining the long list of ethnographers and linguists, going back to the nineteenth century, who had admired the oratorical and dramatic qualities of storytelling but had done nothing about it. In the days when stories were collected by handwritten dictation—which precluded smooth, uninterrupted performances—there were limits to what could have been done. By the time I entered the field the use of portable tape recorders had become standard practice, but the liberation of the performer had yet to be accompanied by a renovation of the text. Field workers were treating recorders as mere dictation machines, allowing them to postpone the creation of prose texts and translations until a later occasion. I had even been advised that as soon as I had finished transcribing a tape, I might as well reuse it!

In recent years there had been at least one promising development in the translation of Native American texts. In 1965, Dell Hymes had set forth methods for recovering poetic structures in texts of chants and songs that had been collected by the dictation method. It was not until 1975 that he turned a similarly detailed and formalist attention to narrative texts, again of the dictated kind, but his early work did make me wonder what I might find if I scanned my texts of Zuni stories for poetic patterns. As things turned out, what I did find was revealed to me not by the eye, but by the ear. Instead of reorganizing my prose texts by means of what I could *see* in them, I replayed my recordings for what I could *hear* in them.

Here it needs to be explained that ever since my undergraduate years I had been going to poetry readings, taking a special interest in poets who were writing what Charles Olson called "projective" or "open" verse. In theory, at least, what these poets put on the page indicated how their work was to be voiced. In particular, their lines were supposed to be measured not by quantitative schemes, but by the breath. Among the practitioners I listened to in Albuquerque was Robert Creeley, who had come there from Black Mountain College. New opportunities to go to readings came when I took a job in the speech (later rhetoric) department at Berkeley in 1967. There I met a woman who shared my interest in poetry, and among the poets we heard together in Berkeley were Robert Duncan and Denise Levertov. In 1968 I began working out new methods for scoring storytelling performances. The woman who was going to readings with me became Barbara Tedlock during that same year, and we have remained together through all the years since then.

The most important step in scripting Zuni stories was finding the lines, and once I did they seemed quite obvious. I treated each definite pause as a line break, with strophe breaks for the longer pauses. In training my ear to hear pauses more accurately, along with changes in loudness, I had the help of Peter MacNeilage, an acoustical phonologist who was then in the speech department at Berkeley. We ran two of my recorded stories through an apparatus that marked a scroll of graph paper with lines whose rises and falls measured pitch and amplitude against a time scale. Wherever there were silences, the lines became straight and horizontal. Today, musicians, sound technicians, and some linguists use computer software to produce similar images from digital sound files. But they can only examine one short segment of sound at a time, whereas we produced continuous scrolls that ran on for as much as half an hour. What was most striking about the results was the contrast between thick, jagged sounds and level silences. There could not have been more graphic evidence that scoring a performance ought to involve more than tuning the ear to the sounds of phonemes and converting them to letters of the alphabet.

The scrolls also called attention to enormous differences in the lengths of sound sequences. Some of the poets I had been hearing and reading produced lines that were fairly consistent in length, as if they were being guided by the organization of the page as much as by the potentials of the voice. But there were other poets, more like Zuni performers, who suddenly changed the pacing of their lines according to what they needed to say at different moments in the same poem. Among them was Charles Olson himself, and I cannot help but think there is a connection between the relative unpredictability of his lines and his desire that poets should work to regain the ground they had lost in the domains of drama and narrative.

The story I chose for my first scripted translation was "The Boy and the Deer," which is also the first story in the present book. Once I had a full draft in hand, I began showing it around and reading it to anyone who would listen. Whenever I presented my work to poets, they understood immediately what I was doing. The same was true of anyone who remembered what it was like to have a parent or grandparent who could tell stories without looking at a book. But no one in Berkeley seemed to have any idea as to where I might try to publish my work. The beginnings of a solution to that problem came from the opposite coast, when I saw the first issue of a New York literary magazine called *Stony Brook* in Moe's bookstore. In its pages I learned of Jerome Rothenberg's interest in a field he would later give the name "ethnopoetics." I wrote to him at his Manhattan address, enclosing a version of "The Boy and the Deer." His response was immediate and warm, and before long we agreed to found a magazine of our own, *Alcheringa/Ethnopoetics*. We billed it as "A First Magazine of the World's Tribal Poetries" and produced the inaugural issue in the summer of 1970, in Santa Fe. In that issue I published a scripted translation for the first time, the one that appears here (in a revised version) as the second part of "When Newness Was Made."

In the fall of 1970 I took a job in anthropology at Brooklyn College, and ever since then I have taught at various institutions in the Northeast. Among the first poets I met in New York was David Antin. When I first showed my work to him he was still writing his poems first and giving readings afterward, but soon he reversed this process, talking to audiences while taping himself and then publishing transcripts. Much of what he had to say took the form of stories, which further set him apart from other poets. For the written versions he chose a format different from mine, marking his pauses with long horizontal spaces within lines and moving from one line to the next only when the width of the margins made it necessary. The first of his works in this form appeared in 1972, in the fourth issue of *Alcheringa*.

It was also in 1972 that The Dial Press, a New York trade house, published the first edition of *Finding the Center*, with the subtitle *Narrative Poetry of the Zuni Indians*. My editor there was Karen Kennerly, who later served for many years as executive director of the PEN American Center in New York. The original designer, many of whose superb ideas have been carried over into the present edition, was Lynn Braswell. She welcomed my desire to use small type for the passages that were spoken in a soft voice, though this created a production problem. Computer typesetting was relatively new at the time, and the compositor insisted (erroneously) that two different type sizes could not be set on the same line. For that reason, lines that combined normal and soft voicing were split into multiple parts, creating a choppy effect. This problem has been smoothed out in the present edition.

Interest in all things Native American was running high in 1972, and this, combined with the fact that it was much easier for innovative work to get attention than it is now, meant that the book was widely reviewed. I am especially thankful for reviews by Alisdair MacIntyre in *The New York Times Book Review*, William Kittredge in *Harper's*, and John Peck in *The Nation*. Each of these reviewers, in his own way, was an ideal reader, not only understanding what was new in the book, but exploring its implications.

My first opportunity to present copies of the book at Zuni came in the summer of 1973. Andrew's eldest son took his copy home and read to his family that evening. Since it was the wrong time of year for tales he chose a true story, the one that appears here as "When Newness Was Made: Part I." The next day he told me that instead of voicing it in English he had translated it back into Zuni, line for line. But there was one thing that puzzled him. What did I mean by "ozone smell"? This was my translation of *k'oli*, a Zuni term referring to the odor given off by electrical sparks or arcs and also by stink beetles, which are used in treating people who have suffered a lightning strike. The odor produced by electricity is indeed that of ozone (O_3), but I soon discovered that readers in general were puzzled by my use of this term. I had rejected "electrical smell" as an alternative because it conjures up technology that did not exist in the world of the story. My solution for the present edition of the book is "lightning smell." This doesn't do away with all possible puzzlement, but it provides a simple description of something that has been a part of Zuni knowledge for a very long time: lightning has an odor that is unforgettable to those who have been close enough to smell it.

In giving my own performances of translated Zuni stories I have found that some lines bring back the memory of the sound of the original Zuni—not just the words, but the way in which they were spoken. When this happens I expand on the script by speaking both the Zuni and English versions aloud. I have given some performances in the same contexts as those in which the writers of poetry and fiction do readings of their work, but my favorite venues have always been those in which verbal art is not the usual fare. Among these have been The Kitchen (a New York experimental music consortium), a gathering of students at the California Institute for the Arts that included painters and sculptors, a typography class at the Rhode Island School of Design, and an auditorium at the American Museum of Natural History that is normally used for lectures.

Since the first edition of this book was published, similar methods of transcription and translation have been applied to tape-recorded narratives and speeches in numerous languages (see the bibliography). In the Amerindian field, major efforts to do the required close listening include those of Nora and Richard Dauenhauer for Tlingit, Allan F. Burns for Yucatec Maya, and Joel Sherzer for Kuna. Other languages whose verbal arts have been scripted are Yup'ik and Inupiaq Eskimo, Dena'ina, Tanacross, Eyak, Central Koyukon, Chipewyan, Lushootseed, Nakota, Navajo, Hopi, Yaqui, Nahuatl, Sierra Popoluca, Yekuana, Shokleng, and Quechua. Meanwhile, I have extended my own work to Quiché Maya. Outside the Amerindian field, the liveliest scripts are those of Peter Seitel for Haya (Tanzania), Isidore Okpewho for Igbo (Nigeria), and Richard and Sally Price for Saramaka (spoken by Suriname maroons). Other scripts have been published for performances in Ungarinyin (Australia), Ngunese (Vanuatu), Hmong (Vietnam), and Persian (Afghanistan).

In 1978, after Dial let the first edition of *Finding the Center* go out of print, the University of Nebraska Press reissued it (with a new preface) in the Bison Books series. The acquiring editor for that edition, which stayed in print for the next twenty years, was Steven Cox, who later became the director of the University of Arizona Press. For proposing this newest edition and for agreeing to an expansion of both the page size and the contents, I offer my thanks to the University of Nebraska Press.

Fourteen designs from Zuni painted pottery appear on the main title page and story title pages of this edition. Most of the choices are new ones, made with greater attention to the meanings Zuni potters assign to their designs than in the case of the original edition. Most of the interpretations given here (see the table of contents) are based on Ruth L. Bunzel's classic work, *The Pueblo Potter.*

Three stories have been added to the ones that appeared in the previous editions, and all the repeated stories have been fine-tuned with various revisions and corrections. Two of the additions, "The Girl and the Little Ahayuuta" and "Nick," were tape-recorded in 1965. The third, "A Story Was Made," was recorded in the summer of 1972, when the first edition was already in press. There is a story behind this last story.

On an evening when Barbara and I were visiting Andrew Peynetsa and his family in Upper Nutria, he was seized by the idea of creating a new tale out of recent events that involved several of the people who were present, including himself. Tales are supposed to be set in the ancient past, but these events struck him as being just like a tale. As for the custom of confining tales to the winter, he thought it was all right to tell this one in the summer "because I'm only pretending it's a tale." Toward the end of his performance he told how the characters had sat around one evening and decided that what had happened to them should be made into a tale. The evening in question was the very one on which we all sat there listening to him. At the close, instead of saying something like, "That's why there's a place called Tree Crescent," he said, "A story was made!"

Introduction

The land around the town of Zuni, in west-central New Mexico, is a high and rocky plateau. Open spaces are bordered by the sandstone walls of canyons and mesas—yellow in some places, red in others, and marked with alternating bands of pink and white in still others. In the lower areas, down to 6000 feet above sea level, are grasslands. Higher elevations, ranging up to 7500 feet, support stands of ponderosa pine, with fir and aspen on slopes that face north or east. In between are scrub woodlands of juniper and nut-bearing piñon pine. Scattered across the grasslands and woodlands are water holes, windmills, corrals, and houses used by Zunis who run sheep and cattle.

Not far east is the continental divide, with the watershed of the Rio Grande on the far side and that of the Colorado on the Zuni side. Running down toward the town of Zuni are two small streams, the Nutria and the Pescado, which join to form the Zuni River before they get there. Along these watercourses are stands of cottonwoods and thickets of willows. Here and there on the flood plains, both above and below the town, are irrigated fields with small clusters of farmhouses on nearby knolls. The more practiced eye can spot the mounds and fragments of masonry walls left by earlier villages and hamlets, abandoned two or more centuries ago. In the upper drainages of countless dry arroyos are the traces of check dams that once diverted the sudden runoff from summer thundershowers into fields now overgrown with weeds and brush.

But this is the description of an outside observer. Except for the ruins and check dams, it consists of a collection of seemingly timeless objects. If we pass through the same landscape with a Zuni storyteller in a talkative mood, what we will get instead is a collection of events, each one read from something seen along the way, and each one taken from a longer story. Such a journey is something like leafing through a book, turning the pages too fast to catch more than fragments of what it contains.

Suppose we enter the present reservation from the east, on State Highway 53. Soon we pass through a farming hamlet that lies along the Pescado River. When we reach the last few houses, our storyteller points out that on the right, on the opposite bank of the river, are the mounds of an ancient ruin whose Zuni name means "Striped House." Long ago, it seems, a flute player named Nepayatamu came by there on his way to the eastern ocean, bringing along a woman who had once attempted to kill him. She had gone so far as to cut his head off, but he had been healed by the songs of a medicine society. Now, as the two of them passed Striped House, she was too tired to go on, so he sucked her into his flute. Then he played it, and what came out was a swarm of white moths.

A few miles farther on, again on the right and across the river, is Yellow House, a ruin today but a living village in the time of tales. In the hills nearby is a hollow where an orphan girl once lived with her grandfather, so old he could hardly see. When she saw the young men from the village hunting rabbits in the snow, she longed for the taste of rabbit meat and decided to go on a hunt of her own. She did bag some rabbits, but when night came she was too far away to get home. She found shelter in a cave near Cliff House, in a canyon whose entrance can be seen on the other side of the highway from Yellow House. But then, when she built a fire, she attracted the attention of Old Lady Granduncle, a cannibal who sometimes stalks children even today.

Not far from the town of Zuni, to the left of the highway, stands the high mesa known as Towayalanne, or Corn Mountain. Any number of stories inhabit the ruins, pinnacles, hollows, and springs all around this mesa, but since we have left a girl trapped in a cave back at Cliff House, what now comes to mind is that her cries for help and the cannibal's threats of doom could be heard even from here. At that time an old woman and her two grandsons were living on Corn Mountain, and it was she who heard the noise. When she told her grandsons about it, the younger one set off at once to rescue the girl. He and his brother, known as the

Ahayuuta twins, are the gods of warfare, sports, and games, and their grandmother is the goddess of childbirth.

Closer to the road and closer to town, but still on the left, are the Badger Hills, rocky and barren. They bring to mind a foolish boy named Pelt Kid, who knew nothing about girls and also knew nothing about figures of speech. His grandmother told him that when he got married, he should search for a "steamy" place in the "hills." So, on his first night with a girl, he left her bed and went off to the Badger Hills, searching everywhere but never finding whatever it was he thought he was looking for.

From this far down the road the mesa known as Big Mountain can be seen on the horizon, ahead and to the right. A boy who lived in a village at the foot of that mesa once climbed it, looking for a broad-leafed yucca with a cluster of long blades at its center. His mother needed the fibers from the blades to tie off the outer edge of the basket she was weaving. She had abandoned the boy when he was born, and it was only recently that they had been reunited. Until then he had been raised by deer, a doe and two fawns who had found him under a tree. Now his deer family was gone, having been hunted down by his human uncles. As he ascended Big Mountain, all he could think about was his old life in the open.

Between Corn Mountain and Big Mountain is a broad valley, and that is where the town of Zuni stands. A century ago all its households, with several rooms apiece, were clustered in three massive buildings, rising in terraces that reached as high as four stories. By now most people live in single-story, single-family, stand-alone houses, spread out over several square miles. These are the only visible houses when we first enter the town and pass the high school, but then, on the left side of the highway, something else comes into view. From a distance it looks like a large terraced building, but closer up it resolves into closely-spaced houses of one or two stories, built on the slopes of what seems to be a hill. In actuality this hill is a mound several stories thick, composed of the rubble, potsherds, and dust from six centuries of occupation.

Amongst the houses on the mound are six kivas, rectangular ceremonial chambers used by the six divisions of the Kachina Society. Twice a year, each division takes its turn at bringing the dead back to town from down the river, where they live in a village beneath a lake. Sometimes they come back in the guise of rain clouds, and sometimes they take the shapes of the singing and dancing gods known as *kokko*, or kachinas. Today, as in the past, a kiva is entered by means of a ladder that descends through a trap door in the roof. Long ago, in the time of tales, even ordinary houses were entered in this way.

On the summit of the mound are two small plazas, Broken Place to the east and Rat Place to the west, connected by a narrow walkway. On the north side of Broken Place is the first in rank of the six kivas, whose ladder figures in a tale about a girl who had a flock of turkeys in her care. She lived at Wind Place, a village about two miles away to the west, but even from there she could tell that a big dance was going on at Broken Place. She heard the drum and saw the crowd of spectators standing on the rooftops, and she wanted to join them. A big tom turkey warned her not to stay away too long, but she got no farther than Rat Place before the dance directors spotted her and invited her to take part. She forgot all about her turkeys until the tom flew to the plaza and alighted at the top of the kiva ladder, creating a public spectacle.

All the stories that have come to mind so far belong to the category of tales, or *telapnaawe*. The question as to whether a tale really happened is not as important as the question of whether the teller can transport the audience into a world whose places are real but whose time belongs to storytelling itself, located in a floating region of the past that becomes present in the imaginations of the listeners. Once a tale has been told it recedes into its own time again, but it waits there, ready to return to consciousness when the teller or listener passes by a certain place, or hears about someone who longs for a life away from the confines of town, or someone who is drawn by crowds but has chores to do. "Past" though a tale may be, its characters did not so much live out their lives in the past of the present world as they go on living and dying in a parallel world.

There are other narratives whose claim on reality rests not so much on the teller's ability to make them seem present as on the notion that they not only happened at real places, but occupy a definite position along the same continuous road of time as the one the listeners travel in real life. At the near end of this road are anecdotes about things that happened earlier today, or last year, or during someone's childhood, or to a grandparent who is no longer living. In the more distant reaches of the road, with roots extending westward and downward into whole worlds that preceded the present one, is a narrative known as *Chimiky'ana'kowa,* "When Newness Was Made." It accounts, among other things, for the fact that the town of Zuni and its people are where they are.

Looking southwestward from the rooftops above the plaza at Broken Place, we can see the ruins of Wind Place on a knoll above the Zuni River. There was a time when the Zuni people, migrating upriver from far in the west, had settled in villages as near to the present town as Wind Place. But then the Ahayuuta twins wanted to find the location of the middle of the earth. They sought help from a water strider, an insect whose four longest legs form a cross when it stands on the surface of water. When they came to the place where a mound now rises at the center of Zuni, they asked the water strider to stretch its legs out flat, all the way to the four oceans. When this was done, its heart rested at the middle of the earth. The people then built a new village, and one of its names is *Itiwan'a,* or Middle Place. The exact middle is located in a dark interior room that adjoins the kiva at Broken Place.

The narrative of the making of newness begins in places so far away they are not of this earth. The first four locations are underworlds, something like the stories in a building. After the ascent to the roof of this building, which is to say the present world, comes a long migration, upstream and eastward. The earliest place names in this part of the story, starting from the Place of Emergence itself, are so far back they cannot be located on a map. Even so, the distance is not like the one in which tales exist, floating in time even though they are fixed in space. Instead, it is a distance that can be numbered. There is first of all the fact that the worlds beneath this one are four in number. Moreover, during their eastward migration the people stayed four days at each of the named places where they stopped—which is understood to mean four years, however long years may have been in those days. In one of the official versions of this narrative, the number of stops required to get to the Middle Place is four times thirteen, or fifty-two.

The near end of the making of newness is not fixed. At the time of emergence the earth was soft and wet, and then it slowly became harder and drier. But there are some events, recent enough to have been remembered by the grandparents of people who are now grandparents, that seem more and more as though they belong to a world of lingering softness as they recede into the past. An episode of this kind might come to mind as we look southward from a rooftop at Broken Place. On the other side of the river is a bare and level strip of ground that runs east-west. That is where the six tall kachinas known as Sha'lako race back and forth when winter is approaching. It is a sacred place, but it was chosen as a campground when the U.S. Army occupied Zuni for six months in 1897-98. The soldiers came because a Zuni named Nick, who had learned to write, had sent a letter to their fort. He called on them to save him from being tried for witchcraft by the Priesthood of the Bow, whose members were responsible for protecting Zunis from external and internal enemies. The resulting invasion dealt a blow to Zuni sovereignty that now looks like one of the steps in the hardening of the world.

Stories like the one about Nick can be told at any time of year and any time of day. The same is true of episodes that occupy an earlier and more established place in the narrative of the making of newness. It is also true of stories people tell about themselves or their contemporaries. But as for tales, they stand apart. It is one thing to introduce a brief description of an incident from some tale into a conversation, which can be done at any time, but it is quite another to bring its characters and events to life with a full performance. A teller of tales may let us know something about Nepayatamu and his flute as we drive past Striped House on a summer's day, but we will have to wait for another occasion to get the whole story.

The proper season for tales begins midway through the Big Wind moon, also called Corn-picking moon, which corresponds roughly with October. On the night when this moon is full the medicine societies meet—including, incidentally, the society that cured Nepayatamu. The members sing songs that send snakes, especially rattlesnakes, into their winter homes beneath the earth. After that the snakes stay out of sight through the Nameless moon, also called Set the Date for the Dancers moon; the Turn-about moon, when the sun's path stops its southward slide and turns back; the Broken Branches moon, when the heaviest snow-fall comes; and the No Snow in the Road moon, when snow that falls on bare ground is quick to melt. Then, midway through the Little Wind moon, roughly corresponding with March, the medi-cine societies meet to sing snakes back to the surface.

Tales, perhaps because they are long and sinuous, are said to have the power to attract snakes. A person who tells tales out of season and then dares to go out walking over the earth may sud-denly be smiled upon by a snake (this is how snakebite is de-scribed). Only when snakes have gone underground for a long stay is it safe for tales to come out in the open. Even then there is a problem with telling them on a winter's day, which is that they have the power to quicken the pace at which time goes by. This is a positive power on a winter's night, when people may wish that both the darkness and the season were shorter, but no one wants to speed up the setting of the sun on a winter's day. So the right time to bring a tale to life is after dark and during the darkest time of year. The best place is at home, with the audience gathered near a fireplace or a heating stove. But since the 1960s, tales have been driven from ordinary household settings. Their places of refuge are the media-free zones provided by medicine society meetings and by sojourns in the country, where some families have unwired houses near their farms or pastures.

The two narrators whose work is represented in this book, Andrew Peynetsa and Walter Sanchez, belonged to a generation in which many people had spent most of their time on farms and ranches while they were growing up. When I first met them, they and their wives still spent half of each year in the farming hamlet of Upper Nutria. Extra help was provided, when needed, by their grown children (and by myself), and during the summer they al-ways had grandchildren staying with them. In their dry-farmed fields they planted corn and beans of all colors, reserving irrigated fields for sweet corn, wheat, and alfalfa. Their wives grew squash, melons, vegetables, coriander, and chili peppers in so-called waffle gardens, using an ancient system of irrigation in which the water from ditches is let into small, rectangular plots laid out in a grid.

Andrew Peynetsa tying feathers to one of the prayer sticks his family will offer on the day of a full moon. Photo by Dennis Tedlock.

Both men kept a pair of work horses, and Andrew ran a herd of rams for the sheep ranchers in the area.

Andrew had long been a passionate advocate of the interests of Zuni farmers and ranchers, and he was serving as chairman of the tribal government's Agricultural Advisory Committee when the stories in this book were recorded. Over the years he had acquired oratorical skills, which he applied in either Zuni or English as the occasion demanded. Both Andrew and Walter participated in the activities of the Kachina Society, as all Zunis do in one way

Walter Sanchez riding bareback on one of his workhorses at the farming hamlet of Upper Nutria. Photo by Dennis Tedlock.

or another. Andrew was also a long-term member of a medicine society. He had particular responsibility for its songs of initiation, which he reckoned as numbering more than six hundred. As a healer, he knew how to treat convulsions by using his hands and speaking powerful words. On an occasion when my wife Barbara and myself had narrowly escaped a fatal accident, we learned that he also knew how to treat shock. Walter, for his part, was well-versed in the songs and rituals of deer hunting.

In most of Andrew's tales the protagonist is from a priestly family or belongs to a medicine society, whereas Walter's tales are about people who are orphaned or otherwise in humble circumstances. Andrew takes great care with his words, in the manner of a poet or an orator, while Walter is driven by his vision of a story's scenes and events. In dwelling on a particular moment, Andrew is apt to construct what amounts to a lyric poem, while Walter is more likely to produce a realistically detailed description. Joseph Peynetsa (Andrew's brother's son) was struck by the difference between them while he and I were transcribing the recordings of their stories. He remarked that Andrew, whose exact words were relatively easy to catch, "brings out his stories not fast, but precisely," whereas Walter "tells it like he really lived it."

If space is to be made for the telling of a tale on a winter's evening, someone present should say to a storyteller, *Telaapi*, which literally means, "Take out a tale." It is as if stories were kept in a bag or jar when they were not being told, or perhaps in a hole in the ground or a crevice in some rocks. If the teller consents, he or she will begin the tale by casting a spell over the audience, whose members will hopefully remain entranced until the spell is broken at the end. The words that begin and end the spell have the sounds of ordinary words, but their meaning is somewhat obscure, as if they themselves were relics from the time of tales. First of all the teller says, *So'nahchi!* Buried in the past of this word, which is never spoken except when a tale begins, may be a phrase something like, *Si ho'na ahhachi*, which would mean, "Now we take it up."

At this moment the speaker pauses long enough to let the listeners respond. They use another word that is heard only when tales are told, saying, *Ee——so*, something like, "Ye——s indeed." The first syllable echoes the ordinary Zuni word for "yes," which is simply *e*. By pronouncing that syllable with a long glide, the listeners not only emphasize their assent but give it particular connotations. Ordinarily such a glide is applied to a word that deals with motion, time, or location, indicating a long duration or distance. In the present case it implies that the audience is agreeing to let the storyteller go on for a long time, or take them some distance away in time or space.

Next the speaker says, *Sonti ino——te*, and again the listeners respond with *ee——so*. *Sonti* is obscure, but behind it could be a phrase something like, *Si onati*, "Now the road begins." The word *inoote* is heard outside of tales and means "long ago," but when it is used to open a tale it becomes *inoo——te*, "lo——ng ago." The gliding effect not only emphasizes that the distance between the time of the telling and the time of the tale is long, but suggests that the two times are not connected together by numbered years or by numbered stops along a road. There are no such glides in the opening lines of narratives other than tales, whether they deal with recent events or claim to be part of "When Newness Was Made."

The phrases used to open a tale would seem to make good candidates for so-called oral formulas, but in fact there is some room for variation even here. Andrew delivers some or all of the words in these phrases loudly (but without shouting), and sometimes he runs through both of them before pausing. Here is the way he opens "Coyote and Junco," using a loud voice (indicated by capitals) throughout. He chants at the same time, keeping his pitches on two distinct levels about three half tones apart:

SO'
    NAHCHI SONTI *INOO——* *TE*

NOW
   WE TAKE IT UP, THE ROAD BE GINS
    LO——NG A GO

Lines delivered in this way sound something like the recitative interludes in an opera. In the Zuni ear they evoke the voice of a town crier making a public announcement from a housetop, the difference being that a crier must shout as loudly as possible, meanwhile lengthening all the syllables to make them carry into the distance. Walter takes a different approach, placing himself on a more level footing with his audience. Sometimes he says *so'nahchi* no more loudly than he would if he were merely continuing a conversation. As for *sonti inoote,* he is perfectly aware of the existence of this phrase, but he chooses to differentiate himself from Andrew by omitting it.

After the words announcing that a tale will be told comes an introduction to the particular tale of the moment. The lines that compose the introduction may be spoken loudly at first, even in Walter's case, and Andrew sometimes chants them. As the lines continue, a more conversational level of speech begins to take over. Here is a passage from the opening of "The Boy and the Deer," in which Andrew chants the first line and renders the next four (each preceded by a pause of a half to a full second) in a normal speaking voice:

HE' SHOKT'AN LHU WAL'AP
taachish
nawe
K'uushina Yalht'an
ky'akwenap.

THERE WERE VIL LAGERS AT HE' SHOKTA
and
up on the Prairie-Dog Hills
the deer
had their home.

The pace here is slow and deliberate, as is usually the case when characters or places are introduced. It is as if they were being given separate billing on a poster or marquee. The present introduction continues with the singling out of one particular villager, followed by a one-line description of what she is currently doing. For the latter line Andrew shifts back to chanting, but without returning to a loud voice:

Shiwan an e'le

a witen te litton lha liiwashap po' ullap.

The daughter of a rain priest

was sit ting in a room on the fourth story down weaving bas ket plaques.

Scattered echoes of chanting are heard among the next few lines, mixed in with a normal speaking voice.

Once a tale is under way, those who have agreed to listen are obligated to stay awake until it is over. Children who are not yet fully grown have been warned that falling asleep would cause them to become hunchbacks. From time to time, when the speaker has followed the end of a sentence with a definite pause, the listeners may signal their continued attention by saying *ee——so*. They are more likely to do this when a statement clarifies the meaning of an event than when it simply moves the action forward. The speaker may elicit their response to such a statement by suddenly turning to one or more of the listeners and establishing eye contact. Ordinarily, this is as close as a storyteller comes to leaving the role of narrator for that of an individual addressing remarks to other individuals. But Andrew, when he was not being recorded, sometimes made bolder moves. Once when he was telling the "The Boy and the Deer," he named the pregnant woman in the story after a pregnant daughter who was listening, and he named the story woman's elder brother, who eventually beats her for abandoning her baby, after one of his daughter's elder brothers. In this way he startled his audience into paying closer attention, but without breaking the rule that in tales, the only people who use the first or second person are the characters, conversing inside their own world. While in the role of narrator, the storyteller neither speaks as "I" nor addresses the listeners as "you."

Whenever the characters enter into dialogue, the performer takes on their roles. The opening of a dialogue, like the opening of the story itself, often involves formalities of a generic sort. In Andrew's "The Women and the Man," for example, there is a series of scenes in which the members of a medicine society summon an animal into their presence with the intention of asking his help in finding a member who has disappeared. The conversation opens with an exchange of greetings in which the two sides address one another as kin, then moves toward the business at hand. In the following excerpt, a mountain lion has reached the point of asking the members of the society to explain what they have in mind:

Itekkunakya s hokti tasha: "SII, hom chaWE
kaw'chi ko' le on akkya hom ton anteshemaaWEE."

The mountain lion now questioned them: "NOW, my
    CHILDREN
for what reason have you summoned ME?"

Here it is not only the wording that is formal, but the use of a loud voice at the ends of phrases, running directly against the natural tendency to let the voice fade as the breath is depleted.[1] Despite such formalities, Andrew varies these scenes in such a way that no two (out of a total of eleven) are identical in either wording or delivery. In the case of an owl, for example, the passage parallel to the one just quoted runs as follows (the dot marks a pause of about two seconds):

Itekkunakya mewishokkwa:

•

"SII, hom chaWE, kaw'chi ko' le on akkya hom ton anteshemaawe."

The owl questioned them:

•

(almost yawning) "NOW, my CHILDREN, for what reason have you summoned me?"

The soft voice of the first of these lines (marked by small type) evokes the stealthy flight of owls, and the two-second pause followed by yawning evokes their apparent sleepiness when they sit motionless on a perch. This particular owl has more to say, but he dozes off before he continues. Andrew represents this lapse as follows:

•

•

•

That is to say, he remains silent for six full seconds, which is a very long time in the midst of a story.

Whatever a storyteller may do by way of acting out the speaking parts of characters, it stops short of full impersonation. That is to say, the individual voice of the actor is never completely masked by the imitation of the characters' voices. Even so, the rendering of their lines does much of the work of conveying their personalities, thoughts, and emotional states. In Andrew's story of "Coyote and

Junco," Coyote opens a conversation with old lady Junco by asking her direct questions rather than giving her the respect of a gradual approach. She answers his first query without hesitation, but their second exchange goes like this:

"*Kwap to' kyawashy'a,*" *le', "Ma'*

•

teshuk'o taap k'ushuts'i," *le' holh anikwap.*

"What're you winnowing?" he says. "Well

•

pigweed and tumbleweed seeds," she tells him then.

The long pause is not the result of the performer's effort to think of the names of the seeds, which he mentioned just a few lines before these, but is rather his representation of old lady Junco's hesitation to go along with Coyote's demands.[2] The next thing Coyote gets out of her is her winnowing song, which he is anxious to take home with him. He takes his leave of her by saying,

"*EE, HO' s HO AKKYA*
ma' s ho anne, yam ho' cha aawan tena'unna."

"YES, I, now I, SO
well I'm going now, I'll sing it for my children."

In the first of these two lines it is not the performer who is stumbling over his words; rather, the performer is representing Coyote as doing so.

A hoarse voice is a distinguishing feature of two of the characters in the present collection of tales, both of them adolescent boys whose voices are in the process of breaking. One of them is the younger of the Ahayuuta twins, who is confident and smart, and the other is Pelt Kid, who is shy and stupid. In Andrew's "The Sun Priest and the Witch Woman," the younger Ahayuuta insists that he should be the one to imitate the call of a mountain lion, which is high and somewhat rough. With ironic modesty he says, "Perhaps I'll know how." His hoarseness erupts twice in Walter's

"The Girl and the Little Ahayuuta," the first time when he has occasion to touch the girl and the second when they eat a meal together at her home and he anticipates staying overnight. In Walter's "Pelt Kid and His Grandmother," Pelt Kid's hoarseness is attractive to girls, but he has no idea why they invite him to go home with them.

There is a difference between Andrew and Walter in the way they represent the voice of an adolescent male. Andrew simply acts the part, speaking in a high and sometimes hoarse manner when he delivers the younger Ahayuuta's lines in "The Sun Priest and the Witch Woman." Walter, whose voice is somewhat rough to begin with, chooses the route of description. He says the kinds of things a novelist would write, such as, "Now he was speaking in a very hoarse voice." Here it would be pointless to argue as to whether Andrew's feigned hoarseness is a substitute for a description, or Walter's description is a substitute for feigned hoarseness. More important is the fact that information central to the understanding of plot and character can be carried elsewhere than in the sheer wording of a story. In a conventional prose version of Andrew's story, the adolescence of the younger Ahayuuta would simply disappear. This is not a trivial matter, since it holds a key to one of the subtler aspects of Zuni concepts of time. As twins, the Ahayuuta brothers are as close as they can come to existing at the same point on the road of time and yet coming one after the other (as even twins must). The elder, who speaks in a normal adult voice, is located just past an important transition in his life, while the younger is in the midst of it. This gives the two of them the ability to overcome the linearity of time, seeing into the past or future from their not-quite-co-presence.

When the action in a story follows a predictable sequence, as in the case of a ritual, it may be unfolded in a slow and orderly manner much like the one used for introductions and formal dialogues. But if there is a need to represent uncertainty, as in the case of a character who is going around hunting, the lines may be divided in a suspenseful way. In the following passage from "The Boy and the Deer," the hunter is the uncle of a boy who was abandoned as a baby and has been living with a herd of deer. The listener is kept waiting through nine lines of extremely uneven

length and two extra-long pauses before the end of a complete
sentence coincides with a pause:

Aateya'kya———— koholh lhana
                            •

ist
an lhuwal'an
an kyak holh
imat lhatakky'an aakya. Lhatakky'an aana
imat paniina s ist
uhsi lak ist
Wi'ky'al'an holh, lesna paniina uhs ist lak
                               •

K'uushin Yalht'an uhsi tewuuli yalhtookwin holh imat ky'alh kon holh
   yemakna.

There they lived o————n for a long time
                         •

until
from the village
his uncle
went out hunting. Going out hunting
he came along
down around
Worm Spring, and from there he went on towards
                         •

the Prairie-Dog Hills and came up near the edge of a valley there.

The tension between line boundaries and sentence boundaries is
resolved when the hunter arrives in the area where (as the audience
already knows) a herd of deer is living.[3] Tension is still present at
this point, but now it is sustained by words alone. The hunter ar-
rives "near the edge of a valley," but has yet to see what might lie
beyond it.

The last six lines of the above passage are delivered in a soft
voice. Performers often speak this way when they combine the
position of a narrating observer with that of a character who hap-
pens to be doing something other than speaking. At one level, the
present lines can be read as a third-person description of the
hunter's actions, spoken quietly because the hunter is quiet. But at

another level, they can be read as an indirect representation of the hunter's thoughts and experiences as he decides where to go next and moves quietly ahead.

As the story continues, the narrator's voice comes even closer to being that of the character being narrated. When the hunter finally gets to the edge itself (rather than being near it), he looks down and

TEWUULI kolh nahhayaye. Nahhayap
lalh holh aksik' ts'an aksh allu'aye
kwan lheyaa k'ohanna.
Muusilili lheya'kwip an lapappowaye.
Lapappow, lesn hish an el'ap, ten aktsik'i
ottsi
ho"i akshappa.

THERE IN THE VALLEY was the herd of deer. In the herd
    of deer
there was a little boy going around among them
dressed in white.
He had bells on his legs and he wore a macaw headdress.
He wore a macaw headdress, he was handsome, surely it was a boy
a male
a person among them.

The loud voice that opens the first of these lines is in maximum contrast with the soft lines that ended the previous passage. The effect is one of surprise, but this is not the performer's surprise. He has known all along where the deer and the boy are, and so has the audience. The surprise belongs to the hunter, and in fact the whole passage (though it is all in the third person) unfolds according to his successive perceptions and his reactions to them. At first he is hesitant as to whether he is really seeing what he thinks he sees, but he reassures himself.

By now it should be apparent that the difference between direct quotation and third-person narrative, or between enactment and description, is not a matter of polar opposition. Just as a performer's voice is still present during the enactment of the speech of a character, so a character's voice can be present when the performer's speech is that of a third-person narrator. Thus the multiplicity of voices in storytelling is not only a matter of contrasts among successive passages in which different characters speak or different narrative modes are employed, but also involves a layering of voices within passages. Such complexities are not the preserve of novelists, but are abundantly present in the productions of storytellers.[4]

As a tale comes to an end, anywhere from five minutes to an hour and a quarter after it began, the spell that was cast by stages at the beginning is undone by stages. An optional part of the undoing is a statement claiming that the story accounts for the origin of something that exists in the present day. Some of these statements seem merely amusing, as when the events of "Coyote and Junco" are said to account for the bad condition of the teeth of coyotes. Others are more serious, as when the events of "The Girl and the Little Ahayuuta" are said to account for the fact that the Ahayuuta twins and their grandmother, who once lived together, are now given offerings at three widely-separated shrines. But statements like these do not so much make a tale into an explanation of the real world as they use what is already known about that world to make a tale seem real.[5]

Just before or just after the origin statement comes the sentence, *Le'n inoote teyatikya,* "This happened long ago," which is not so much a claim to factuality as it is a reminder that the events belong to another kind of time. Then comes a final sentence that completes the undoing of the spell, *Le—— semkonikya.* The first of these two words, which would ordinarily be pronounced *leewi,* means "that's all." The glide does two things at once, implying that the story was long and providing a fast-forward shift into the present. The final word, like the opening *so'nahchi* and *sonti,* is heard only when tales are told. Behind it would seem to be a two-word phrase, *semme konikya,* combining an archaic noun meaning "word" with a verb meaning "it was short." So the overall effect of the closing is something like, "That's a——ll the word was short."

As in the case of the opening, there are variations in the closing. Andrew sometimes incorporates the penultimate phrase, *Le'n inoote teyatikya,* into the beginning of his origin statement, saying,

Le'n inoote teyatikkow akkya, which changes "This was lived long ago" into "Because of the one who lived this long ago." There are still more variations if we consider the manner in which the closing phrases are voiced. Andrew often makes a point of sounding breathless at the end of *le*——, leaving it hanging over a pause in which a gasp for air can be heard, and then pronounces *semkonikya* with an emphatically final drop in pitch. Walter, unlike Andrew, never uses a loud voice in his closings, and he runs the last two words together without a pause.

Even as the last word of a tale is being spoken, the teller and listeners begin to stretch, straightening their arms and raising them over their heads. At the same time, they should stand up straight. These actions, like staying awake, are said to prevent hunchback. They also maximize the difference between the posture of the humans present and that of snakes, as if to make doubly certain that the telling of a tale did not bring the human and snake worlds closer together.

Entering and leaving a story that forms part of "When Newness Was Made" involves different moves from those involved in taletelling. For the part of the story of newness that begins with an ascent into the light of the present world and runs as far as the finding of the Middle Place, there is a canonical version that is properly performed only once every four years.[6] The narrator is a kachina named Kyaklo, who repeats his story, verbatim, for audiences in each of the six kivas. He speaks with the utmost formality, but unlike a tale-teller, he uses the first and second persons to join himself with his audience. As his first line he says, *Nomilhte ho'n chimiky'anapkya teya,* "In truth this is how our newness was made," and as his last he says, *To'no tek'ohannan yanikchiyattu,* "May all of you be blessed with daylight." Each line is chanted in a monotone except for its last syllable, which is held long enough to carry a brief rise to a higher pitch and a fall back to the original one, after which there comes a pause.

Listeners respond to Kyaklo from time to time, but not as they would to a tale-teller. Instead they say, *Hacchi,* "Certainly," or *Eleete,* "Just so." What they are hearing is the oral equivalent of an authoritative text. It does not earn their attention, but rather demands it. When Andrew was a child, he and Joseph's father learned this the hard way. They asked their maternal grandfather for a tale one night, but they wouldn't have done so if they had known what was coming. He didn't know any tales, but he went ahead and recited what he did know, which was Kyaklo's story. He kept them awake all night, hitting them with a stick whenever they fell asleep.

Kyaklo's version of "When Newness Was Made," along with a similar but somewhat less formal version in the keeping of rain priests,[7] has served as a source for countless unofficial reinterpretations of the story. These are told in the same settings as tales and draw upon some of the same skills, focusing on the story rather than the reproduction of its original wording. In opening and closing such a narrative, the speaker does not use the cryptic words that serve to fence off the imaginal world of a tale from the surrounding conversation. *Ma' imati,* "Well then," is the typical beginning line, and at the end comes, *Leewi,* "That's all." Like Kyaklo, the performer may use "we" or "you" even when speaking directly to the audience, as Andrew does in his rendition. There are statements of origin, as in a tale, but they may occur at various points within the story rather than being saved for the end, and there may be many more of them.

All the lines in Kyaklo's narrative, whether they belong to the characters or the narrator, are chanted in the same way. In reinterpretations by storytellers, his insistently authoritative voice is replaced by a multiplicity of voices. Echoes of Kyaklo's chanting remain in Andrew's version, but they take the same form as the chanted lines heard in tales. In rendering the dialogues, Andrew enjoys some of his finest moments as a storyteller. There is, for example, the scene in which the Sun Father first meets the Ahayuuta twins, who are standing at the place where his light struck the foam of a waterfall and brought them into existence. As Andrew interprets this encounter, the twins, who are young and have something of the character of tricksters, and their father, who is the highest and most dignified of the gods, are not quite sure how to address each other. For the twins' opening line Andrew chooses a formal greeting that would normally go as follows: *Ho'n tacchu, ko'na to' tewanan teyaye,* "Our father, how have you been passing the days?" But he has the twins render this greeting shyly (in a soft voice) and uncertainly (they insert the word "father" only after a false start). The Sun Father begins his reply with standard wording, but he moves rapidly from the gentleness of a soft voice to the high formality of a phrase-ending loud voice:

> "*Ko'na, tacchu, ko'na to' tewanan teyaye.*" "*K'ettsanisshe, hom chaw aaCHI.*"

> "How, father, how have you been passing the days?" "Happily, my CHILDREN."

If the Sun Father were to continue his reply with normal wording, he would next say, *Kesh to'n iya,* "Are you coming now?" What Andrew has him do instead is to refer to the fact that the twins, instead of having arrived where they are by traveling from some other location, are standing at their place of origin. The twins, for their part, abandon their soft voice and play along with his choice of wording:

> "*Kesh ton uuwa'kya,*" *le' holh aach anikwa.* "*Ma' s hon uuwa'kya.*"

> "Have you sprouted now?" he asked them. "Yes we've sprouted."

In the official versions of this same scene, no exchange of greetings takes place. The Sun Father simply tells the twins, who are already in his company when the story opens, what he wants them to do.

There are many other differences between Andrew's version of "When Newness Was Made," which he told before the fireplace in his farmhouse at Upper Nutria, and the recitals that take place during religious rituals. There are also differences between his version and other published versions of the unofficial kind, which are different from one another.[8] For example, only in his telling is the surface of the earth populated, in turn, by people from each of the four underworlds, with each group perishing as the next one emerges.[9] The relationship between ritually sanctioned versions and individual performances such as his is analogous to the relationship between text and interpretation in a written tradition, but there remains a difference.

Just as it is possible to talk or write about a text outside the text itself, so it is possible, in an oral tradition, to talk about what was said in a performance outside the performance itself. This is easiest to do soon after a story is told, when it is still fresh in mind. If a story comes into a conversation far from the time of its telling, as when the sight of a certain landmark or the behavior of a certain person brings it to mind, the mention of a few details can make it clear which story or episode is being talked about. But moments like these produce a discourse like that of footnotes or commentaries or citations, rather than constituting a hermeneutics. In an oral tradition, the only serious way to undertake the hermeneutical task of understanding a story is to perform it.

In the course of performing "When Newness Was Made," Andrew incorporates some of his understandings into the story itself, as when he dramatizes the meeting between the Sun Father and the Ahayuuta twins. But there are also moments when he calls attention to his acts of interpretation, making remarks such as, "That must have been the way it was." In the case of tales, where there is no hierarchy between official and unofficial versions, the convergence between acts of narration and acts of interpretation comes closer to being complete. As one of Andrew's sons-in-law put the matter, "You're right with that story, like you were in it."

NOTES

[1] For more on this mode of delivery, see D. Tedlock (1983: chap. 6).

[2] Dramatic moments such as this one disappear in the recasting of this story by Hymes (1980). In his search for verse structures in the version of the text and translation I published in the original edition of the present book, he reorganized the lines on the basis of the words and phrases alone, as if he were dealing with a conventional prose text. The result has the visual appearance of lyric verse arranged in stanzas, but it has little to do with the way a narrative performance unfolds in time. For a further discussion see D. Tedlock (1983: 56-61).

[3] For a detailed study dealing with the variable interaction between pause phrasing and syntactic phrasing in oral narrative, see Woodbury (1987), whose example is a Yup'ik Eskimo tale.

[4] Bakhtin, in setting up the multivocal novel as an advance over the univocal epic, ignores the folktale; see the essays on "Epic and the Novel" and "Discourse in the Novel" in Bakhtin (1981). Narratives of personal history can also be spoken with a rich multivocality, as in the case of a Nahuatl performance analyzed by Hill (1995).

[5] For a general exposition of the poetics of verisimilitude in Zuni stories, see D. Tedlock (1983: chap. 5).

[6] An outline of this version is given in Stevenson (1904: 72-89).

[7] For this version see Bunzel (1932a: 549-604).

[8] A survey of published versions is given in Benedict (1935: I, 255-61); see also The Zuni People (1972: 129-37).

[9] This aligns Andrew's version more closely with the fourfold creations and destructions of Mesoamerican traditions.

Guide to Reading Aloud

Where a juniper tree stood, the child
    was crying.

      •

The deer
the two fawns and their mother
    went to him.

Pause at least half a second each time a new line begins at the left margin, and at least two seconds for each dot separating lines. Do not pause within a line (not even at the end of a sentence) or for indented lines.

She tried to catch it.
It sprinkled them all with its wing powder.
THEY WENT CRAZY.

Use a softer than normal voice for words in small type and a louder than normal voice for words in capitals.

She worked o———n for a long time.

Hold vowels followed by dashes for up to two seconds.

KERSPLASHHHHHH

Hold repeated consonants for up to two seconds.

aaaaaaAAAAAH THE RAIN CAME

Produce a crescendo for repeated vowels that change from lower case to capitals.

ta ^{la}^{a}$_{a}$$_{a}$$_{a}$

Produce a glissando for ascending or descending vowels.

THE ^{HEART} OF THE ^{EARTH}

Chant split lines, with an interval of about three half tones between levels.

Over there *(points north)*
was Yellow House.

Tones of voice, gestures, audience responses, and other details are indicated by italics.

a, e, i, o, u — Vowels should be pronounced approximately as in Spanish.

aa, ee, ii, oo, uu — Double vowels should be held a bit longer than single ones, like the long vowels in Greek.

ch, h, k, l, m, n, p, s, sh, t, w, y — These consonants should be pronounced as in English, except that p and t are unaspirated.

lh — This is like English l and h pronounced simultaneously, something like the Ll in Welsh "Lloyd."

' — The glottal stop is like the tt in the Scottish pronunciation of "bottle." When it follows other consonants it is pronounced simultaneously with them.

cch, hh, kk, ll, llh, mm, nn, pp, ss, ssh, tt, ww, yy, " — Double consonants are held a bit longer than single ones, like the double consonants in Italian.

′ — Stress is always on the first syllable except in words marked with accents.

Note. In songs (shown in boldface capitals), the pauses, loudness, lengthened sounds, glissandi, and pronunciation of Zuni words are as indicated in this guide. The tempo follows the stresses in the words.

THE BOY AND THE DEER

NOW WE TAKE IT UP.
(audience) Ye———s indeed.

NOW THE ROAD BEGINS ^LO———NG A^ GO.
(audience) Ye———s indeed.

THERE WERE ^VIL^LAGERS AT ^HE'^SHOKTA
and
up on the Prairie-Dog Hills
the deer
had their home.

•

The daughter of a rain priest
was ^sit^ting in a ^room^ on the ^fourth^ story ^down^ weaving ^bas^ket
    plaques.
She was always sitting and working in there, and the Sun came up
every day ^when the^ Sun came up
the ^girl^ would sit ^working^
at the place where he came in.
It seems the Sun made her pregnant.
When he made her pregnant

though she sat in there without knowing any man
       her ^{bel}ly grew large.
She worked o———n for a time
weaving basket plaques, and
her belly grew large, very very large.
When her time was near
she had a pain in her belly.
Gathering all her clothes
she went out and
went down to Water's End.

                      ●

On she went until
she came to the bank
went on down to the river, and washed her clothes.
                      ●

Then
after washing a few things, she had a pain in her belly.
                      ●

She came out of the river. Coming out, she sat down
by a juniper tree and strained her muscles:
the little baby came out.
She dug a hole, put juniper leaves in it
then laid the baby there.
She went back into the water
gathered all her clothes
and carefully washed the blood off herself.
She bundled
her clothes
put them on her back
and returned to her home at He'shokta.
                      ●

And the DEER
who lived on the Prairie-Dog Hills

were going down to DRINK, going down to drink at dusk.
The Sun had almost set when they went down to drink and the little baby was
      crying.
"Where is the little baby crying?" they said.
It was two fawns on their way down
with their mother
who heard him.
The crying was coming from the direction of a tree.
They were going into the water

                                        •

and there
they came upon the crying.
Where a juniper tree stood, the child
was crying.

                                        •

The deer
the two fawns and their mother went to him.

                                        •

"Well, why shouldn't we
save him?
Why don't you two hold my nipples
so
so he can nurse?" the mother said to her fawns.

                                        •

The two fawns helped the baby
suck their mother's nipple and get some milk.
Now the little boy

                                        •

was nursed, the little boy was nursed by the deer
o———n until he was full.
Their mother lay down cuddling him the way deer sleep
with her two fawns
together

lying beside her
and they SLEPT WITH THEIR FUR AROUND HIM.
They would nurse him, and so they lived on, lived on.
As he grew
he was without clothing, NAKED.
His elder brother and sister had fur:
they had fur, but he was NAKED and this was not good.

•

The deer
the little boy's mother
spoke to her two fawns: "Tonight
when you sleep, you two will lie on both sides
and he will lie in the middle.
While you're sleeping
I'll go to Kachina Village, for he is without clothing, naked, and
this is not good."

•

So she spoke to her children, and
there
at the village of He'shokta

•

were young men
who went out hunting, and the young men who went out hunting
    looked for deer.
When they went hunting they made their kills around the Prairie-
    Dog Hills.
And their mother went to Kachina Village, she went o————n
    until she reached Kachina Village.
It was filled with dancing kachinas.

•

"My fathers, my children, how have you been passing the days?"
    "Happily, our child, so you've come, sit down," they said.

"Wait, stop your dancing, our child has come and must have
    something to say," then the kachinas stopped.
The deer sat down, the old lady deer sat down.
A kachina priest spoke to her:
"Now speak.
You must've come because you have something to say." "YES, in
    TRUTH
I have come because I have something to SAY.
There in the village of He'shokta is a rain priest's daughter
who abandoned her child.
We found him
we have been raising him.
But he is poor, without clothing, naked, and this
is not good.
So I've come to ask for clothes for him," she said.
"Indeed." "Yes, that's why I've come, to ask for clothes for him."
"Well, there is always a way," they said.
Kyaklo
laid out his shirt.
Long Horn put in his kilt and his moccasins.

                            •

And Huututu put in his buckskin leggings
he laid out his bandoleer.

                            •

And Pawtiwa laid out his macaw headdress.

                            •

Also they put in the BELLS he would wear on his legs.

                            •

Also they laid out

                            •

strands of turquoise beads
moccasins.
So they laid it all out, hanks of yarn for his wrists and ankles

they gathered all his clothing.

When they had gathered it his mother put it on her back: "Well, I must GO
but when he has grown larger I will return to ask for clothing
again."
That's what she said. "Very well indeed."

Now the deer went her way.

When she got back to her children they were all sleeping.

When she got there they were sleeping and she

lay down beside them.

The little boy, waking up

began to nurse, his deer mother nursed him

and he went back to sleep. So they spent the night and then
(with pleasure) the little boy was clothed by his mother.
His mother clothed him.

•

When he was clothed he was no longer cold.
He went around playing with his elder brother and sister, they
would run after each other, playing.
They lived on this way until he was grown.
And THEN
they went back up to their old home on the Prairie-Dog Hills.
After going up
they remained there and would come down only to drink, in the
evening.
There they lived o———n for a long time

•

until
from the village

his uncle

went out hunting. Going out hunting

he came along

down around

Worm Spring, and from there he went on towards

•

the Prairie-Dog Hills and came up near the edge of a valley there.

When he came to the woods on the Prairie-Dog Hills he looked down and

THERE IN THE VALLEY was the herd of deer. In the herd of
   deer

there was a little boy going around among them

dressed in white.

He had bells on his legs and he wore a macaw headdress.

He wore a macaw headdress, he was handsome, surely it was a boy

a male

a person among them.

While he was looking the deer mothers spotted him.

When they spotted the young man they ran off.

There the little boy outdistanced the others.

•

"Haa——, who could that be?"

So his uncle said. "Who

could you be? Perhaps you are a daylight person."

So his UNCLE thought and he didn't do ANYTHING to the
   deer.

He returned to his house in the evening.

•

It was evening

dinner was ready, and when they sat down to eat

the young man spoke:

"Today, while I was out hunting

when I reached the top

of the Prairie-Dog Hills, where the woods are, when I reached the top, THERE
   in the VALLEY was a HERD OF DEER.

There was a herd of deer

•

and with them was a LITTLE BOY.

Whose child could it be?

When the deer spotted me they ran off and he outdistanced them.
He wore bells on his legs, he wore a macaw headdress, he was dressed in white."
So the young man was saying
as he told his father.
It was one of the boy's OWN ELDERS
his OWN UNCLE had found him.
     (audience) Ye—s indeed.
His uncle had found him.

•

Then
he said, "If
the herd is to be chased, then tell your Bow Priest."
So the young man said. "Whose child could this be?
PERHAPS WE'LL CATCH HIM."
So he was saying.
A girl
a daughter of the rain priest said, "Well, I'll go ask the Bow Priest."
She got up and went to the Bow Priest's house.
Arriving at the Bow Priest's house
she entered:
"My fathers, my mothers, how have you been passing the days?"
     "Happily, our child
so you've come, sit down," they said. "Yes.
Well, I'm
asking you to come.
Father asked that you come, that's what my father said," she told
     the Bow Priest.
"Very well, I'll come," he said.
The girl went out and went home, and after a while the Bow Priest came
     over.
He came to their house
while they were still eating.

•

"My children, how are you
this evening?" "Happy
sit down and eat," he was told.
He sat down and ate with them.
When they were finished eating, "Thank you," he said. "Eat plenty," he
was told.
He moved to another seat

•

and after a while
the Bow Priest questioned them:
"NOW, for what reason have you
summoned ME?
Perhaps it is because of a WORD of some importance that you
have summoned me. You must make this known to me
so that I may think about it as I pass the days," he said.
"YES, in truth
today, this very day
my child here
went out to hunt.
Up on the Prairie-Dog Hills, there
HE SAW A HERD OF DEER.
But a LITTLE BOY WAS AMONG THEM.
Perhaps he is a daylight person.
Who could it be?
He was dressed in white and he wore a macaw headdress.
When the deer ran off he OUTDISTANCED them:
he must be very fast.
That's why my child here said, 'Perhaps
they should be CHASED, the deer should be chased.'
He wants to see him caught, that's what he's thinking.
Because he said this
I summoned you," he said. "Indeed."
"Indeed, well

perhaps he's a daylight person, what else can he be?
It is said he was dressed in white, what else can he be?"
So they were saying.
"WHEN would you want to do this?" he said.
The young man who had gone out hunting said, "Well, in four
    days
so we can prepare our weapons."
So he said.
"Therefore you should tell your people that in FOUR DAYS
    there will be a deer chase."
So
he said. "Very well."

            •

(sharply) Because of the little boy the word was given out for the
    deer chase.
The Bow Priest went out and shouted it.
When he shouted the VILLAGERS
heard him.
(slowly) "In four days there will be a deer chase.
A little boy is among the deer, who could it be? With luck
you might CATCH him.
We don't know who it will be.
You will find a child, then," he SAID as he shouted.

            •

Then they went to sleep and lived on with anticipation.
Now when it was the THIRD night, the eve of the chase

            •

the deer
spoke to her son
when the deer had gathered.
"My son." "What is it?" he said.
"Tomorrow we'll be chased, the one who found us is your uncle.

When he found us he saw you, and that's why

•

we'll be chased.
They'll come out after you:
your uncles.

•

(excited) The uncle who saw you will ride a spotted horse, and
    HE'LL BE THE ONE who
WON'T LET YOU GO, and
your elder brothers, your mothers
no
he won't think of killing them, it'll be you alone
he'll think of, he'll chase.
You won't be the one to get tired, but we'll get tired.
It'll be you alone
WHEN THEY HAVE KILLED US ALL
and you will go on alone.
Your first uncle
will ride a spotted horse and a second uncle will ride a white horse.
THESE TWO WILL FOLLOW YOU.
You must pretend you are tired but keep on going
and they will catch you.
But WE
MYSELF, your elder SISTER, your elder BROTHER
ALL OF US

•

will go with you.
Wherever they take you we will go along with you."
So his deer mother told him, so she said.
THEN HIS DEER MOTHER TOLD HIM EVERYTHING:
    "AND NOW
I will tell you everything.
From here

•

from this place
where we're living now, we went down to drink. When we went
    down to drink
it was one of your ELDERS, one of your OWN ELDERS
your mother who sits in a room on the fourth story down weaving
    basket plaques:
IT WAS SHE
whom the Sun had made pregnant.
When her time was near
she went down to Water's End to the bank
to wash clothes
and when you were about to come out
she had pains, got out of the water
went to a TREE and there she just DROPPED you.
THAT is your MOTHER.
She's in a room on the fourth story down weaving basket plaques,
    that's what you'll tell them.

•

THAT'S WHAT SHE DID TO YOU, SHE JUST DROPPED
    YOU.
When we went down to drink
we found you, and because you have grown up
on my milk
and because of the thoughts of your Sun Father, you have grown
    fast.
Well, you
have looked at us
at your elder sister and your elder brother
and they have fur. 'Why don't I have fur like them?' you have
    asked.
But that is proper, for you are a daylight person.
That's why I went to Kachina Village to get clothes for you

the ones you were wearing.
You began wearing those when you were small
before you were GROWN.
Yesterday I went to get the clothes you're wearing now
the ones you will wear when they chase us. When you've been
    caught
you must tell these things to your elders.

•

When they bring you in
when they've caught you and bring you in
you
you will go inside. When you go inside
your grandfather
a rain priest
will be sitting by the fire. 'My grandfather, how have you been
    passing the days?'
'Happily. As old as I am, I could be a grandfather to anyone, for
    we have many children,' he will say.
'Yes, but truly you are my real grandfather,' you will say.
When you come to where your grandmother is sitting,
    'Grandmother of mine, how have you been passing the days?'
    you will say.
'Happily, our child, surely I could be a grandmother to anyone,
    for we have the whole village as our children,' she will say.
Then, with the uncles who brought you in and
with your three aunts, you will shake hands.
'WHERE IS MY MOTHER?' you will say.
'Who is your mother?' they will say. 'She's in a room on the
    fourth story down weaving basket plaques, tell her to come
    out,' you will say.

•

Your youngest aunt will go in to get her.
When she enters:

(sharply) 'There's a little boy who wants you, he says you are his
    mother.'
(tight) 'How could that be? I don't know any man, how could I
    have an offspring?'
'Yes, but he wants you,' she will say
and she will force her to come out.
THEN THE ONE WE TOLD YOU ABOUT WILL COME
    OUT:
you will shake hands with her, call her mother. 'Surely we could
    be mothers to anyone, for we have the whole village as our
    CHILDREN,' she will say to you.
'YES, BUT TRULY YOU ARE MY REAL MOTHER.
There, in a room on the fourth story down
you sit and work.
My Sun Father, where you sit in the light
my Sun Father
made you pregnant.
When you were about to deliver
it was to Water's End
that you went down to wash. You washed at the bank
and when I was about to come out
when it hurt you
you went to a tree and just dropped me there.
You gathered your clothes, put them on your back, and returned
to your house.
But my MOTHERS
HERE
found me. When they found me
because it was on their milk
that I grew, and because of the thoughts of my Sun Father
I grew fast.
I had no clothing
so my mother went to Kachina Village to ask for clothing.'

SO YOU MUST SAY."

•

So he was told, so his mother told him. "And
tonight
(aside) we'll go up on the Ruin Hills."
So the deer mother told her son. "We'll go to the Ruin Hills
we won't live here anymore.
(sharply) We'll go over there where the land is rough
for TOMORROW they will CHASE us.
Your uncles won't think of US, surely they will think of YOU
ALONE. They have GOOD HORSES," so
his mother told him. It was on the night before
that the boy
was told by his deer mother.
The boy became
very unhappy.
They slept through the night
and before dawn the deer
went to the Ruin Hills.

•

They went there and remained, and the VILLAGERS AWOKE.
It was the day of the chase, as had been announced, and the people
    were coming out.
They were coming out, some carrying bows, some on foot and
some on horseback, they kept on this way
o———n they went on
past Stone Chief, along the trees, until they got to the Prairie-Dog
    Hills and there were no deer.
Their tracks led straight and they followed them.
After finding the trail they went on until
when they reached the Ruin Hills, there in the valley
beyond the thickets there
was the herd, and the

young man and two of his elder sisters were chasing each other
by the edge of the valley, playing together. Playing together
they were spotted.
The deer saw the people.
They fled.
Many were the people who came out after them
now they chased the deer.
Now and again they dropped them, killed them.
Sure enough the boy outdistanced the others, while his mother and
    his elder sister and brother
still followed their child. As they followed him
he was far in the lead, but they followed on, they were on the run
and sure enough his uncles weren't thinking about killing deer, it
    was the boy they were after.
And ALL THE PEOPLE WHO HAD COME
        KILLED THE DEER
                    killed the deer
                            killed the deer.
Wherever they made their kills they gutted them, put them on
    their backs, and went home.
Two of the uncles

                            •

then
went ahead of the group, and a third uncle
(voice breaking) dropped his elder sister
his elder brother
his mother.
He gutted them there
while the other two uncles went on. As they went ON
the boy pretended to be tired. The first uncle pleaded:
    "Tísshomahhá!
STOP," he said, "Let's stop this contest now."
So he was saying as
the little boy kept on running.

As he kept on his bells went telele.
O———n, he went on this way
on until

                            •

the little boy stopped and his uncle, dismounting
caught him.

                            •

When he caught him,
(gently) "Now come with me, get up," he said.
His uncle
helped his nephew get up, then his uncle got on the horse.
They went back. They went on
until they came to where his mother and his elder sister and brother were lying
and the third uncle was there. The third uncle was there.
"So you've come." "Yes."
The little boy spoke: "This is my mother, this is my
elder sister, this is my elder brother.
They will accompany me to my house.
They will accompany me," the boy said.
"Very well."
His uncles put the deer on their horses' backs.
On they went, while the people were coming in, coming in, and still
        the uncles didn't arrive, until at nightfall
the little boy was brought in, sitting up on the horse.
It was night and the people, a crowd of people, came out to see the boy as he was
        brought in on the horse through the plaza
and his mother and his elder sister and brother
came along also
as he was brought in.
His grandfather came out. When he came out the little boy and his uncle
        dismounted.
His grandfather took the lead with the little boy following, and they went up.
When they reached the roof his grandfather

made a cornmeal road
and they entered.
His grandfather entered
with the little boy following
while his
uncles brought in the deer. When everyone was inside

•

the little boy's grandfather spoke: "Sit down," and the little boy spoke to his
    grandfather as he came to where he was sitting:
"Grandfather of mine, how have you been passing the days?" he
    said.
"Happily, our child
surely I could be a grandfather to anyone, for we have the whole village as our
    children." "Yes, but you are my real grandfather," he said.
When he came to where his grandmother was sitting he said the same
    thing.
"Yes, but surely I could be a grandmother to anyone, for we have many children."
    "Yes, but you are my real grandmother," he said.
He looked the way
his uncle had described him, he wore a macaw headdress and his
    clothes were white.
He had new moccasins, new buckskin leggings.
He wore a bandoleer and a macaw headdress.
He was a stranger.
He shook hands with his uncles and shook hands with his aunts.
"WHERE IS MY MOTHER?" he said.

•

"She's in a room on the fourth story down weaving basket
    plaques," he said.
"Tell her to come out."
Their younger sister went in.
"Hurry and come now:
some little boy has come and says you are his mother."

(tight) "How could that be?

I've never known any man, how could I have an offspring?" she said.

"Yes, but come on, he wants you, he wants you to come out."

Finally she was forced to come out.

The moment she entered the little boy

went up to his mother.

"Mother of mine, how have you been passing the days?"

"Happily, but surely I could be anyone's

mother, for we have many children," his mother said.

So she said.

•

"YES INDEED

but you are certainly my REAL MOTHER.

YOU GAVE BIRTH TO ME," he said.

•

Then, just as his deer mother had told him to do

he told his mother everything:

•

"You really are my mother.

In a room on the fourth story down

you sit and work.

As you sit and work

the light comes through your window.

My Sun Father

made you pregnant.

When he made you pregnant you

sat in there and your belly began to grow large.

Your belly grew large

you

you were about to deliver, you had pains in your belly, you were
    about to give birth to me, you had pains in your belly

you gathered your clothes

and you went down to the bank to wash.

When you got there you
washed your clothes in the river.
When I was about to COME OUT and caused you pain
you got out of the water
you went to a juniper tree.
There I made you strain your muscles
and there you just dropped me.
When you dropped me
you made a little hole and placed me there.
You gathered your clothes
bundled them together
washed all the blood off carefully, and came back here.
When you had gone
my elders here
came down to DRINK
and found me.
They found me

                                        •

I cried
and they heard me.
Because of the milk
of my deer mother here
my elder sister and brother here
because of
their milk
I grew.
I had no clothing, I was poor.
My mother here went to Kachina Village to ask for my clothing.

                                        •

That's where
she got my clothing.
That's why I'm clothed. Truly, that's why I was among them
that's why one of you

who went out hunting discovered me.
You talked about it and that's why these things happened today."
    (audience) Ye——s indeed.
So the little boy said.

•

"THAT'S WHAT YOU DID AND YOU ARE MY REAL
    MOTHER," he told his mother. At that moment his mother
embraced him, embraced him.
His uncle got angry, his uncle got angry.
He beat
his kinswoman
he beat his kinswoman.
That's how it happened.
The boy's deer elders were on the floor.
His grandfather then
spread some covers
on the floor, laid them there, and put strands of turquoise beads on them.
After a while they skinned them.
With this done and dinner ready they ate with their son.

•

They slept through the night, and the next day
the little boy spoke: "Grandfather." "What is it?"
"Where is your quiver?" he said. "Well, it must be hanging in the
    other room," he said.

•

He went out when he was given the quiver and wandered around.
He wandered around, he wasn't thinking of killing deer, he just
    wandered around.
In the evening he came home empty-handed.
They lived on

•

and slept through the night.
After the second night he was wandering around again.

• 23 •

The third one came

and on the fourth night, just after sunset, his mother
spoke to him: "I need
the center blades of the yucca plant," she said.
"Which kind of yucca?"
"Well, the large yucca, the center blades," his mother said. "Indeed.
Tomorrow I'll try to find it for you," he said.
(aside) She was finishing her basket plaque and this was for the
      outer part.
      (audience) Ye——s indeed.
So she said.
The next morning, when he had eaten
he put the quiver on and went out.
He went up on Big Mountain and looked around until he found a
      large yucca
with very long blades.

•

"Well, this must be the kind you talked about," he said. It was the center
      blades she wanted.
He put down his bow and his quiver, got hold of the center blades, and
      began to pull.
(with strain) He pulled

•

it came loose suddenly
and he pulled it straight into his heart.
There he died.

•

He died and they waited for him but he didn't come.

•

When the Sun went down
and he still hadn't come, his uncles began to worry.
They looked for him.
They found his tracks, made torches, and followed him

until they found him with the center blades of the yucca in his
    heart.

                                    •

Their
nephew
was found and they brought him home.
The next day

                                    •

he was buried.
Now he entered upon the roads
of his elders.
THIS WAS LIVED LONG AGO. THAT'S A———LL THE
    WORD WAS SHORT.

NOTES

Narrated by Andrew Peynetsa on the evening of January 20, 1965, with
Walter Sanchez and myself present; the responses (marked *audience*) are
Walter's. The performance took half an hour.

He'shokta: a small village that was composed of several one-story
masonry room blocks, located on a terrace below the cliffs of the mesa
known as Big Mountain. It was occupied in the eighteenth and early
nineteenth centuries.

Rain priest: the young woman's father is a *shiwani,* occupying one of
several ranked priestly offices that belong to specific clans. Rain priests
abstain from violence, whether physical or verbal. During the summer
rainy season they take turns going on retreats lasting either four or eight
days, fasting and praying for rain in a dark room that represents the
fourth and deepest underworld (see Part I of "When Newness Was
Made").

Basket plaques: flat wicker baskets used as trays. The weaving of the weft proceeds spiral-wise from the center.

Birth of the boy: describing this afterwards, Andrew said, "She drops him like an ewe, by a juniper tree." The mother abandons the boy because, according to Joseph Peynetsa, "she was supposed to be a priest's daughter, meaning that she's not supposed to have a child out of wedlock; a priest's family sets an example for the people." Water's End is several miles from He'shokta; Andrew said, "She went that far so no one would know what she was doing."

Kachina Village: this lies beneath the surface of a lake and comes to life only at night; it is the home of all the kachinas, the ancestral gods of the Zunis. Kachinas are impersonated by the Zunis in masked dances.

Kyaklo: one of the priests of Kachina Village; his face is bordered by a rainbow and the Milky Way, his ears are squash blossoms, rain falls from his eyes and mouth, and he is unable to walk. His shirt is of white cotton cloth with an embroidered border.

Long Horn: another kachina priest; he has a long blue horn at the right side of his head, his long left eye extends out onto his left (and only) ear, and he walks with stiff stomping. His kilt is of white cotton cloth with an embroidered border; his moccasins are of a type called *ketomaawe*, decorated with red, blue, and yellow flaps.

Huututu: deputy to Long Horn; he lacks Long Horn's asymmetry and walks less stiffly. His bandoleer is decorated along its entire length with small conch shells.

Pawtiwa: the chief priest of the kachinas; he has a blue face, blue beak, large furry ears, and his eyes are formed by a black, two-billowed cloud; he is tall and moves in a stately manner. His headdress is a tall bunch of macaw tail feathers worn upright at the back of the head. In pre-Columbian times live macaws were traded from Mexico.

Bells: these are sleigh bells on leather straps. Similar bells, made of copper, were traded from Mexico in pre-Columbian times.

"Daylight person": living human beings are *tek'ohannan aaho"i* or "daylight people"; all other beings, including animals, some plants, various natural phenomena, and deceased humans (kachinas), are *ky'apin aaho"i* or "raw people," because they do not depend on cooked food. The boy is partly daylight, since his mother is daylight, and partly raw, since his father is the Sun and since, as Andrew pointed out, "he was the half-son of the deer mother, because she gave him her milk."

The uncles and their horses: the first uncle, the one who catches the boy but kills no deer, rides a spotted horse. The second uncle, who follows the first one but neither touches the boy nor kills deer, rides a white horse. A third uncle kills the boy's deer mother, sister, and brother. The color of his horse is not specified, but one of Andrew's sons later made a point of telling me it was black.

Bow Priest: in charge of hunting, warfare, and public announcements; he shouts announcements from the top of the highest house.

The deer mother's clairvoyance: twins, whether they are daylight or raw people, are said to be able to predict the future. Deer are nearly always born as twins (hence the boy has two foster siblings).

Deer chase: Joseph liked this episode best, "because the boy is fleeing, and yet he knows he'll be brought back by his uncles, where, in truth, he belongs." He added: "The way my own grandfather told this story, when they caught the boy he was so strong they could hardly subdue him." After the chase the surviving deer scatter all over the countryside the way they are now, and, as Andrew put it, "From there on after, there's no chasing deer like that."

The boy enters his house: in the "long ago," houses were entered through a trapdoor in the roof; the boy and his grandfather go up an outside ladder to reach the roof and then down a second ladder into the house. Just before they enter the grandfather makes "a cornmeal road" by sprinkling a handful of cornmeal out in front of them, thus treating the boy as an important ritual personage.

"We have the whole village as our children": as a rain priest, the boy's grandfather prays for the entire village, and everyone there addresses him and his family as if they were kin. But the boy insists that they are his "real" kin, not just metaphorical kin.

The mother is beaten: according to Andrew, the uncle did this with his riding whip.

The treatment of the slain deer: Joseph commented, "When deer die, they go to Kachina Village. And from there they go to their remake, transform into another being, maybe a deer. That's in the prayers the Zunis say for deer, and that's why you have to give them cornmeal and put necklaces on them, so that they'll come back to your house once again." He added, smiling, "I suppose the boy didn't eat the deer meat, because he said, 'This is my mother, my sister, my brother.'"

Yucca plant: this was the broadleaf yucca, or Spanish bayonet, with sharp, stiff blades up to a yard long. To finish her basket plaque the boy's mother needed to make a rim for it, bending over the projecting rabbit-brush stems of the warp and tying them in place with fibers stripped from yucca blades. Joseph commented, "When you find this yucca while sheep herding it's always tempting to take it out, but it caused a death in a story, so you're afraid to take it out."

The boy's death: asked whether the boy's mother was responsible for this, Joseph said, "No, I wouldn't say that. I think he was really unhappy. He never stayed home: he went out hunting, but he never thought of killing a deer. Probably he was lonesome, and used to being out in the wilds." Andrew said, "Yes, his mother got blamed, because she sent him to get the yucca; he wasn't just going to do that. Her folks said she shouldn't tell him to get it and that his uncles should go and get it. Probably he had it in his mind to kill himself, that's the way I felt when I was telling it. All that time he was with his deer folks, and all that time he had it on his mind. He never did grow up with his family, but with those deer, in the open air, and probably he didn't like it in the house."

"He entered upon the roads of his elders": that is, in Andrew's words, "The boy went back to the deer forever." He was able to do this because death made him a completely "raw" person; he was no longer partly "daylight."

THE HOPIS
AND THE FAMINE

NOW WE TAKE IT UP.

NOW THE ROAD BEGINS ^{LO}—NG A_{GO}.

THERE WERE ^{VIL}LAGERS AT ^{HO}PI

AT ^{LUU}HAY

A RAIN PRIEST, A YOUNG MAN, HAD HIS FIELDS

AND AT ^{HO}PI THEY WERE GOING TO HAVE THE

^{FEA}THER-CARRYING DANCE.

They were going to dance
and the dancers were meeting for practice.

They were ^{li}.ving this way, meeting for ^{prac}.tice
and the young man always went to his fields, that's the way he
    lived.

The day before the dance

•

when the young man returned from his fields
his wife
was with her lover.

It seems

•

she had a lover.
She went with her lover to his house and there she washed and
    combed his hair
and when the young man came home to his in-laws his wife was
    not there.
Her elders told him she had gone out to the neighbors
to fix their hair.
When the young man
had eaten he went over to the neighbors.
His wife
was fixing her lover's hair.
He found out.
He found out.
The young man got angry.
He got angry when he found out and returned to his own house.
He took out his bundle of feathers.
And this
was the day before the dance.
The young man took out his bundle of feathers
and went to his fields at Luuhay.
When he got there he started work on his prayer sticks.
He worked on his prayer sticks until he finished.
Finishing them, making them good
he painted the sticks with clay from the place where Newness Was
    Made.
When he had finished them, made them good
he went into his field
into the center of his field.
There in the center

                                        •

he planted the sticks.
Famine was to come.
All waters

were to end.

                          •

He sent in the prayer sticks
so that
there would be no rain, but
for his own fields there would be enough to plant yearly.
And at Hopi they danced and danced and danced until it was
     finished.
The next year
the people planted
what seeds they had.
They planted until there were no more, and by the fourth year
the earth was completely HARD.
The earth was completely hard
and so
the people
dispersed because of hunger.
Some went to Acoma
and some to Laguna
because of hunger.
The young man's
wife, who had a lover
got married to her lover.
THEY LEFT HER TWO SMALL CHILDREN
WITH THEIR OLD GRANDMOTHER AND THEIR OLD
     GRANDFATHER
TO STAY
while they went to Acoma because of hunger.
And the young man was getting along well in his fields.
JUST AS HE HAD WANTED IT
it was a time of famine
there was nothing to eat.

                          •

It had been a year since the people left, it had been a year.
His two children were still small then, they were
on the cradle board.
After four years

•

(sighing) there was really
nothing.
The young man thought, "I'll go to my
village and see whether my children
are alive
or perhaps dead.
Who could be alive after all this?" he thought, and the young man
left his fields. After leaving his fields he went on to Hopi.

•

And the
grandfather and the grandmother
and the sister and her
younger brother
these four
were barely able to live, but still living, and the very old Hopis
were all in one kiva, LYING AROUND ALMOST DEAD
        FROM HUNGER.
They were lying around this way
when the young man came.
On their roof, in the sun
together with their grandfather
the two small children
sat there.
(straining to see) When he was far off, "Someone is coming."
So the little boy said. "Where is he?" "There he comes."
"Well it must be someone who eats well," their grandfather said.
"Indeed."
He came closer.

"It looks like our father."
"Where is he now?" "Well, there he comes."
"Yes, that's him."
They were all sitting there this way
when their father came.
Their father
came closer and it really was him.
"Yes indeed that's our father.
Perhaps he's living well
and that's why he's coming."
They were sitting
sitting there when he came up.

•

(shyly) "My father, my children, how have you been passing the
    days?"
"Happily, our
child, so you've come." "Yes."
"Where's
their grandmother?"
(weakly) "She's inside
making parched corn for the children
one more time
with the last remaining ear of corn," so
their grandfather said. "Indeed.
Let's go inside."
The young man
and his two children and his
father
went down inside to their grandmother
who was making parched corn with THE LAST REMAINING
    EAR OF CORN.
They were going to be hungry.

They were already hungry.

●

When they entered:
"My mother, how have you been passing the days?" "Happily, my child, so you've come." "Yes.
(shyly) I've come
to see you
because it's been a long time
since I left you. That bad thing happened to me
so I left you, and it's been a long time so I wanted to see my
    children
and I thought of coming to see you, and you
are barely able to live."
(weakly) "Well, there's nothing left, only this last ear of corn
which I'm parching for the children, then we'll probably starve,"
    she said.
"That's why I've come.
Is anyone else around?"
"No.
There is no village.
Everyone has left for Acoma because of hunger," she said.
"Indeed."

●

"There might be someone else around:
there might be old people
gathered in the kiva.
Perhaps a few of them are still alive," she said.

●

"VERY WELL, I'LL BE BACK," he said.
The young man then
went back to his fields.

●

The young man

went into his fields and picked some CORN.
After picking CORN
he got together a sack of cornmeal and
ears of sweet corn and
melons and
rolls of paper bread.
After gathering these

•

he went back a second time
to leave them with his small children.
Then they ate.
They were safe now.
The next day
the young man
came again
and spoke to his son. His son had been growing.
"My son," he said. "What is it?"
"I'm going to take you with me."
So he said.
His grandfather said, "Very well, you
may go with your father."
The boy went back with his father.
They went on together
until they came to his cornfield.
The boy was amazed.
There was so much in the field
all over the plot
tall corn
melons, watermelons
all of them grown.

•

The father took his son into the field
and built a fire to ROAST him some CORN.

When he had roasted some corn the boy ate the corn.
He filled himself. "Are you full?" "Yes."
"Now you'll have plenty to eat," he told him.
Again he picked some corn. After picking corn
he put some venison with it
put some paper bread with it.
"Take this back with you.
Leave it and then you can come back here," he said. "All right."
The boy carried the load on his back and went to his village.
He was taking it to his grandfather, his grandmother, his sister.
When he brought it into the house:
"My father asked me to go back." "You may go."
So his grandmother told him, and he went back.
He went along WHILE HIS FATHER
WAS SHELLING SOME CORN FOR HIM.
He put the kernels in a sack.
He said to his son, "NOW
you must go back
you must take these corn kernels with you.

                              •

With this sack of kernels on your back you must go o————n
     until
you reach the village.
You must take these kernels to each house
to each dwelling
to each door.
                 ALL OVER THE VIL
You must go   LAGE
leaving kernels in every place. If you are lucky and have some
     kernels left over
then you must take these home.
If nothing is left, then that's the way it will be."
So his father told him.
"Indeed." "Yes, that's what you must do.

Just before
you reach the village
you must start singing," he told him.
"When you finish the song
you must give the ik'oku call," he told him.
"Indeed." "Yes."
HIS FATHER SANG FOR HIM. He sang
o———n until, when he finished the song
he gave the ik'oku call.
And he sang and sang and sang and gave the ik'oku call.
"DO YOU KNOW IT NOW?" he said. "Yes

•

I know it."
But the little boy
did not ask his father what the song SAID.

•

As he was leaving his father said, "When
when you get near there you should start your song, so your
grandmother and your grandfather
and your elder sister will hear you."
"All right."
AS THE LITTLE BOY WENT ALONG HE CARRIED THE
    SACK OF KERNELS ON HIS BACK.
He carried his kernels until he CAME NEAR THE VILLAGE.
When he came near he sang:

LOHO$^{\text{HO-}}$ O-O-O IHI$^{\text{HI-}}$I-I
HAW$_{\text{'U-U}}$ HAW$_{\text{'U}}$
HA-A-$^{\text{A-AAA}}$A HAW'U-U
HA-A-$_{\text{A-}}$
$_{\text{A-}}$A HAW'U-U
HAW'U-UHA

WU ^{HA-} A- A _{WU}

WUSHA- _{AKKYEWA}

WU- UTTIMA

HU _{WINI} WA- A-A-A

U ^{LEWA} ANI _{TI-I}

WUT _{TIYAMA ANI _{TI-} I}

YU- _U YE _{SHE} KI ^{WE} E ^E EE

U-UWI U-UWI U-U ^{WI} HU

HU- _U LI _I I _I

WHEN HE FINISHED HE GAVE THE IK'OKU CALL.
WHEN HE GAVE THE IK'OKU CALL
HIS
grandfather and his grandmother
(frowning) heard him.

•

THEY WERE NOT HAPPY.
AND THE SECOND TIME HE SANG, HE WAS SINGING
    VERY NEAR.
IN THE SONG HIS GRANDMOTHER WAS WUTTIMA
HIS GRANDFATHER WAS SHAKKYEWA
AND THE LITTLE BOY WAS HUWINIWA:
HE WAS CALLING HIS OWN NAME.
HE WAS TELLING HOW THE FAMINE HAD STARTED IN
    THE SONG.
When he sang this

his elders became unhappy.
The third time he sang it
THERE AT THE KIVA
THE OLD HOPIS
WERE LYING AROUND ALMOST DEAD
WHEN THEY HEARD IT.
There was one
who was listening.
"A^{HA}A_A."
"What is it?"
"Someone is saying something."
And soon he ENTERED THE VILLAGE and sang.
He sang
and when he sang the Hopis listened to him.
WHEN HE FINISHED SINGING he gave the ik'oku call.
"AHA^{HA}A_A
SO THAT'S WHY WE'RE ALMOST DEAD.
BECAUSE OF THAT PERSON
we're almost dead.
TÍSSHOMAHHÁ.
Our children don't know any better.
So that's why
(sighing) there's a famine.
For it is said
that when the wife of a rain priest is taken
there will be a famine
there will be an earthquake:
SO IT IS SAID and
THAT'S WHY WE'RE ABOUT TO DIE."
So the old Hopis were saying
LYING AROUND THINKING, lying around while the little
     boy went from house to house

giving out corn kernels. He went on and on a————ll over the
village
going around until
when he got home
he had a few left over.
He entered. When he entered, "My
grandmother, my grandfather, my
elder sister, how have you
passed the day?" "Happily, our son, so you've come home now."
    (seriously) "Yes, I've come home
and I've done what my father told me to do
and these
I will take
inside there
where the corn used to be stored.
Father said
these will multiply themselves magically.
When we don't have enough parched corn, when we aren't full
you
must go inside
where the corn is
and bring out AS MUCH AS YOU WISH
for there will always be enough.
So
my father told me
so he said."
"Indeed."
"Yes indeed."

                                        •

And so
he told his grandmother, his grandfather, and his elder sister.
    "Indeed.

THIS IS THE WAY IT WILL BE, but now I must go back again,"
he said.
"Very well, you may go back."
"Do you have enough food now?" the boy said. "Well
well, we have enough food now.
You might be given further instructions."
Again the boy went back to his father.

●

After spending the night, he went back to his father.
"My father, how did you pass the night?" "Happily, so you've
come."
"Yes." "Have you given out the corn kernels?" "Yes."
"Were they all gone?"
"No, I had a few kernels left and took them home."
"So finally everyone got some."
His father
took some corn and roasted it in the coals for him
he roasted the corn.
The little boy ate the roasted corn
until he was full, and he brought him a melon which he also ate
and
he set out a roll of paper bread and some venison which he also
ate, until he was full.
"Are you full?" "Yes."
When he had cleared away the meal:

●

"TOMORROW
I will work on some prayer sticks," the young man said. "Indeed."
"Yes, I will work on some prayer sticks tomorrow.
How IS it?
Does your grandfather still have some food left?"

●

"Yes, they have some food left:

that's what they told me."
So he told his father.
"You must take some more corn to them
and then you can come back here to stay with me.
Then
you will stay here with me about four nights
and then you may go back," his father told him.
"Indeed." "Yes, that's what we must tell your elders so they won't
    wait for you," he said.
"All right." So his father gathered some CORN
a sack of cornmeal
some corn, some rolls of paper bread, some venison
some melons.
When all these had been gathered they took them there
to his house.
Now they had enough food
so the boy
and his father told them.
"Very well, we won't expect you until then."
When this had been said THEY LEFT, AND THE NEXT DAY
he worked on his sticks, the RAIN PRIEST.
He made the sticks.
It was about noon when he finished the sticks.
He painted them with clay from the place where Newness Was
    Made, and when he had finished
the young man spoke:
"Son." "What is it?"
"You must sit at the door," he said.
"All right."
"And I will go to the center of the field
with the prayer sticks
and give the prayer sticks to the Uwanammi."
There

in his shelter there
at the end of the field
he brought out
his sacred bundle.
When he brought it out

•

HE SANG A STRING OF PRIESTLY SONGS.
He sang priestly songs.
He kept on singing, singing these until he had sung them four
    times.
He told his son, "Look outside and see if anyone
is coming up," but
he did not say, "See if the clouds are coming up."
The boy went out
and looked all around. *(aside)* "No one is coming up."
And he sang and sang
and the second time he sang, he asked him
to look again.
The fourth time he sang
when he had sung the first part
he told his son, "Look outside and see if anyone is coming up."
(aside) It THUNDERED.
It thundered.
"Are they coming up?" "Well now
the clouds are getting very dark." "They're the ones I'm talking
    about," he said.
"THE CLOUDS ARE SWELLING," the boy said.
He sat down again and sang, and the rain came
aaaaaaAAAAAAH
ALL OVER HOPI IT WAS REALLY RAINING.

•

That's how it happened.
It rain-rain-rained and

all his fields were full of WATER.
THE OLD HOPI MEN WERE ALMOST DEAD
THEY WERE BARELY ALIVE, alive
when it rained. When the rain passed
the next day
he said to his son, "Son." "What is it?"
"SOME PEOPLE ARE LYING INSIDE THE KIVA *(aside)*
    ALMOST DEAD.
You must take them this sack of cornmeal
five melons
and this sack of cornmeal.
You must take this sack to them
and feed them. You will break the melons, take out
the flesh and FEED THEM and THEY WILL GET WELL.
They will go to their own homes, bring back corn kernels
parch the corn
FILL THEMSELVES and then go home again," so
so he told his son, *(aside)* and that's why he was supposed to take
    these things to them.
He took the food, and when he got there
he went inside.
They were almost dead.
When he entered, "My grandfathers, my fathers, how have you
    been passing the days?"
(weakly) "Happily, our child.
So you've come in," they said. "Yes.
I've come in, I've come in to FEED you.
My father
told me to, that's why I've come.
That's why I'm here." "Tísshomahhá, our child.
(sighing) It's because of your PARENTS that we're ALmost
    DEAD.
It's because of your parents that we're almost DEAD.

Who was singing, was it you?" they said.
"Yes, it was me." "Indeed.

•

Are you HUWINIWA?" they asked him. "Yes."
"Haa——, so it's your father
who is a rain priest
for the old ones spoke of this.
So that's why this was done, and that's why
we're about to die."
"You will NOT die.
You must get up," he told them. *(hoarsely)* "Why, we can't even get
    up, *(aside)* you must feed us lying down," they said.
THE LITTLE BOY BROKE A MELON AND TOOK OUT
    THE FLESH
AND MIXED THE FLESH
WITH CORNMEAL TO MAKE DOUGH, AND WENT
    AROUND FEEDING THEM, FEEDING THEM UNTIL
when he had used a couple of melons to make dough
they were full. "ARE YOU FULL?" "Yes, we've eaten
but we must get WARM, we'll lie here until we get WARM."
He went out to get some kindling and when he came back in
he built them a fire.
He said, "My fathers, grandfathers of mine
you will get well, get well and WARM YOURSELVES
and you will go to your own houses, and each of you will bring
    corn kernels back here
and in this fire
you will parch
your corn kernels.
THEN YOU WILL EAT ALL YOU WANT
and go back again to your own houses."
"Indeed.
How could it be? We don't have anything, that's why

we're almost dead," they said.
"IN YOUR HOU
SES

there is COR
N.
Because of the thoughts of my PARENT your houses have HEARTS again.
There are stacks of corn and you need no longer be hungry, and you must bring some kernels here:
THEN you will eat until you are FULL.
You will be safe, you will not die," the little boy said.
"Tísshomahhá, our child
is this true?" "YES IT'S TRUE, I'm not lying.
That's why I've come, but now I must go back. May you have a good night."
"By all means may it be the same with you."
The little boy went out
AND FINALLY THEY ALL GOT UP AND WARMED THEMSELVES UNTIL THEY WERE ALL WARM.
(with pleasure) THEY BROKE A MELON AND ATE, AND THE SECOND TIME THEY BROKE A MELON THEY WERE ALL FULL.
THEY WALKED AROUND.
They could do that now.
They talked about what they'd been told:
"HA' AA
MAMA,
IT MUST BE TRUE."
And after talking, they went to their own houses.
Just as he had told them, there was plenty of CORN, stacked where the corn had been stored before.
There was corn of every kind.
When they had eaten they went back to their houses again
and the little boy went on back

to his father, and arrived there.

•

The marks where the water had run were all around, and
far away there at
Acoma
the mother of the two children
said to her new husband, "Why don't you go to our
children's land. Perhaps
our children are dead.
Perhaps our elders are dead
for we came here a long time ago."
So
his wife told him. "Yes, I should go."
And then the young man set out from Acoma.
He arrived.
HE RAN ALL THE WAY AND SPENT FOUR NIGHTS
    BEFORE
HE ARRIVED AT HOPI. It was about noon when he came
and again they were up on their roof:
all of them were sitting there.

•

The young man was coming.
(straining to see) "Someone is coming," they said. "There he comes, running. Well,
    whoever it is
must eat well to move that way."
When he got closer they said
"Well, we know who it is. It's our mother's husband."
That's what the two children said. "Indeed."
"Let no one speak to him," they said.
His elder sister went in
and the little boy went in. When they went in, they spoke to their grandmother:
"Our mother's
husband is coming.

When he gets here and comes inside, don't speak to him, for it's his fault
that we almost died of hunger.
Our mother didn't know what was right.
You mustn't speak to him, and we'll see what he does."
They were inside, and only their grandfather was sitting outside.
And soon their mother's husband climbed up.
When he climbed up

•

he came
to where their grandfather was sitting.
(with overdone friendliness) "Father of mine, how have you been
    passing the days?"
He didn't answer him at all.

•

He climbed down
and entered.
The two children were with their grandmother
and she was parching corn for them.
When he entered:
"My children, my mother, how have you been passing the days?"
No one spoke to him.

•

He spoke to them repeatedly.
The young man went out and
went among the houses.

•

He went around the village
and the smoke was coming out wherever the old people were.
He went all around before
he went back to his Acoma.
They lived on until the boy
went back to his father
and while he was there

he was told the ways of a rain priest, they lived this way
o————n until the next year
and his mother's new husband, who had come visiting
had told the Hopis at Acoma about the good land and the marks
    all around where the water had run
and then
they were talking about going back to Hopi. And the boy had his
    own
cornfield.
He had a big cornfield.
And one by one they were coming back, and the mother
had made shirts for her children, pants for them:
she had made everything for them to wear.
And they left Acoma and went o————n spending several nights,
    and on the fifth day
THE HOPI PEOPLE CAME BACK TO HOPI.
The mother and her new husband went there
to clothe their children, but no one spoke to them.
They went out and went to their own house
the house of the husband.
O————N ONE BY ONE ALL THE HOPIS WHO HAD
    LEFT BECAUSE OF HUNGER WERE COMING BACK,
    COMING BACK.
They went into their houses
and the storeroom doors would not open
there was so much corn.

•

The old Hopis
were the ones who
told what had happened, the old ones told it and the others told
    one another.
They told one another

•

about that person
about the rain priest's
wife
who didn't know what was right and who almost caused them to
    die, the old Hopis told the others.
And the rain priest lived on
until he told his son, "Now, my SON, this is the way you will live."
After saying this he sang the priestly songs, he untied everything
    for him.
When he brought his elder sister, he told both of them about
PRAYERS:
he untied these for them.
How to WORK WONDERS:
how to cause great floods and STOP them
how to do EVERYTHING, to cause FAMINES:
he untied everything for them.
And they understood clearly.
The corn grew old. When the corn grew old
their father said to them, "My children." "What is it?"
"You must go back to your own house.
You will tell your grandfather to summon the Bow Priest.
He will announce that the people will come
here to my fields and haul corn to your house four times.
All the people will come and they will haul it to your house four
    times
and they will take whatever is left in the field for THEIR OWN.
That will be theirs.
When you

•

go back
you will live this way.
Now you have TAKEN MY PLACE.
You will think of all the prayers I have lived by

and the sacred bundle, that's the way you will live.
The wonders, the rituals
whatever I have known
you will live by
and in the future
we do not know what will happen
to you
and I will return to my village
I will return to my home
and there perhaps
I will find another wife. I will find another wife and
you two will replace me
for you are young, and you must do this.
When you go back you must tell the Bow Priest
that there will be a corn harvest on the fourth day."
THAT'S WHAT HE TOLD THEM.
Then, taking their sacred bundle with them
and their paint, they returned to their house.
When they got there they told their grandfather
their grandmother
of all the things their father had told them, of how they were now
both
rain priests

•

and of the things their father had untied for them.
"We must summon the Bow Priest." Their grandfather summoned the
    Bow Priest.
The Bow Priest came.
Then the two children told him, "Now
we have become persons of value
and four days from now
there will be a corn harvest at Luuhay.
You will haul it for us four times

including the melons, four times, then you
will bring in
what is yours."
That's what they asked.
"Very well."
The Bow Priest went out and shouted his announcement.
On the fourth day

•

they went out to gather the corn.
When they arrived there was lots of tall corn.
Just as they had been told, they hauled it four times
and then they hauled their own.
That's the way it was lived there.
That's why the Hopis knew how to WORK WONDERS:
how to THROW one another off the CLIFFS
how to ROAST one another
how to cause FAMINES, how to cause great FLOODS and STOP
    them.
That's how these things were untied.
That's how they came to be such knowledgeable people. This was
    lived long ago. That's A———LL THE WORD WAS
    SHORT.

NOTES

Narrated by Andrew Peynetsa on January 20, 1965, later during the same evening on which he told "The Boy and the Deer." He said that the present story was borrowed by the Zunis from the Hopis and that the song is in the Hopi language. But most of the details of the story fit the Zuni way of life as well as they do the Hopi. The performance took thirty-five minutes.

Luuhay: according to Andrew, this is northeast of the Hopi villages of First Mesa.

Feather-Carrying Dance: a social dance, no longer performed at Zuni.

Hair washing: this is done on the eve of almost any major ceremonial occasion.

Prayer sticks: these consist of a series of feathers tied to willow sticks. The sticks are painted with "clay from the place where Newness Was Made," the kind Zuni priests brought with them as part of their sacred bundles when they emerged from the underworld (see Part I of "When Newness Was Made"). Prayer sticks are planted in the ground as offerings to the raw people.

The famine: in causing this, the rain priest uses his normally benevolent powers to do his people harm. Priests are regarded with suspicion, for, as Joseph Peynetsa puts it, "They get to a place where they know too many prayers, and they say, 'Let me try this, maybe it'll work.'"

The grandparents: these were the maternal grandparents of the two children. The priest calls the grandfather "father" rather than using the term for "father-in-law."

Cradle board: a board to which a swaddled infant is snugly laced with thongs.

Kiva: a rectangular ceremonial chamber, sometimes partially underground, entered through the roof by a ladder.

Foodstuffs: "sweet corn" is the familiar yellow corn. "Parched corn" is usually made from black corn; it resembles popcorn but the kernels are only cracked, not burst. "Paper bread" is usually made from blue corn; the watery dough is spread on a stone griddle, and the resulting flat bread is in sheets thin enough to be translucent.

The ik'oku call: a tight, high-pitched whine, most commonly heard from some of the kachinas.

The Uwanammi: rain-bringing raw people who live on the shores of the four oceans.

Sacred bundle: one of the principal sources of a priest's power, brought from the underworld when Newness Was Made. Laymen are not supposed to know exactly what these bundles contain.

"The marks where the water had run": small eroded channels and alluvial deposits of sand, clay, or leaves and twigs.

The children become "persons of value": this refers to their possession of powerful knowledge rather than to material wealth. The boy becomes the priest proper, while his sister becomes the female assistant some priesthoods require.

The harvest: in former times, the villagers took care of a rain priest's fields.

"How to throw one another off the cliffs": according to Andrew, in one of the religious societies at Hopi, "When someone was initiated, he was thrown down to try him out." "How to roast one another" also refers to an initiation trial.

THE GIRL WHO TOOK CARE OF THE TURKEYS

Now we take it up.
(audience) Ye———s indeed.
There were villagers at the Middle Place

                          •

and
a girl
had her home
there
at Wind Place
where she kept a flock of turkeys.
At the Middle Place they were having a Yaaya Dance.
They were having a Yaaya Dance, and
during the first day
this girl
wasn't
drawn to the dance.
She stayed
with her turkeys
taking care of them.
That's the way
she lived:
it seems

she didn't go to the dance on the FIRST day, that day
she fed her turkeys, that's the way
they lived
and so
the dance went on
and she could hear the drum.
When she spoke to her turkeys about this, they said
"If you went
it wouldn't turn out well: who would take care of us?" her turkeys
    told her.
She listened to them and they slept through the night.
Then it was the second day
of the dance
and night came.
That night
with the Yaaya Dance half over
she spoke to her big tom turkey:
                                •

"My father-child, if they're going to do it again tomorrow
why can't I go?" she said. "Well
if you went, it wouldn't turn out well."
So he told her. "Well then
I mustn't go."
So the girl said, and they slept through the night.
They slept through the night, and the next day
was a nice warm day, and
again she heard the drum over there.
Then she
went around feeding her turkeys, and
when it was the middle of the day, she asked again, right at noon.
(tight) "If you
went, it wouldn't turn out well.
There's no point in going:

let the dance be, you don't need to go, and our
lives depend on your thoughtfulness," the turkeys told her.
"Well then, that's the way it will be," she said, and
she listened to them.
But around sunset the drum could be heard, and she was getting
    more anxious to go.
She went up on her roof and she could see the crowd of people.
It was the third day of the dance.
That night she asked the same one she'd asked before
and he told her, "Well, if you
must go

                        •

then you must dress well.
YOU
must go around
just four times:
you must THINK OF US," he told her.
"You must think of us, for if
you stay all afternoon, until sunset
then it won't turn out well for you," he told her. "Well
well, I'll certainly do as you say: why should I stay there
for a long time?
They get started early and I'll
do as you say," she told her
her
tom turkey.
"Let's get some rest," they said, and they went to sleep, but the girl
    JUST COULDN'T GET TO SLEEP.
So
she got up and built a fire in the fireplace then
she made some yucca suds.
She washed her body all over and then went back to bed, but she couldn't
    sleep, she was so anxious, she was

EXCITED

about going to the dance, she was so excited. She passed the night.
THE NEXT DAY
the sun was shining, and
she went among her turkeys and spread their feed.
When she had fed them she said, "My
fathers, my children, I'm
going
to the Middle Place.
I'm going to the dance," she said. "Be on your way, but think of
    us.
Well
they'll start when you get to those
tall weeds, so
you'll get to the dance in plenty of time," so
her children told her. "Then that's the way it will be," she said,
    and she LEFT. *(pained)* It was getting so hot.
It was so hot when
she entered the village.
They noticed her then.
They noticed her when she came up.
She went to where
Rat Place is today, and
when she entered the plaza, the dance directors noticed her.
Then they asked her to dance.
She went down and danced, and she didn't
didn't think about her children.
Finally it was midday, and when midday came she was just dancing
    awa———y until
it was late, the time when the shadows are very long.
The turkeys said, "Tísshomahhá! our mother, our child
doesn't know what's right."
"Well then, I must GO

and I'll just warn her and come right back
and whether she hears me or not, we'll
LEAVE

•

before she gets here," the tom turkey said, and
he flew away.
He flew along until he came to
where they were dancing, and there

•

he glided down to the Priest Kiva and perched on the top
  crosspiece of the ladder, then he sang:
KYANA^A^A^A^A^A^A TOK TOK KYANA^A^A^A^A^A^A TOK TOK
YEE-E-E HU^LI HU^LI HU^LI TOK TOK TOK TOK
THE ONE WHO WAS DANCING HEARD HIM.
  LHA^PAA——
  HE FLEW BACK to the place
where they were penned, and
the girl ran all the way back.
When she got to the place where they were penned, they sang
  again, they sang and FLEW AWAY, GOING ON
until they came to what is now Turkey Tracks, and they glided
  down there.
When they glided down they stood there and made their tracks.
WHEN SHE CAME NEAR they all went away
and she couldn't catch up with them.
Long ago, this was lived. That's why there's a place called Turkey
  Tracks. That's a——ll the word was short.

NOTES

Narrated by Walter Sanchez on January 20, 1965, immediately following Andrew Peynetsa's "The Hopis and the Famine." The response is Andrew's. The performance took seven minutes.

Wind Place: Pinnaawa, a village that was composed of two-story house blocks grouped around several courtyards, located on a knoll above the Zuni River. It was occupied in the fourteenth and fifteenth centuries.

The keeping of turkeys: since pre-Columbian times, this has been done as much for the feathers as for the meat.

Yaaya Dance: in part, a social dance; revived in 1969 after a lapse of twenty years. A Douglas fir is cut and set up in the center of the plaza; the dancers move around it in concentric rings.

"My father-child": an abbreviated form of "My father, my child."

"Our lives depend on your thoughtfulness": Joseph Peynetsa said, "Just because there's a dance doesn't relieve you of any responsibilities. If you've had your pleasure, it doesn't mean you have to stay out all day. It's like people who own sheep, maybe they like to see a lot of things that go on, but because they depend on them for their livelihood, they can't just let them stay in the corral and go hungry."

Yucca suds: soap is made from the tuberous root of the yucca plant.

Rat Place: in the Middle Place (Zuni), a small plaza immediately west of the central plaza, connected to it by a narrow alleyway.

Priest Kiva: the main kiva at Zuni, on the north side of the central plaza. The Rain Priest of the North is supposed to live next to it.

"The top crosspiece of the ladder": not a rung but a stay, high enough to clear a person standing on the top rung.

The turkey's song: the "words" are meant to represent the sounds of a tom turkey, especially in the case of "TOK TOK" and "HULI HULI," but "KYANAA" suggests *kyanaye*, which would mean, "Spread out the seeds!"

SUSKI TAAP SILO

COYOTE AND JUNCO

SO'   NAHCHI SONTI   INOO——TE
                                    •

SHOP   LHUWA   YAL,'AN
SIL   OKYATTSIK   KY'A   kwappa
taachi   SUS ki
suski lak A'l Iimulh'an holh cha'liye.
Cha'lappa
taachi sil okyattsik holhi
kyawashey'a,
teshuk'o
taap k'ushuts'i, holh kyawashey'a.
Ill'anna wolun holh lesna
kyawashnan allachelhky'akkya.
Allachelhky'ap taachi suski
suski s
lhat allu'ya, yam cha'l aawan lhat allu'ya laks:

silo kyawashennankwin tecchi.
"Kop to LEYE'A," le anikwap, "Ma' ho kyawashey'a," le'.

NOW WE TAKE IT UP, THE ROAD BE GINS LO——NG A GO

•

WHERE THE BOT TLE GOURD STANDS ON TOP
OLD LADY JUN CO has her HOME

and Co YO te
Coyote has his children there at Sitting Rock.
He has his children
and as for Old Lady Junco
she's winnowing,
pigweed
and tumbleweed seeds, it seems she's winnowing.
With her basket, this way *(holds out his hand palm up, bouncing it up and down)*
she winnowed by tossing them in the air.
She's tossing them in the air and Coyote
now Coyote
he's going around hunting, going around hunting for his children
    there:
he reaches the place where Junco is winnowing.
"What're you DOING?" he says to her. "Well I'm winnowing,"
    she says.

"Kwap to' kyawashy'a," le'. "Ma'

•

teshuk'o taap k'ushuts'i," le' holh anikwap. "Hayi.
Kop to ikwe'a," le'. "Ma' hom luk kyawashnakya tenanne," le'.

"AAMA HOM'AAN TENA'U
akkya ho' yam
chaw o tenna," le'.
Sil okyattsik s yam
suski aan tena,

YUUWA^{HINA} YUUWA^{HINA}
YUUWA^{HINA} YUUWA^{HINA}
YU^{HINA} YU^{HINA}
PHHH PHHH
YU^{HINA} YU^{HINA}
PHHH PHHH

le' holh i.
"EE, HO' s HO AKKYA
ma' s ho anne, yam ho' cha aawan tena'unna."
Suski aakya lak Wiimayaawan holh lottikyap, NIISHAPAK'O
     ALLAHIPPA
taa yam tenan okky'a.
Ikya, ina:
"Hanatte, tom'an tena'u, niishapak hom
tenan okky'anapkya," le'.
Taa s an tene,
tenan yaanikwatinan taa s aakya.
Lak teshoktaawan holhi
taa s isk'on yeyye an a' kwachu.

"What're you winnowing?" he says. "Well

•

pigweed and tumbleweed seeds," she tells him then. "I see.
What's that you're saying?" he says. "Well this is my winnowing
    song," she says.
"COME ON, SING IT FOR ME
so I can
sing it for my children," he says.
Old Lady Junco now
sings it for Coyote,

YUUWA^{HINA} YUUWA^{HINA}
    YUUWA^{HINA} YUUWA^{HINA}
      YU^{HINA} YU^{HINA}
(blowing)   PFFF PFFF
      YU^{HINA} YU^{HINA}
(blowing)   PFFF PFFF

she says.
"YES, I, now I, SO
well I'm going now, I'll sing it for my children."
Coyote went this way, and when he came near Oak Arroyo
    MOURNING DOVES FLY up
and he loses his song.
He came back, he's coming back:
(muttering) "Quick! Sing your song, it was mourning doves, my
song, they made me lose it," he says.
And now she sings for him,
he learns the song and now he's gone.
This way, where a field is planted then
and now there's a gopher hole, he breaks through.

Taa s yam tenan okky'a.
Taa s kwiliky'annan iy:
itekkunan
taa an tene.
Haa'iky'annana s anne, taa s Wiimaya holh tecchippa,
K'ECCHO ALLAHIP taa s yam tenan okky'a.
Aawitenaky'annan iya s iyappa
sil okyattsik les kwikkya, "Aa lak to iyappa
kwa' s ho tena'shukwa," le' kwana s. A' ky'amon teshuna
a' ky'amon awana, yam
sil ucchun ullunan, an sil a unan kyala''u.

"Shemak yamante ko' ley ona." Silo yam ky'akwen kwato.

Suski s aawitenaky'annan iya.
Inan s,
"Hanatte tom'an tena'u, taa s an tenan okky'an akkya, iya," le
    anikwa.
Kwa' silo peyena'ma.
"Hanatte," le anikwap, kwa' pena.
"Too———PA" le'.
"Aawitenaky'annan ho'— penap— kwa' hom'an to' tena'ma, tom
    ho' uttenna," le an.

                            •

"Kwiliky'annan, kwii———LI" le'.
"Hanat tom'an tena'u," le' holh.
Kwa' tenap, "Haa———I," le' holh, "ALHNAT ho' PENUWA,"
    le'.

                            •

Suski s, HANAT TENA'U, le' an.
Kwa' tena.
Silo suski a'u.
Sil uttep, KWAAM a' ky'amon sil utte.

And now he loses his song.

And now he comes back for the third time:

he asks for it

and she sings for him.

Now for the third time he goes, and when he reaches Oak Arroyo,
BLACKBIRDS FLY UP and now he loses his song.

When he came for the fourth time

Old Lady Junco said, *(in a tight voice)* "Aw, here you come

but now I won't sing," she says. She looks around for a round rock

she finds a round rock, she

puts her junco-blouse on it, she makes her junco-rock look
smooth.

(in a tight voice) "Go ahead and ask, it's up to you." Junco goes inside her
house.

Coyote now comes for the fourth time.

When he comes,

(muttering) "Quick! Sing your song," now he's lost his song, so he's
back, he tells her that.

But Junco doesn't speak.

"Quick!" he says to her, but she doesn't speak.

"ONE!" he says.

"The fourth time I, uh, speak and you don't sing for me, I'll bite
you," he tells her.

•

"Second time, TWO!" he says.

"Quick! Sing your song," he says.

When she doesn't sing, "THREE!" he says, "I'll SPEAK for the
LAST TIME," he says.

•

Coyote says, "QUICK! SING IT," to her.

She doesn't sing.

Coyote bites Junco clear through.

He bites Junco, CRUNCH! He bites the round-rock Junco.

Liilh lu
    no ky'anna
    koo yo'nashky'an, akkya luk yo'na yalha kwaye.
    "Luhappa ten hish tom ho' leyanna." "Ay ay," le' kwana.

Sani yam cha'likwin tecchip, kyaakyamash koo an chawe
    yashekkya tekkwin tecchi.
Le'n inoote teyatikkow akkya, kwa' suski liilhno aawo'nawamme,
    LEE————— SEMkonikya.

Right ^{these} here *(points to molars)* here

all his teeth come out, the whole row of teeth comes out.

(in a tight voice) "This is exactly what I wanted to do to you." "Ay!
Ay!" he says.

When the prairie wolf returned to his children, by the time he got
there his children were dead.

Because of the one who lived this long ago, coyotes have no teeth
here *(points to molars)*, that's A———LL THE WORD was
short.

NOTES

Narrated by Andrew Peynetsa on January 20, 1965, immediately after Walter Sanchez did "The Girl Who Took Care of the Turkeys." The performance took four minutes; Andrew learned this story from a man who had a reputation for telling only very short stories.

Coyote: Joseph Peynetsa commented, "These Coyote stories make it sound like he's an outcast and nobody thinks too much of him. So he's the eater of any kind of food, like bugs, roots, berries."

Blackbirds: these are Brewer's blackbirds.

Junco shirt: Old Lady Junco is an Oregon junco, and her "shirt" is the hood-like area of dark gray or black that covers the head, neck, and part of the breast of this species.

Prairie wolf: at this point Andrew uses *sani,* an esoteric term for coyote, rather than *suski,* the ordinary term; therefore I have used the less common of the two English terms for this animal.

The ending: asked whether this story teaches a lesson, Joseph said, "It just teaches how the coyote is being very foolish. It doesn't teach anything like a human being might do."

THE GIRL AND
THE LITTLE AHAYUUTA

NOW WE TAKE IT UP.
(audience) Ye———s indeed.

•

THERE WERE VILLAGERS AT YELLOW HOUSE.
There were villagers at Yellow House
and in a hollow at the foot of the hills
around there
a girl and
her grandfather were living together
at about this time of the WINTER.
At this time of winter
there was a lot of snow.
There at Yellow House, every day, the young men
went out during the day
to pull the rabbits out, they went out, went out hunting and in the
      evening
they always brought back long strings of rabbits.
They brought them back, but that girl
lived with her grandfather and her grandfather was very old.
Because of this
he couldn't go out to kill rabbits.
This girl

this girl was very hungry for rabbit meat.
She thought of going hunting herself
and she asked her grandfather about it
one night
she said, "Grandfather
TOMORROW
I would like to go out hunting rabbits.
Every day at dusk
the people who live up there
bring home strings of rabbits.
I've been thinking about going hunting tomorrow.
I like the taste of rabbit so much
so I've been thinking about it," she told her grandfather.
It was because her grandfather was so old.
"Tísshomahhá! daughter
this can't be, you're a girl.
The cold is dangerous.
The snow is deep.
You shouldn't go out at a time like this.

•

IT ISN'T YOUR PLACE," he told his
daughter, his granddaughter.
"Even so, I want to go.
I, tomorrow, that day
I will go out hunting rabbits."
So she told her grandfather.
"Tísshomahhá! daughter
what about the things you'd need to wear in the cold?
We don't
have them.

•

Well, my daughter, you must think whether
there's anything warm to wear in this cold weather.

HOW WILL WE GET IT?" he told his daughter. "But wait, I'm
going in the next room," then she went in the next room and
got a pelt there
and brought it out. When she brought it out:
"You'll have to make snow boots for me with this," she said. Her
      poor grandfather was very OLD.
She handed it to her grandfather and he was feeling it.
"Well then
tonight, I'll
make you
good snow boots, they'll be warm."
So her grandfather told her. When her grandfather had told her:
      "Now then
you must spray this and then wait

                              •

until the water soaks in
then come here
in front of me and put out your foot, because
I have no sight, and if I didn't know what your foot was like
they wouldn't turn out right, I need your foot size to make your
      snow boots," he told his daughter.
She quickly went where the water was kept, took some in her
      mouth, and sprayed the pelt.
When she'd sprayed it all over, she folded it up.
She folded it up, and when the water had soaked in, a little later
she told her grandfather, "Well, I've
done what you told me, I've already done it.
I think it's all damp now," she said. "Well then, bring it right
      here."
She brought the pelt to her grandfather
and handed it to him.
Feeling the pelt, he said, "Perhaps this will do," and he kept the
      pelt.

Her grandfather pulled out a short stool and spoke to her:
"Now, daughter, come over
and place your foot here
so we can mark the pelt around it, measure your foot, and this
    very night
they'll be finished," he told his
daughter.

                              •

She pulled out a stool for her grandfather and her
grandfather sat down on the stool. He sat there and his
granddaughter stood before him and
put her right foot out
on the other stool
and her grandfather asked her, "Which one
am I measuring first?"
"This is my
right foot you're about to measure," and when he'd measured two
    finger widths away from her foot
enough of the big pelt was left over.
"This sole
is good enough
now let's try the other one," he told his daughter. She set out her other foot
    for him.
"Is this the left one?" he said. "Yes, this is the left one."
She set out her left foot and he marked the
pelt all around it. When it was marked: "Well then
do we have any cordage?
I need that to sew them up," he told his granddaughter.
"What kind?" "Well, the narrow yucca blades
and they should be about this long (indicates about two feet).
Give me that kind, I'll
use them because they're rough and strong.

I'll use them to sew for you," he told her. "Well, there are some of
     those around
there were some left over
when I last made tamales." "Well then, get them."
So she went in the other room
and a moment later she brought them out and showed them to
     him, and
her grandfather was VERY OLD
so he felt them. They were long.
"Well THIS, this is the kind I was telling you about," and then
he took one out of the bundle and stripped it until he had only the
     center fiber.
It was a long one.
"Well, I'll use this for sewing," he told his
daughter.
He sewed on until, when he was almost finished, his
cord ran out. When it ran out:
"How much more do you need? Did it run out?" "All I need is an
     arm's length to finish it."
She got more yucca. "Well, it'll probably take one more fiber to
     finish it.
Why don't you strip it for me the way I did the other one, so I can
     finish?
About this long *(indicates about eighteen inches),*" her grandfather
     told her, and his
granddaughter started to
strip it.
She finished. When she had finished
he started up again where he'd left off.
He finished it. When he'd finished: "Now then
try it on, perhaps it'll be all right," he said.
His
daughter tried on the snow boot.

(tight) "Well
well, it's a little too large," she told him.
"It's fine for it to be a little too large
because you'll have to use strips of fur
to wrap your feet in before you put it on.
You have to put them on tight," he told her.
So he told his granddaughter.
"There's some cord left over, well
it can be used too.
If you stripped about three more of these
then I could use them
to finish the other boot.
I could finish it this very night," he told his
granddaughter.
She took them
and stripped the edges of the blades until the center fiber was left.
"What did you do next, grandfather?" she said.
"Give it to me, I'll have to do that part myself."
So she gave one to her grandfather
and when he twisted the fiber of the narrow yucca
it was almost like a ligament, a deer's ligament.
It came out long.
Her grandfather pulled it tight, then he said, "Well, it's quite long.
But we'll need another one," he said, and his
granddaughter got to work again and she
started to strip it
the yucca
and she gave it to her
father.
When this was done: "Maybe this will do for finishing the other
    one.
You'll have to put the first one on so it won't get hard," he told his
daughter. "Very well then."

And she put on the one that was already finished.
"And when you
dress yourself tomorrow, you must make your clothes snug.
Because there's a lot of snow, not just a little," he told his
daughter. Then
he started on the other one and kept on, kept on sewing
and when he was almost finished
his yucca cord ran out. "Well, my
sewing cord is gone.
Another like the last one I made should finish it, about an arm's
    length.
NOW THEN, LOOK OUTSIDE and see how far in the NIGHT
    it is."
So he told his granddaughter, then his granddaughter looked
    outside. "Well now
Stars-in-a-Row
has almost gone down." "Ah, then
I'll be able to finish this."
So he told his daughter. *(excited)* The girl came back inside and she
    was ALL EXCITED
because she never got to eat rabbit, and the young men
came back every evening with them, long strings of them.
That's why she'd made up her mind to go hunt rabbits.
That's why
snow boots were being made for her.
"There's only a short way to go, so
I'll be able to finish before Stars-in-a-Row goes down, I should be
    able to finish."
"Well, here it is," and she gave
the stripped yucca to her grandfather so he could twist it.
He felt it and said, "This should finish it."
He felt for the place where he'd left off and started up again until
    he was done.

He had some cord left over when he finished.
Then he
tied it off and he was finished.
The boots were finished.
"So
daughter, they're finished.
Now then, try this one on, because
you must think about keeping warm, these will be warm and your
feet won't get cold."
So he told her, then his
daughter, the girl, granddaughter, went in the other room again
     and she
found some rabbit skins
old ones
that he had there
and she took them out and sprayed them, then
she wrapped her feet with them, one side then the other side.
She tried the snow boots on again
and they just fit her.
"So
they fit you well
but you'd better spray them and fold them up
and put them away.
Well, we should go to bed
but first you need to make yourself some provisions for tomorrow
you need to make lots of
provisions, and
I'll be waiting for you here
so you must think about me, you
must think," he told his granddaughter.
"Very well, I'll go do that, there's still time."
She went in the other room and got out
a small dish

of corn flour.

●

Then she made some tortillas, and
she kept on making them till she had a tall stack, then her dough was
    gone.
"Well, perhaps this will do."
So she told her grandfather. "Well, it'll do, since I'm
never very hungry
so
if I can't eat
I'll wait for you, and if you're lucky enough
to make a kill and get back in time, then we
can eat together, for when you eat by yourself the food doesn't
    taste good," her grandfather told her.
"Yes, that's the way it is." "Now you can make
your preparations
get everything ready.
Back there where
my
cornmeal pouch is, inside it you'll find
a fire drill.
That's something
we'll have to get ready tonight," he told his daughter.
"Where is it?" she said. "It's right THERE
just as you go in, my
cornmeal pouch, the things inside.
It's the fire drill, get that thing I use to start a fire, get that.
So then tomorrow, if you
don't get back by evening
you can start a fire, I'll show you how," he told his daughter.
So she went in and there
by the antlers was his cornmeal pouch
hanging there.

"Perhaps this is it," she said.
She took it down
and brought it to him. "Is this it?"
"Yes, THIS is it, this is my
cornmeal pouch. Now look inside that small pocket and see if all
my fire-making things
are there. Perhaps they're still there, well then hand them to me,"
    he said.
So his poor daughter

                    •

opened it
and took out
the fire drill and the platform the sparks fall from.
She took them out
then: "Is EVERYTHING THERE?"
her grandfather said, his sight wasn't good, he was so old.
When he'd taken them: "THESE are the ones.
When evening comes
when the sun is going down, think of your home
and if it's too far away you must think about the cold
and if you can't make it back
you must think of shelter for the night, even before
sunset you must think about this. First, you
have to find a sheltered place and you
make a clearing there.
If you don't want to carry this pouch
you can leave it there.
Get some bark
find some mountain mahogany and
peel the bark and have it ready.
Before the sun goes down
you'll gather some wood and have it ready.
Before the sun goes down, even if it's about to set

you must turn this fire drill toward the sun
so it will blossom.
Then you'll pass a good night," he told his
granddaughter. "Yes, may it be so."
So she said. Then her grandfather instructed her:
"There is the FAST KIND:
their tracks will not be numerous, well, their
tracks will be far apart, but the other kind, the cottontail rabbits
will make tracks closer, closer together.
Where the surface of the snow is clear
the tracks of the fast kind will be farther apart.
Their tracks won't show whether
they've gone into a hole.
But the kind you're going after tomorrow is the cottontail.
When you find his tracks in clear snow
they're the tracks that are closer together.
Those are the tracks you must follow, and if you're lucky
the tracks will lead into a hollow in a tree
or a crevice in the rocks.
If they go inside
well that's what I'll
prepare you for."
So he had a STICK, it was
the length of both arms. He asked her to get it.
"You put this in the hole, and if he's TOO FAR IN
you won't be able to touch him with it, but
if you're LUCKY he'll only be a SHORT WAY INSIDE
and you'll put your arm in. This is the way
rabbits are hunted in winter," he told his daughter.

•

"Very well, I'll
keep all this in mind as I go around."
So she told him.

"But it is not
by strength alone
that you can go against these raw people
so I will give you
the cornmeal pouch."

•

SO HER GRANDFATHER TOLD HER, he spoke
to his daughter: "TOMORROW
when you leave your home here
you'll go along, and as you go you
must watch for your Sun Father.
When he is up this far *(thrusts out an arm a little above the*
horizontal), then, beside a tree or a bush

•

you
must ask for daylight.
Well, it doesn't matter how far he has gone, how far the Sun has
gone
it could even be just as he reaches the place where he goes in.
But when you ENTER upon the ROADS of the RAW PEOPLE
THEN, WITH THESE WORDS, YOU
WILL OFFER THEM PRAYER MEAL," he told his daughter.
So he told her, he spoke it, spoke it, *(turning to a listener as if*
expecting him to speak) come on, speak.
(listener shakes his head, refusing to take the part of the girl's
grandfather)
(to the listener) Your word is short.
When he had finished: "You must give thanks in this way
my daughter, you must do this.
Now let's go to bed," he said.
They
went to sleep, they slept o———n until the next morning.
The next day, early in the morning, they got up and his

daughter
got herself ready
for she was very anxious.
When she'd built up the fire
she went in the next room
and there

•

she got a little bowl
of water
and she
put it by the fire
and made some meal cakes.
When they'd eaten well:
"Daughter, you must be sure
to remember
that the cold is dangerous, and if you can't get home
by tonight
then, while our Sun Father is still up
you must think, as you go along, about where you will shelter for
   the night.
Over there

•

in the village there are young men, and these young men, around
   sunset
that's when
they bring back their strings
of rabbits
and for this reason
you have decided to do the same.
I won't say no to you, for you are at the beginning of your life.
If you have to stay overnight
you must think of your happy return.
But now you must go fix all your provisions

you must get ready:
if you're going to spend the night
you
must think of making yourself ready," he told his
granddaughter. "You told me that last night.
Well, I think probably I
have all I need to last me, I'm ready," she said, and
she'd made tortillas
and these
were in a tall stack.
She wrapped some up.
When she'd wrapped them:
"My grandfather, my father, I'm going now, may you
have a happy day."
So she told her father. "My daughter, may it be the same with you
may you be happy," he told his daughter.
She went out. When she went out she stood on the roof, and over
        there *(points north)*
was Yellow House, where the young men lived, and
it was to the south of Yellow House
in a hollow below there
that the girl lived with her very old grandfather.
Every evening those young men
brought in strings
of rabbits
and for this reason the girl
had made up her mind
and so her snow boots had been made, and now, the next day
she got herself ready and went out.
She went
southward
she went on, she went on until
she found a cottontail's tracks, and when she found the cottontail's tracks

they went on and on until they entered a yucca thicket.
When she came to the yucca thicket: "Oh yes, my father, this is what
    you told me about."
And then
it seems
she put her hand inside her dress
she
took out her cornmeal
and
spoke the way her grandfather father had told her.
She asked that this would bring her daylight
that the day would not be wasted, that she
would enter upon the roads of the raw people, that the raw people
    would enter her house
holding their waters, forever bringing in their roads as they lived.
And when the poor girl had SAID this
she sprinkled the cornmeal. After sprinkling the cornmeal she
    went on her way.
When she found some more tracks
a jackrabbit ran out, STOPPED for an instant, and then made a
    long jump.
"This is the fast kind you told me about.
Then it's just as well that you be on your way."
And she went on a short distance until
she came to a thicket, and there
she saw the tracks of a cottontail:
his marks were going along there.
"This must be the one."
Then the girl FOLLOWED him, FOLLOWED him until she
    came to some ledges.
When she found where he'd gone inside, she looked all around
and there weren't any tracks
there weren't any tracks coming back out.

"Well, this is what you told me about."
She took her stick and stuck it in.
When it was in: "You must be just a short way in." There was rustling.
"Well, this must be what you meant."
And the girl put her hand in. She put her hand in
she almost had him, but he huddled himself together.
"Well there you are," and then the girl lay down, and she stretched her
    arm until she caught his feet.
She pulled him out, but she didn't know how to kill a cottontail,
    this was something her
grandfather hadn't explained. She pinched the cottontail's nose
    until
finally she managed to KILL him.

•

When she'd KILLED him she laid him on the ground.
She put her stick back in
and there was another one
and she worked the stick.
"This is what you told me to do."

•

She lay down on her side
put her hand in
until her hand stopped
and again she pulled one out.
When she'd pulled out this one, she had two cottontails.
"Well
at least I've killed two.
I didn't think I could do it
in such a short time." The girl
was SO HAPPY, she kept thinking she might see more of them,
    this was her thinking.
Carrying the two, she went
eastward.

She went down until she saw more tracks going along
and these tracks
were distinct in the clean snow.
They went northward to where
he had jumped
and when she got there the jump was too long.
"Well
this isn't the right kind, this is the fast kind you told me about."
Well then the girl went back to where she'd first seen these tracks.
When the girl got there, some new tracks went on and on this way
    (points south)
the tracks headed this way, southward, they
were headed this way.
"This is what you told me about."

                    •

Well she
WENT ON AND ON until she came to some ledges, and there
his tracks went inside, they went inside.
They went in underneath.
"Well, maybe you're inside."
And THEN, just as her
father had told her to do
she PUT HER STICK IN and there was rustling.
The girl then
put her hand in
and again she TOOK ONE OUT, and again, just as she had done
    it the first time
she pinched his nose and
BURIED HIM
in the snow
and when she finally managed to kill him she put him down.
    There were now
three cottontails.

When there were three cottontails
she PUT HER STICK IN AGAIN, AND AGAIN there was
    rustling.
And then she
broke away some dirt from the edge of the hole and put her hand
    in
and now he was not far in, and again she pulled one out.
This was now her fourth cottontail, this was the count.
When this was the count it was dusk. "Well
this is what you told me to do."
And she started across there
and came to Line of Pines
and on to Cliff House, the girl crossed a ravine.
After crossing she came
to the rocks, to a small cave there.
When she entered it there was a small dry clearing.
"I think this is a good place.
This is what you told me about."
And then
she gathered wood. After gathering wood
the girl brought it inside.
The bark of the mountain mahogany was very loose.
She peeled some off and
brought it inside.
She put that on the ground.
Oh, her grandfather had told her this:
"Before you start a fire
you must present the fire drill to the sun so
you'll have a better chance of getting it lit," her grandfather told
    her. "Oh yes
that's what you told me."
When she remembered this
the sun was still up *(turns and points west, a little above the horizon).*

After she did it
she took her fire drill back inside
and was trying to get a piece of bark started.
For the third time she tried, and about the fourth time she had the
        edge of it glowing.
She took it outside
instead of blowing on it, since
there was a light breeze and sssssso came the flame.
She went back inside
and soon the fire was going, the fire was really going.

                                          •

Now she took off her snow boots and laid them aside
then she
opened up her provisions.
It was very dark by the time she started eating, she ate until she had enough.
"Well
(almost yawning) I'm sleepy, I'll lie down," so
she's thinking.
Now she warms herself, and she takes some of the wood she
        gathered and puts it on the fire
the fire blazes up.
Now
there's a voice.
Now there's a voice
and she hears it.
"Perhaps
you are
someone from the village who's lost the way
and you're calling out.
Well, I'll answer you, and
perhaps I could depend on you for the night."
That's how the poor girl felt.
She quickly put on her snow boots, then

she went out in the clearing to the edge of the firelight.
(as if from a distance, and very high)
hoooooooooooolhaaaaaaaaaaaaaaaaaaaaaaaaa_a

a_a_ay it said.

(calling out) "Come over here, I'm spending the night here," the
    girl said.

•

And then
there was another call then:
hoooooooooooooooooolhaaaaaaaaaaaaaaaaaaaaaaaaaaaaa_a

a_a_ay it said.

(calling out) "Come over here, I'm spending the night here," the
    girl said again.

•

The girl went inside and PUT MORE WOOD ON, the fire was
    really blazing, then it came CLOSER.
It came closer
calling
hoooooooooolhaaaaaaaaaaaaaaaaaaaaaaaaaaaaaaaaaaaa_a

a_a_ay it said.

The girl heard it very clearly now.
(gasping) "Hiyáhha! this is why you
warned me.
Why did I answer?
So this is why you told me
that I shouldn't have a fire late at night.
Well, I asked for it," she said, and the girl
was SCARED, and at the spot where she'd eaten she had the four
    rabbits
her four rabbits there on the ground.

•

She could hear her coming now: it was Old Lady Granduncle.

She had a crook
and the little shells tied to it were chinking as she came.

●

After a time she came to the edge of the light.
She had bulging eyes and was carrying a basket.
She was speaking in a strong voice as she came.

●

THEN SHE CAME UP
to the fire.

●

"Why is it
that a girl like you spends the night away like this?
ToNIGHT
I shall have
MEAT
I shall eat salt."
THAT'S what
Old Lady Granduncle said, speaking in a strong voice.
The poor girl was frightened and didn't say a thing.
Then
she got back in where she'd been before, and
there was just enough room for the girl to get in

●

and when she got in as far as she could, the fire was going out, the
    light was dim.
Old Lady Granduncle
could see her rabbits now.
"WHAT are those tasty TIDBITS there?" "Well my RABBITS."
"COME ON, THROW ONE OUT TO ME," she told her.
"I had a hard time killing them

●

so why should I
throw one out to you?"

"If you don't throw one out to me right now
then I'm going to eat you," she told her.
The poor girl now
got so frightened
that she threw the smallest rabbit out to her.
Holding it like this *(dangles an imaginary rabbit above the mouth)*,
    HASHÁN!
she swallowed it.
She looked in again:
"WHAT tasty tidbits are THOSE?" "Well my rabbits again."
POOR THING, SHE HAD ONLY FOUR RABBITS TO GIVE
    HER.

•

NOW, here she was giving her the THIRD ONE
and over there at CORN MOUNTAIN
the Ahayuuta twins lived with their grandmother.
This GRANDMOTHER of theirs was about to go to bed, and
    then
she stepped outside, and far away, near
Cliff House, all this was going on, and the girl was in a cave.
Now
she was going outside to pee when she heard the girl crying,
the chinking sound there, the strong voice there.

•

The Ahayuuta grandmother got excited and KOLÓN! she went
    inside.
"Grandsons
someone is crying somewhere.
And there's a chinking sound, and somebody's speaking in a strong
    voice.
'Tonight
what I shall do
is eat you.'

Somebody's talking that way," she said. "Aha—
at Yellow House village
just below there to the south
is a girl
who lives with her grandfather, and this
grandfather
is very
weak, very old.
The young men bring in rabbits every evening, and so
she decided to do the same.
SHE WENT OUT HUNTING.
It must be HER."
SO THE LITTLE AHAYUUTA SAID, and he got himself ready,
    he
put it on, put on his quiver.
His elder brother said, "Well now, go ahead
by yourself, younger brother.
With luck you can take care of it before the night is over.
Go ahead, but you'll have to HURRY," he told his younger
    brother.
"Well then, that's the way it will be."
And
as soon as he got outside he started to run.

                            •

He runs along below Blackweed Row, and then
as he runs along, the girl cries out again:
"Grandfather
come
come help me
I'm about to die.
She says she'll eat me.
Grandfather come help me." *(rasping)* The old lady answers in a
    strong voice:

(sharply) "How could your grandfather come, your grandfather is
    old and he can't see.
How
could he come and help you?"
So says the old lady.
The poor girl is crying.

•

THE LITTLE AHAYUUTA RUNS, and he circles around to the
    south of them
going along
until he sees them there
and then
he sits down on top of a cliff.
As he sits down, the poor girl speaks
again: "Grandfather
come and help me.
For some reason she wants to eat me."
So she keeps saying, and the old lady gets mad again:
(sharply) "You've got an old grandfather who can't see.
How could anybody
help you?"
So Old Lady Granduncle told the girl.
"Then I'LL HELP YOU," the little Ahayuuta says now.
He's sitting on top of a cliff and the old lady glances around.

•

AND NOW, now she runs against the cave entrance and hits it, a
    rock gives way
she's about to get inside.
She chips the rocks away, and again the girl
speaks:
(weakly) "Grandfather
come and help me.
For some reason I'm going to die tonight.

Come on now, grandfather, help me," she said.
Again the little Ahayuuta spoke:
"I'LL HELP YOU
I've come to help you," he told her.
The old lady stopped and looked up, she looked up.

                            •

When she looked up she said:
"Well then, TONIGHT
you've come to help her.
Well then, tonight
if you are going to help her
then we shall have a CONTEST tonight," she said.
(firmly) "Well, go ahead and test me, if
you are strong
then go ahead and hook me and pull me down
then perhaps you
can eat both of us, tonight you might eat."
So
the little Ahayuuta told Old Lady Granduncle.
He was up there on a narrow ledge
sitting up there, the little Ahayuuta was sitting there.
Then she hooked him with her crook
she pulled down on it
she pulled, but because he was a person of the raw kind
he was stuck on tight.
(with strain) She PULLED and she pulled, and she failed.
"Ahwa! I'm tired," she said.

                            •

"If you're really going to eat us, come on, COME ON AND TRY
     THE OTHER ARM.
Perhaps you can pull me down by the other arm," so
he told her, the Ahayuuta told the old lady.
He stretched out his arm. When he stretched out his arm

she hooked him by the right hand.
Old Lady Granduncle *(with strain)* pulled
she pulled
and she failed.
"Aha——

•

well now, it must be that this girl is the lucky one tonight, now
    that I have entered upon
entered upon your roads.
(sharply) I had thought that
you would know everything," he told her, "but no.
I'm not holding on very tight here, but you couldn't pull me
    down."

•

Then Old Lady Granduncle told the little Ahayuuta: "YES, in
    truth
you must be stronger than I
since I
couldn't pull you down, I failed,"
she said.
"You FAILED
and tonight
what I shall do
is kill you.
(sharply) You made
threats against me.
Tonight
what I shall certainly do
is kill you."
So he said, then the little Ahayuuta slid down.
HE SLID DOWN and stepped forward
while Old Lady Granduncle stood at the edge of the light.
He placed an arrow and shot her. When he placed an arrow and shot her

she fell down.
When she'd fallen he went to the girl.
(kindly) "Tísshomahhá! my child
my mother
all this
cold is very dangerous.

•

But I have entered upon your road.
Well, tonight
you were lucky that I entered upon your road.
You have nothing to fear now:
you can go back inside again
for the night.
I'll keep watch over you."
So the little Ahayuuta told the girl
he told her.
The girl's
rabbits had been eaten.

•

"WHAT IS IT
that she took from you to eat?" he said. "Well, I had four rabbits:
she ate them," she told him.
He went to where the old lady was lying.
He turned her so her head was toward the east.
She was lying on her back, and he took his stone knife and sliced her belly open.
When he sliced her belly open
THERE WERE THE POOR GIRL'S SNOW BOOTS. *(audience
laughs)*
HE TOOK THESE OUT
but left the rabbits in.
"Let THOSE be HERS.
You shouldn't
cry about it, but put your things on again, you

can have a good sleep while I stand guard for you here.
You won't have anything to fear.
The one who tried to eat you is finished
so there's nothing to fear, may you
have a good rest."
So he told the girl.
The poor girl
put on her snow boots and put some wood on the fire to make it bright.
She lay down but she COULDN'T GO TO SLEEP.
She STILL HADN'T SLEPT *(turns west and lowers his arm below
    the horizon)* when Stars-in-a-Row went down.
She didn't go to sleep and the little Ahayuuta
knew it.
"Tísshomahhá! daughter, mother, you haven't gone to sleep," he
    said. "No."
"YOU'RE AFRAID OF ME, BUT I WON'T DO ANYTHING
    TO YOU.
The one who tried to kill you is dead.
I've saved you.
What is there
to be afraid of? I've
rescued you.
You'll last the night."
So he told the girl. "Tísshomahhá! is it true?"
"It's REALLY TRUE: because of my thoughts
nothing will happen.
There
is the one you were afraid of, and now she lies dead, you have nothing to
    be afraid of."
Then the poor girl lay down and finally went to sleep.
The Ahayuuta watched the girl as she
slept though the night. The night passed, then
just before dawn

the little Ahayuuta

fixed the fire and had it going. Because it had taken her a long time to fall asleep

she slept on and on until finally she woke up, the girl woke up.

"Are you awake now?" "Yes, I'm awake now."

"Then you can

eat your

meal," he told her. The poor girl

had saved some meal cakes.

She ate these, she ate well.

"Have you had enough?" "Yes, I've had enough."

(kindly) "Let's go now.

Your father

is very sad, because

the weather is cold and there's a lot of snow.

It isn't a girl's place to be out like this

but you've been out overnight

you've passed the night

and got some sleep

(sharply) but your father hasn't slept the whole night."

So the little Ahayuuta told the

girl he'd saved, so he told her. "Is that true?"

They went a little way, and BECAUSE HE WAS A PERSON OF
        THE RAW KIND

he pulled out some rabbits for her, pulled them out. They went
        on, went on

until they had two strings of rabbits.

"Well now, if we

carry them this way

they'll be too heavy.

Wait now, let me fix them the way I think they should be."

The TWO OF THEM WENT ON AND ON until

they came near the village. Before they got there

they came to some dead wood.

When they got there

he cut the wood, he cut it and laid out two sticks, these two

he laid out side by side

and then across these two

he laid the rabbits, facing in alternate directions

and in this way he made a LADDER OF RABBITS.

It was done

and it was good, and because he was a wonder worker, he

made it so it wasn't heavy.

"Now then, try it on

to see if it's all right, or if it's heavy, because we still have some
     way to go."

So he told the girl. The girl did this *(bending forward at the waist)*, standing up,
     while the little Ahayuuta put it on her, and now he was speaking in a
     very hoarse voice. *(audience laughs)*

When she'd first met him, he spoke in a normal voice, but now he
     was being SILLY.

He put four ladders of these rabbits

on the girl's back

and because he was a wonder worker he made it so they weren't at all heavy for
     the girl.

"Well, we'll let this be enough

and now we can go on over there," he said.

They watched the Sun until he was JUST ABOUT

to go in, and they arrived at the girl's

house JUST as he was going in, and they all went in.

When they went in

they entered upon the road of their grandfather.

"Daughter, have you come now?" *(with relief)* "Yes, we've come."
     "Thanks be.

So you've come, it's good that you've come back. Ever since you
     left

I haven't eaten.

And, 'All raw PEOPLE, holding your waters, holding your seeds
enter here into my house upon your Pollen Ways':
I've been saying that
and now you've COME BACK." "Yes, we've COME," she said.

•

The little Ahayuuta came in and said, "My grandfather, my father, how
      have you
been passing the days?" "Happily, so you've come now."
"Yes, we've come."
And THERE THE TWO OF THEM
entered upon the road
of their father, their grandfatherly father.
Then
they untied their rabbits
and spread them out.
When they'd spread them out
the girl went in the next room. Going in the next room
she brought out ears of corn and put one alongside the breast of each
      rabbit. When she'd done this:
"Have you done it?" he said.
"Daughter, have you done it?" he said. "Well, I've
done it," she said.
"Now then, come over here and help me stand up," he said, and
the girl went to help her grandfather stand up.
When he came to where they'd spread them out, her father said,
"Daughter
our prayer meal:
where is it?" he said. "Well, I've got it here," so
his daughter said.
Then
she handed it to her grandfather. He held it
and the little Ahayuuta was sitting there
on the woodpile.

As he sat there, her grandfather spoke a prayer:
(almost monotone, but with a higher pitch on stressed syllables)
•
"NOW in truth, ON yesterday's day, when our Sun Father by
   whom we LIVE, FROM his holy place
CAME out standing
ENtered upon our roads, MY child here
HOLding holy meal
SENT this with prayer upon the Pollen Way; RAW people:
WHEN SHE ENTERED upon your roads, she ended your
   daylight; RAW people:
HOLding your waters
HOLding your seeds
YOU are first upon the Pollen Way; OUR child
STANding last behind you
SENT there the Pollen Way.
OUR father
THERE at the place where he sets has a small space to go
OUR children, RAW people, HOLding your waters, HOLding
   your seeds
BRING in your Pollen Ways, FLESH by which we live, FLESH
   of white corn, HOLY meal, strong meal
WE give these into your hands; FORever
HERE into our houses, HOLding your waters, HOLding your
   seeds
YOU will live the entering Pollen Way; BY your flesh, *(normal
   voice)* by your EVER presence we shall live."
That's what her father said.
He sprinkled the meal on the rabbits, and the little Ahayuuta said,
   "Just SO, in truth, that is the way you shall live," THAT'S
   HOW HE RESPONDED
TO HER FATHER, STANDING THERE.
IN THIS WAY HE COMPLETED IT. After completing it

he sprinkled them too. After sprinkling them:
"Well
let's eat, I haven't eaten since yesterday, since you left," so
the grandfather told his daughter, and his
daughter went in and

•

got out the flour and boiled some water. After boiling water
she made meal cakes. After making meal cakes
she served dinner and they ate. While they were eating the little
    Ahayuuta said, "Ah
this is what I really wanted," he said, in his
very HOARSE VOICE.
He was speaking in a hoarse voice, and they ate until they were full.
The little Ahayuuta said to her, to his
well, to his wife:
"Don't you have relatives?" he said.
"Yes indeed, we
have relatives."
"Then go and tell the Bow Priest
to come.
Ask him to come
here
and I will speak to him.
Well, summon him," the little Ahayuuta
told the girl.
"Very well, I'll GO."
And it was in a hollow that they
had their house.
She went out and WENT UP to the village, to the house of the
    Bow Priest. There was a noise.
"Oh, somebody's coming," they said. "Yes, yes," they said.
A moment later she entered. When she entered
she stood by the ladder: "My fathers my

mothers, how have you
been?" "Happy."
When they got a look at her
it was the girl who lived with her old grandfather.
"Our child, you've
come. There must be a word of some importance
there must be something to say, for you wouldn't enter upon our
    roads for no reason
you wouldn't enter here," the Bow Priest told the girl.
"Yes, in truth, you
must make it known to all your children
that tonight they will come

                                •

they will come to my house, where we have something
that will make all of you happy." *(with pleasure)* "Very well
    indeed," he said.
As the girl left she said, "My fathers, may you have a good night,"
    the girl said and she left. The Bow Priest went out
and shouted the announcement, then everyone gathered where the
    girl and the old man were.
They gathered at their place, *(begins scraping the arm of his chair
    with his fingernails)* where the rabbits were being skinned for
    them.
They skinned them until *(stops scraping)* everybody in the village
    got some: because of
the thoughts of the little Ahayuuta
all the villagers got some. When they got theirs there were some
    left over
for the girl and her grandfather. With some left over, the people
    dispersed. When they'd dispersed

                                •

his
wife said, "Well, let's

go in the next room, that's where I sleep," she said.
"You two go in the next room and, well, I'll
sleep in here, you
get some rest," their
father said, then she fixed a bed and their father lay down.
The two of them went in the other room. When they went in
he sat down. He sat there until
his wife finished making the bed, then the little Ahayuuta said, "I'm so thirsty.

                                      •

I'm so thirsty, get me
some water to drink, I'm so thirsty."
So then the girl
went back to get him some water, and he TOOK HIS
        FOREHEAD IN HIS HAND
and there, he
pulled off his homely Ahayuuta self, he pulled it off and SAT
        DOWN on it.
He was sitting on it when the girl
came back with his water. He was facing her
and she didn't give him his water. "Come on, give me my
water," he said.
(tight) "WHERE'S THE ONE WHO CAME HOME WITH
        ME?" she said to him.
(tight) "Who's the one who came home with you?" he said. "The
        one who came home with me, you aren't
him." "Yes indeed, that's me," the little Ahayuuta said.
"That's ME," he said.
"He wasn't LIKE YOU. He was UGLY," she said. (audience
        laughs)
(laughing) So she told him.

                                      •

Again the girl asked him.
"Yes, that's me," he said, for the second time.

"That's me.
This person
who
came home with you, do you really love him?" he said. "Yes,
  certainly:
because of his thoughts, my life was saved.
Last night
there
where I was spending the night
the old lady was about to eat me, and because of his thoughts
I was saved.
I really do love him," she said.
"I'M the one who saved you, I'm the ONE," he told her, for the
  third time
the third.
"No, he wasn't like you, he was
well, he was ugly."
That's what the girl told him, and she REFUSED HIM THE
  WATER, she wouldn't give it to him.
"Do you REALLY love him?" he said. "Yes, certainly
I love him. Because of his thoughts I regained the daylight."
So she told him.
He raised up a little and showed her his costume.
"HERE he is, I only impersonate him.
And we are not just one.
My elder brother is with our grandmother.
Last night
when my grandmother went out to pee
Old Lady Granduncle was there
running up against the rocks of your cave, and because of the noise
our grandmother came in and told us about it.
My elder brother sent me
and I went there.

THIS is the one," he said, and HE PULLED OUT HIS
    COSTUME AND TOSSED IT OVER TO HER.
HE TOSSED IT TO HER and when the girl saw it: "Hiya! so it
    was you
so this is the way you are."
THERE SHE GAVE HIM THE WATER AND HE DRANK IT,
    AND THERE THE LITTLE AHAYUUTA GOT
    MARRIED.
He got married, and when
he'd stayed two nights, after he'd stayed his first two nights
he thought about going out hunting, on the third day he went
    hunting, and on that day he told his
father and his
wife:
"I'm
going out hunting.
Well now
the sun has only gone a short way.
I'll go hunting
over this way."
So
he told his
grandfatherly father.
His wife said, "I'll fix you some provisions." "Aw—
I'm going right now:
the sun is already up.
I'll be back in a short while," he told his wife.
The little Ahayuuta put on his quiver
and started on his way up.
He went on up, and some time later he killed a deer.
He killed a deer, gutted it, and before the sun
went down, he carried the deer home.

He was carrying the deer on his back when he came, and the
   villagers
noticed him.
"That
girl who lives alone with her
old grandfather must've married someone.
He brought home a deer
he brought a deer and went inside," they were saying.
And the little Ahayuuta took his deer inside.
His wife, when she heard a noise, his wife said:
"Perhaps that's you." Her grandfather
had told her this:
"Daughter
granddaughter
I THINK
he's not
one of the people who live at Yellow House, he's not
not one of them.
He must be some
wonder worker, because he saved you out there, and the way he
   speaks:
perhaps he's not a person of the daylight kind.
But
but let's wait awhile
and IF HE'S THAT OTHER KIND OF PERSON he'll surely
   bring
(smiling) SOMEONE OF HIS OWN KIND WITH HIM," HE
   TOLD THE GIRL.
Her father was the first to guess it, he guessed it.
SURE ENOUGH, before
the sun had set
the little Ahayuuta brought a deer, there was a noise.
"Daughter, go out.

You must
take the holy meal and bring their Pollen Way in, you must bring them in."
So he told his daughter. His
daughter then
took some cornmeal and went up.
"So you two have come now." "Yes we've come now," he said.
She brought in their Pollen Way.
The little Ahayuuta came in with his deer.
It was a very large deer with very large antlers.
Yet he was so small: how could he have carried it?
He brought it inside on his back.
When he got down inside:
"My father, how have you been?" "Happy, so you've come, be
    seated," he was told.
His wife
helped take the deer off his back and lay it out with the head toward the
    east.

•

"You must do the same thing you did the first time, you must lay
    an ear of corn alongside his breast, and we shall ask for
    daylight."
So her
father told her.
The poor girl did this
and they sprinkled the deer and asked for daylight.
They ate.
When they had eaten
when they had eaten well:
"Now let's
skin him."
The little Ahayuuta then

•

took out his stone knife and cut it, shikoko

shikoko, he skinned it
he skinned it until he was finished.
Meanwhile
the Bow Priest was notified again.
He called the priests to a meeting
the daylight priests were notified, and they were the ones who
did the BUTCHERING.
When the BUTCHERING was done
they hung the

•

meat on yucca fiber ropes that were
strung across.
Some of it was given to them and they
took it home
and for four days the little Ahayuuta was bringing in the deer this way.
They lived ON this way
until
the little Ahayuuta had been there eight nights
and on a night like this one he told his father:
"TOMORROW, on that day
what I shall do
is enter upon the roads of my grandmother and my elder brother
for I am a person of another kind."
So he told his
grandfather, he told the girl's grandfather.

•

"Very well, on tomorrow's day
what you must do
is enter upon the road of your grandmother.
I had guessed
that you were not a person of the daylight kind.
The daylight people
live around here

and the raw people cannot enter upon their roads
to live in the SAME PLACE with them.
You are THAT OTHER KIND OF PERSON
and it is because of your thoughts
that we now have so many provisions
to live by," he told him.
(gently) "Tomorrow
what I shall do
is enter upon the roads of my grandmother, my elder brother."
So he told his father, who
told the girl, "Daughter." "What is it?" "Get my bundle of feathers."
She got her grandfather's bundle of feathers
and he cut some sticks.

●

He cut eight sticks
and feathered them. When he'd made them, finished them
they passed the night. The night passed
and on the next day
just as the sun came up
and they had eaten
the little Ahayuuta spoke:
"Well, I'm going now.
What I shall do
is enter upon the roads of my grandmother
and my elder brother.
I'll
enter upon their roads," he said. His
wife said, "I'LL GO ALONG WITH YOU," she said. "Indeed?
If you went along it wouldn't turn out well
for I am another kind of person.
The way I
was a husband to you:
really THAT'S what

you should think about, find someone who will provide for you as
    I did:
you must keep that in mind.
Because of my thoughts
you now have
the flesh
of the raw people.
This will be ever present because of my thoughts
as you live."
SO HE TOLD THE GIRL. When he'd told her, the girl asked
    him
FOUR TIMES
and still he refused. *(sadly)* "Well then
well then, go by yourself."
So she said. Then her
father, grandfather
told her: "Daughter
don't think of following him, don't speak of it, for he
is truly
of a different kind," he said.
Then he told them his name:
"I AM THE AHAYUUTA," he told them.
His wife asked him, "WHAT IS THE AHAYUUTA?" she said.
"Well, I am the Ahayuuta
and my other name is UYUYUWI," he said.
And her father spoke: "Daughter, because of him there is a———ll
    the EARTH.
YOU MUSTN'T ASK ANY QUESTIONS. It is good

                            •

that he should return
to his own land," he told her. He took the sticks he'd cut
the bundle of prayer sticks, and
gave it

to his child, the Ahayuuta.

By his word he gave it.

Her grandfather spoke a prayer to the Ahayuuta

while the Ahayuuta stood there and answered. The prayer said that
there would be waters on the earth forever, that ALL OVER
the wide earth
the raw people would enter the house upon the Pollen Way
    forever
that by means of their flesh, their skins, by their
EVER presence we would live: these were the words he spoke,
    while
the little Ahayuuta answered, "Just so, in truth."
WHEN HE HAD FINISHED HIS WORDS
the Ahayuuta stepped forward:
"My father
my child, may you live happily," he said. "By all means may it be
    the same with you, may you be happy."
When this was done THE AHAYUUTA LEFT.
WHEN THE AHAYUUTA LEFT he went toward the place
    where he'd killed the old lady, he went that way.
ON HE WENT until he came to the place where he'd saved the
    girl. There
the Ahayuuta
skinned that
the Ahayuuta skinned Old Lady Granduncle
then he sewed her skin up like a sack with yucca. He got some
    yucca fiber and sewed until it was done and
when it was sewn he made it STAND UP.
When he'd made it stand up: "Ah, this should work." And there
he put it on his back. When he put it on his back
he climbed up Corn Mountain, up past
the Place Where Rainbows Are Kept, with this thing on his back.
    When he reached the top he made this

old lady stand up, he tested it there

he tested it

and it was working. When it was working

HE STARTED OFF, and when he'd gone some distance the

    Ahayuuta began to call out *(as if from a distance, very high):*

"Grandmaaaaaaaaaaaaaaaaaaaaaaa   help   some   cha

                            come   me,   one is   sing

    meeeeeeeeeeeeeeeeeeeeeee_e."

His grandmother was making porridge.

AFTER A MOMENT HE CALLED AGAIN and his

    grandmother heard him.

                       •

When she looked outside he called again:

"Grandma   help   some   cha   meeeeeeeeeeeee

       come   me,   one is   sing   e_e,"

he said.

"Atiikya! grandson, you big fool," she said.

Then she

TOOK HER STIRRING STICKS, and she painted the left side of

    her face with ashes and the other side with soot

and then his grandmother ran outside. He was getting closer

and he'd rigged that

dead old lady

so it LOOKED LIKE she was RUNNING after him.

He was fooling his grandmother.

His grandmother came down and *(rasping)* killed her, killed her.

"Come on, DON'T KILL THE POOR THING, SHE'S BEEN

    DEAD A LONG TIME," he said. "Atiikya! grandson, you

    big fool."

SO SHE SAID, AND THEY WENT ON UP.

They went on up to the house and passed the night. They passed

    the night

o——n they went by, four of them, a third, and on the fourth,
    on that night
their grandmother spoke to them:
(seriously) "If we continue to live together here, it won't turn out
    well for US.
Tomorrow, on that day, we
shall go
to the separate places which will be our shrines.
You, the ELDER BROTHER
will go to Hanging Wool.
You, the younger brother, will go to Twin
Mountains
and I WILL GO over there to the Middle Place
to the north side of it.
There, at the solstice, the Yellow One plants his feathers."
So it was that their grandmother told them where they would live
    forever.
"So it will be that whenever someone from the Middle Place wants
    to bear a child
I will not be far away and she can enter upon my road
there.
That will be my shrine," she told
her two grandsons.
They PASSED THE NIGHT
and on the following day
just as
the sun came up
they went to their separate shrines. This was lived long ago. That's
    a——ll the word was short.

NOTES

Narrated by Walter Sanchez on January 22, 1965, with Andrew Peynetsa and myself present. The performance took an hour and five minutes. Walter had learned this story just a few nights before, having heard it told by an old man who had a large cornfield near Yellow House.

Yellow House: Heshota Lhupts'inna, a village that was composed of two- and three-story terraced masonry house blocks grouped around a pair of plazas, located on a knoll beside the Pescado River. It was occupied in the thirteenth and fourteenth centuries.

The making of the snow boots: while we were working on the translation of this passage, Joseph Peynetsa remarked, "Walter always has to go into every little detail, like he was actually there."

Stars-in-a-Row: Orion's belt, which sets in the west well after midnight in the middle of winter.

Fire drill: a pointed stick rotated rapidly between the hands, held vertically while the pointed end is inserted in a conical socket on a small plank. The socket is near enough to the edge of the plank's upper surface to have a break in its wall; thus the socket is open not only from the top but from the side. The sparks, actually red-hot specks of wood, fall from the side of the plank while the drill is rotated.

"Come on, speak": with these words, Walter was trying to get Andrew to play the role of the girl's grandfather by saying an appropriate prayer. Walter considered Andrew to be more skilled at praying than himself, and he might have picked up some new lines if Andrew had consented. For his part, Andrew, as a member of a medicine society, felt it would be improper for him to compose a prayer for an imaginary occasion in a story.

Raw people: all the living beings who do not depend on cooked food, including, in this story, the rabbits, the Sun Father, Old Lady Granduncle, the Ahayuuta twins, and the deer. Human beings, on the other hand, are cooked or daylight people; their life is given to them by the Sun Father and Moon Mother.

Prayer meal or holy meal: a mixture of cornmeal with crushed turquoise, coral, and shell. The waters of the raw people consist of all forms of precipitation and of their own bodily fluids; they bring fecundity. Their seeds are their powers of fecundity, and their Pollen Ways are the courses of their lives, marked out by pollen which is again their fecundity.

The rabbit hunt: while we were working on this passage Joseph remarked, "He's telling it like he really lived it."

Old Lady Granduncle: both she and her husband (who does not appear in the present story) are the subject of masked impersonations whose purpose is to frighten children into better behavior. Both are armed with bloody knives, and both have baskets on their backs for carrying their victims away. Either one goes by the name Aatoshle, which is the plural of toshle, an archaic kinship term probably meaning "maternal grandmother's brother."

Ahayuuta twins: the gods of war, gambling games, and sports. They are the sons of the Sun Father (see "When Newness Was Made," Part I), and their grandmother is the patron of childbirth. When Uyuyuwi, the younger brother, speaks to the girl with the hoarseness of an adolescent male, he means to be flirtatious. In the homely state in which he normally appears, he is dirty and has messy hair full of lice.

Bow Priest: a warrior and town crier. The daylight priests, who are forbidden to kill anything, spend much of their time on religious retreats, praying for rain.

Hanging Wool, where the elder brother Ahayuuta went, is about three miles southeast of Zuni, while Twin Mountains, the destination of the younger brother, is about five miles northwest. The shrine of their grandmother used to be just outside Zuni (or the Middle Place) to the north, but in recent decades the town has expanded all around and beyond it. The Yellow One who "plants his feathers" (prayer sticks) at this shrine is the Salimopiya of the north, one of six warrior kachinas.

THE WOMEN
AND THE MAN

NOW we take it up.
Now the road begins LO——NG AGO.
THERE WERE ^{VIL}LAGERS AT THE ^{MID}DLE PLACE

       •

at KYAKIIMA
the K'UUCHININA PEOPLE had their home
and
at SHUUN HILL
the PAYATAMU
had their home.
At Shuun Hill the eldest of the Payatamu brothers
went out every day
to bring out the Sun.
He started out from Shuun Hill
went on to Kyakiima, and then

       •

at Mats'aakya
at the Rock
of the Sun
he brought his father out, that's the way
they were living, and he went every day
and the K'UUCHININA PEOPLE:

those women were the only people living there
at Kyakiima.
They had been killing wood gatherers.
They were making basket plaques
living this way
when the eldest of the K'uuchinina sisters spoke:
"Tomorrow morning
I'll go out and wait for the one who always comes by here."
So she told her younger sister
told all her younger sisters.
"It's up to you," they told her.

•

And at Shuun Hill, Payatamu started on his way. Payatamu started
    on his way
to bring out his Sun Father, and as he went along
there at Kyakiima
where a rock stood
the telele of his bells could be heard, well, she could hear him
    coming.
When she heard him, she made a bundle with her white blanket
putting in her SPEARHEAD
putting in her abalone shell.

•

She put the bundle on her back
and went down to wait for the young man.
She waited near the big rock at Kyakiima
where the young man always came past.
She waited there, and a short time later
the young man came.
When he came, "Where are you going?" she asked him. "I'm going to
    bring out my Sun Father."

•

(high and tight) "He's going to come out ANYWAY.

Why don't we go to my field?" she told him.
"Well, I won't go.
I didn't come just to go anywhere, but to bring out my Sun
    Father."
So he said. "Indeed.

•

But he's going to come up ANYWAY
just the way he's BEEN coming up," she said. "No, it's because of
    me that he comes up."
So he told her, and they kept on arguing this way until
after a time, the young man said:
"Well then
if that's the way you feel
I won't go."
So the young man said, the girl got the better of him.

•

"We'll go over there where our field is,"
she said, then she took the young man to the field, and the SUN
    HAD NOW COME UP, HE HAD COME UP
and was high now, while the woman took the young man to her fields, there at
Hanging Mealbag, where they had their fields.

•

That's where he was led, the girl
led the young man there.
They had their cornfield there, their cornfield.
They had a shelter there.
The Sun went HIGHER AND HIGHER
until it was about noon. It was about noon
when they came to the shelter, and the girl spoke: "NOW
THIS DAY
we'll play hide-and-seek.
Whoever is found
must be KILLED," the girl told the young man. "Indeed."

"Yes, so you go ahead," she said. "Indeed?
Why should I go first?
You're the one who wanted this, you should go first.
You should be first:
since you're the one who wanted this, I won't go," the young man
said.
"Very well indeed."

•

The girl then
entered her field. Entering her field
she came to the middle and then passed one cornstalk, she went
past the cornstalks:
a second, a third, and when she had passed a fourth one
she fastened herself to a cornstalk and became
AN EAR OF CORN.
When she had fastened herself on, "NOW," she said.

•

The young man
entered the field
and went on, went on until
he came near the end of her footprints.
He passed a cornstalk, the first cornstalk, then went on past the
fourth cornstalk.
When he got there, the footprints ended.
There were no more footprints.
He went ALL OVER the field and couldn't find her.
He came back and said, "Oh no
SHOW YOURSELF, for I can't find you." "Aa— pity on you
you haven't been very smart, here I am, FASTENED ON," she
said.
She came out of the EAR OF CORN.
The girl came out.

•

When they got back to the shelter she said, "Now it's your turn, so
    GO," she said.
(weakly) "Well, I'll
try."
So the young man said.

•

The young man entered the field
and did what the girl had done, going past the CORNSTALKS, on
    past the FOURTH cornstalk
but he didn't turn into anything.

•

He stood facing south
and it was already noon, his father was right at the middle.
"Tísshomahhá! my son, surely you'll
you'll be KILLED now.
So he said, and THE YOUNG MAN STEPPED FORWARD,
    TOOK OUT HIS CORNMEAL, and sprinkled it
toward his father. The cornmeal made a road and he followed it
    up. When he got there to his father, he said, "My father, how
have you been?" "Happy, my CHILD.
Tísshomahhá!

•

There will be a lot of TROUBLE now, she will SURELY find you
    and KILL you, just as she SAID.
Even so, sit behind my back," he told his son.
Payatamu
now sat with the Sun, sat behind his back.
"NOW."
Then the girl came out of the shelter. She followed the young man's footprints
    where he had passed among the cornstalks, she went on
until she came to where he had stood.
(nasal) "Haa—, so you're trying to find safety."
She unwrapped her abalone shell. When she unwrapped her abalone shell

she took milk from her own breast

from her own breast she took milk

and filled the shell with it.

The Sun

was reflected in it. The Sun was reflected in it

and she saw Payatamu's macaw headdress sticking out from behind
   the Sun.

(almost laughing) "Haa—, even though you tried to find a safe place.

Hurry on down, for I've found you," she told him.

He came out.

"Well

that's all.

Because of this we'll be harming a———ll the villages: I must go in
   AT ONCE

for I've been coming up because of you.

SHE'S GOING TO KILL YOU, surely she's not just talking,
   she'll kill you," the Sun told his son.

"Now you must go back down

and I will go right in," he told his son.

"I'm going now, and may you pass a happy evening." "May it be the same with
   you," he said.

THE YOUNG MAN CAME DOWN.

•

He came down

and these

were the people who'd been killing

the wood gatherers

until now:

that's what they'd been doing.

•

THE YOUNG MAN CAME ON DOWN until

he came to where the girl was standing.

• *132* •

She led him along until they came to the shelter.
She unfolded her white blanket
and there was a large spearhead inside. It was WRAPPED.
She unwrapped it and got hold of his forehead.
"Now, look at your Sun Father for the last time," she said.

•

She made the young man look up and she
cut through his throat.
Tenén! his body fell dead.
She held his head while the blood ran, ts'ok'ok'oo— until all the
     blood had drained out
then she set it down
and now she went looking for a place to BURY him.
She went through her field
until she came to its end, where water had run through and left a
     deposit of juniper leaves.
There she dug a hole. When the girl had dug a hole
she carried the young man's body there and buried him.

•

She returned to her shelter, and when she picked up his head the blood
     wasn't dripping.
She wrapped it in her white blanket and, putting it on her back
the girl went home.
She carried the head, Payatamu's head
going on until
she reached the house where she lived with her younger sisters.

•

"SO YOU'VE COME NOW," they said. "Yes, I've come now.
    JUST AS I INTENDED
I've killed him.
Because of him
we'll be able to continue working.
Each morning he'll be of great value to us," the girl said.

•

They got together and started working on their basket plaques, and they
    put the young man's head in a water jar.

•

During the day his headdress would quiver, o——n until, in the
    evening
it would become still:
this was a SIGN for them.
Then they slept through the night.

•

The elder brother Payatamu hadn't come home, and FOUR
    DAYS HAD PASSED.
When four days had passed

•

the Payatamu
men said
"Our elder brother hasn't come home and the days have gone by.
Our Sun Father hasn't come up.
What should we do about this?"

•

So they said.
Their society chief spoke: "Well now
let's try something, even though it might not HELP:

•

we'll ask our grandfathers
to come here.
Perhaps
one of them might find him
for us."
So their society chief said.
"Indeed."
"Which one should it be?" he said.

"Well now, our grandfather
who lives in the north, the mountain lion:
let's summon him."

•

Their society chief
summoned the mountain lion.
There in the north he arose, the mountain lion.

•

Coming on and o———n, he arrived at Shuun Hill.
He entered:
"My fathers, my children
how have you been passing the days?" "Happily, our grandfather,
    so you've come now."
"Yes." "Now sit down," they said, and they
set out their turquoise seat for him and he sat down.

•

The society chief sat down facing him.
The mountain lion now questioned them: "NOW, my
    CHILDREN
for what reason have you summoned ME?
You would not summon me for no reason.
Perhaps it is because of a WORD of some importance that you
    have summoned me.
You must make this known to me
so that I may think about it as I pass the days," the mountain lion
    said.
"YES, in TRUTH

•

our elder brother
who always went to bring out his Sun Father, has been gone these
    four days
and hasn't come back.
We don't see our Sun Father anymore.

That's why we summoned YOU.
You must look for him for us," so
they told the mountain lion. "Indeed.
Very well INDEED.
I will TRY
but it's different at NIGHT:
we're used to the day," the mountain lion said.
"So that's why you summoned me." "Yes, that's why we
    summoned you."
"Very well indeed, I'll GO.
I will try," the mountain lion said, and he left.
When he left the mountain lion went around, went around, went around
and didn't DISCOVER him. He didn't FIND him. There wasn't
    even
a SCENT of him, he couldn't find out ANYTHING.

·

A long time passed, and when the mountain lion failed he came back.
When he came back
he entered:
"My fathers, my children, how
have you been?"
"Happy, our grandfather.
Sit down," they told him. He sat down.
They questioned him.
He hadn't found him.
There was no way to find him.
"During the day
we know more," he said. "Indeed. Very well indeed, you must go
    there
and lie down behind the altar.
When our elder brother has been found
then you may go home and rest," so
they told the mountain lion.

He lay down behind the altar, the mountain lion.
And
the society chief said, "WELL NOW
who should be summoned next?" he said.

                                •

"Well, perhaps his younger brother
the bear."

                                •

"NOW, the one whose direction is there
toward the evening, the bear:
enter upon our roads," so
the society chief said.
After awhile he came, the bear.
The bear came and entered.
"My fathers, my children, how have you been passing the days?"
    "Happily, our child
our grandfather, so you've come." "Yes, I've come."
"Sit down," they said.
A seat was set out and he sat down.
The society chief got up and sat down facing him.
Then the bear questioned them: "NOW
for what reason have you
summoned ME?
Perhaps it is because of a WORD of some importance that you
    have summoned ME.
You would not summon me for no reason," the bear said. "YES, in
    TRUTH
our elder brother
who always went to bring out his Sun Father, has been gone these
    four days and hasn't come back.
You must look for him for us.
That's why we summoned you," so
the society chief told the bear. "Indeed.

Very well INDEED.
I will TRY.
During the DAY it's different, we know MORE
but at night
we don't know," he said.

                                    •

"VERY WELL, I'M GOING," he said, and the bear got up, the
      bear left and went around.
He went all around, but he couldn't find him.

                                    •

After a long time passed the bear came back and they questioned
      him, and he didn't know.

                                    •

"Then you must go behind the altar
where you will find your elder brother," they told him. There
      behind the altar
was the mountain lion, lying down.

                                    •

The bear lay down there. "Now then
think about it: who
should be summoned next?"

                                    •

"OVER THERE
in the coral's direction
the badger
is the one who is wise," they said, and the badger was summoned.
And the badger came.
The badger came

                                    •

and entered: "My fathers, my children, how have you been passing
      the days?" "Happily, our grandfather, so you've come." "Yes,"
      he said.
"Sit down," they told him.

He sat down.

Again the society chief sat down facing him.

Then the badger questioned them: "NOW

my CHILDREN

for what reason have you summoned ME?

Perhaps it is because of a WORD of some importance that you
    have summoned me.

You must make this known to me, so that I may think about it

as I pass the days," so

the badger said.

"YES, in TRUTH

our elder brother, who always goes to bring out his Sun Father

has been gone these four days.

Our elder brother hasn't come back.

You must look for him for us, that's why we summoned you," they
    told him. "Indeed.

Well, I will TRY.

But at night one doesn't know, it's during the day that we are
    wise," the badger said.

"Well, I'm

going, I will try," he said.

"I'm going, may you

have a good night." He left.

                    •

He went around, went around, but he couldn't find him.

He came back, and again they questioned him. "I didn't find him."

"Very well, then you must go lie down behind the altar."

And the badger went around behind the altar

where his two elder brothers were lying

and he lay down there.

Again they were THINKING.

They were thinking. "Well now

it should be the one with WINGS," they said.

The eagle was summoned.

The eagle was summoned: "Now, the one whose direction is the zenith

the one who is our father, the eagle

enter upon our roads."

The eagle CAME DOWN. He came down until

he arrived there at Shuun Hill.

He entered the Payatamu house.

LHU^{KW'EE}E_E_{ENN} he entered.

He sat down on the stone seat.

"My fathers, my children, how have you been passing the days?"

"Happily, our child, so you've come." "Yes."

The society chief got up and sat facing him, and

he questioned them: "NOW

my fathers, my CHILDREN

for what reason have you summoned ME?

Perhaps it is because of a WORD of some importance that you
    have summoned me.

You must make this known to me

so that I may think about it as I pass the days," so

the eagle said. "YES, in TRUTH

our elder brother

who always went to bring out the Sun, his Sun Father, has been
    gone four days and hasn't come back.

You must go look for him for us, that's why we summoned you."
    "Indeed.

Well, I will TRY.

But it's different at NIGHT:

in the day we know more," the eagle said.

The eagle left.

And the eagle went around, went around looking for him, but he
    couldn't, couldn't find him.

Again he came.

The eagle was told, "Well
you must go now
if he can't be found."
The eagle then left.
Again they thought about it.
The VULTURE was summoned.
The vulture was summoned: that one
is good at SMELLING ROTTEN THINGS, that's why he was
     summoned.
He was the next to come, and he questioned them and he was told the
     same thing as before:
that he couldn't be found.
The vulture said, "Well, I will try. During the day we are wise
but at night we don't know," he said.
The vulture went out and went around circling, around and arou——nd
but he couldn't find him, and a long time passed.

•

Again

•

he came. When he came
he entered, tired.
They questioned him. "He can't be found."
"Very well indeed, you must go now.
But these, our fathers, our
grandfathers, must wait until our elder brother has been found,
     then they may go home and rest."
The vulture went out and went his way.

•

Again they were THINKING.

•

They were thinking, and
they thought of

the coyote

the one who is the true coyote.

He was the one who was summoned, and he came. He entered and greeted them,
and he sat down.

Then

he questioned them

and was told that their elder brother hadn't returned, and that they
wanted him back

and so they had summoned him. "I will try.

At night

it's hard at night, and in the day also, but I'll try," said the coyote.
He left

and went around looking. He went looking without finding him.

•

Again he came.

"Wait now

you must lie down by the door," he was told. THE COYOTE
LAY DOWN THERE BY THE DOOR, not at the altar.

That other coyote

the JUNIPER coyote

was summoned next.

He came, and

he was jittery.

He entered

and greeted them.

He sat down, but he couldn't keep still.

He questioned them. "Our elder brother, who went to bring out our
Sun Father, hasn't come back, and these four days have
passed.

You must look for him for us, that's why we summoned you,"
they said. "Indeed.

Well, I will try.

During the day we are wise, but at night we don't know," he said.
   He went out and

                              •

IT WAS NO USE, but he went around, went around anyway.
Again he came.
Again, "He can't be found."
Again, this one left.
Or rather, he lay down behind the door.
Again they were thinking.
"Well now, someone with wings.
Why not the crow?"
THE CROW WAS SUMMONED, the crow came, the crow came
   and sat down.

                              •

He questioned them, the crow:
"For what reason have you summoned ME? Perhaps it is because
   of a WORD of some importance that you have summoned
   me,"
the crow said. "Yes, in truth, our elder brother, who
went to bring out our Sun Father
has been gone these four days, and you must look for him for us,
   that's why we summoned you," they told the crow. "Indeed.
I will TRY.
It's different at NIGHT:
during the day we know more," the crow said.
"Well, I'll try," he said, and the crow left.

                              •

He went around, went around, but he couldn't find him.
Again he came.
He was questioned. "I don't know."

                              •

"Very well, you must go and rest," they told him.
The crow left.

Again they were THINKING, again

•

they were thinking. "WELL NOW, there is our father who lives at
    the nadir, the SHREW."
So their society chief said. The shrew was summoned.

•

The shrew came.
He came
and entered:
"My fathers, my
children, how have you been passing the days?" "Happily
our grandfather, so you've come." "Yes." "Sit down," he was told,
    and he sat down.
The society chief again sat down facing him.
Then
the shrew questioned them: "NOW
my CHILDREN
for what reason have you summoned ME?
Perhaps it is because of a WORD of some importance that you
    have summoned me.
You would not summon me for no reason," so
the shrew said. "YES, in TRUTH
our elder brother
who went to bring out our Sun Father, has been gone four days
    and HASN'T COME BACK.
You must look for him for us
that's why we summoned you" he said.
"Indeed.
Very well indeed
I will TRY.
These, my elder brothers, have FAILED, so how could I
    SUCCEED?
The way I get around is POOR

it's PITIFUL.
Even so, I will try," the shrew told them.

            •

THE SHREW LEFT.
When he LEFT

                        •

HE FOLLOWED THE SAME ROUTE PAYATAMU HAD
    TAKEN, the shrew went on, went o———n until
he came near the K'uuchinina People
near their house, where the rock
was standing.
At the place where they had talked there were still footprints.
There were the footprints:
"Well, this is where you came."
Looking around, he saw their sparks flying out, the sparks from
    the K'uuchinina house.
The shrew went up this way. Going up
he climbed the ladder to their doorway

                        •

and LOOKED INSIDE:
they were all around their fire
around their fire, working on their basket plaques.
PAYATAMU'S HEAD WAS INSIDE A WATER JAR, sitting
    there.
"Haa—, HERE he is.
Why, this
didn't happen very far away
and yet my elder brothers couldn't find him,"
the shrew said, and AS SOON AS HE HAD SEEN THE HEAD
he went down, GOING ON until he came to where Payatamu
    had talked with the girl.

HE FOLLOWED THEIR TRACKS, GOING ON AND ON
    AND O——N until he arrived at the CORNFIELD, the
    shrew arrived there.
When he arrived at their cornfield
at the place where Payatamu's head had been cut off
flowers were blooming there, tenatsali flowers.

                                •

"Haa—, so this is where
he was killed,"
he said, and he went on until he came to the place where he was
    buried:
there were a lot of flowers.
"Haa—, he's lying here, not far away, but they couldn't find him.
So THIS is the place."

                                •

He went straight back
went back

                                •

and got there after a long time.
He entered: "My fathers, my children, how have you been?"
    "Happy, our
grandfather, our child, so you've come now." "Yes."
"Sit down," he was told, and he sat down.
The society chief sat down facing him.
"NOW
our GRANDFATHER
our CHILD
you've gone out to look for our elder brother.
Has he been FOUND NOW?" the society chief said.
"He has been FOUND.
He lies not far away, yet my elder brothers here couldn't FIND
    HIM.
Even so, he has been found.

However
how are we going to get his head?"
So said the shrew.

•

"Indeed.
Yes indeed."

•

"WELL NOW, THERE IS OUR GRANDFATHER:
let's summon the HAWK, who is very FAST. Perhaps if we had
    him here we could get it."
So said the shrew. The hawk was summoned.
The hawk came, he came in
    LHUUU$_U$$_{USU}$
    and lit on a stick on the wall.
He lit there
then came down to the seat and sat on it.
"My fathers, my children, how have you been passing the days?"
    "Happily, our child, so you've come now."
"Yes."

•

The society chief went over
where the hawk was sitting.
The hawk questioned him: "NOW, for what reason have you
    summoned ME?
You would not summon me for no reason.
Perhaps it is because of a WORD of some importance that you
    have summoned me," the hawk said.
"YES, in TRUTH
our elder brother
who always went to bring out our Sun Father
has been gone these four days.

•

We have summoned

our grandfathers here, but they couldn't find him.
The last of our grandfathers to be summoned, the shrew
has just found him, but there is no way to get his head, no one
    knows how to do this.
He has said that you are very FAST and should be summoned, so
    we have summoned you."
"Very well indeed, it shall be done," he said.

                              •

Again
the shrew spoke: "If he's alone it won't work.

                              •

YOUR GRANDFATHER, THE OWL, should be summoned,"
    he said
the shrew said.
When the shrew
had told them, THE SOCIETY CHIEF SUMMONED THE OWL.
The owl was summoned and after a time he entered, the owl entered.
"My fathers, my children, how have you been passing the days?"
    "Happily, our child, so you've come now." "Yes."

                              •

He sat down, sat down.
As SOON as he sat DOWN he fell ASLEEP.
He was sleeping
when the society chief sat down facing him.
The owl questioned them:

                              •

(almost yawning) "NOW, my CHILDREN, for what reason have
    you summoned me?

                              •

                              •

                              •

Perhaps it is because of a WORD of some importance that you
　　have summoned me, for you would not summon me for no
　　reason," he said.
"YES, in TRUTH, our elder brother, who went to bring out our
　　Sun Father
has been gone these four days:
that's why we have summoned your elder brothers. He has been
　　found now
but there is no way to get his head, and if you were included in this
　　your medicine might help:
that's what the shrew said, and that's why we summoned you."
　　"Indeed.
VERY WELL INDEED, it shall be DONE."
"Now, let's GET READY."
　　　　　　　　　　　•

The four Payatamu men then
　　　　　　　　　　　•

took PLAIN blankets
two of them.
He led them out, the SHREW.
There were the HAWK and
the OWL
and the Payatamu men.
The shrew led them, they went o———n until
they came to where Payatamu had talked to the woman.
　　　　　　　　　•

"This is where they talked, this is where
the two of them talked.
　　　　　　　　　•

Up ahead:
we must go up there, where the K'uuchinina People have their
　　home," he said.
That thing

that OWL ROOT

was given to the shrew
and when the root was given to the shrew, the shrew
went up with the root
and spit the root
on the women.
The women became sleepy, they became sleepy now.
They said, *(high and breathy)* "Ah'ana, I'm so sleepy."
"Ah'ana, I'm so sleepy."
"Well, let's go to bed now.
It must be the end of the day now, he's become still," they said.
They put their head
which was in a water jar
on the wall, they put it on a shelf.
The shrew saw them.
They made their BEDS, the girls made their beds and went to
   SLEEP.
The shrew went in, he went in
where their
jar with the head in it was. There were flowers around the head and
   the shrew pulled the flowers out, he pulled all of them out.
He took these outside and gave them to the Payatamu men, saying, "You must
   take all of these, so that his
his flesh will be whole," he said.

•

He spoke to the hawk: "Now
you must go in," he said. "Very well indeed."
The hawk went in

   lhuuu_uukwa

   he went in.
He took it out, he took the head out quickly.

(high) "Hiyáhha! who has stolen our head?" they said
but he had already taken it out.
The Payatamu men
took their
elder brother's head
wrapped it in a blanket
and went down, they went on down
to the place where he had been killed, with the shrew in the lead.
He led them on
until they came to the CORNFIELD, came to the cornfield.

                            •

WHEN THEY GOT THERE
where he had been
killed, lots of flowers were growing.
Lots of flowers were blooming.
"NOW, you must pick all these flowers. When you have picked all
        the flowers, all of them
you
will put them in a bundle."
When they came to where he lay, there were EVEN MORE
        flowers, SO many.
They picked all the flowers until they were all in a bundle, in the
        blanket.
When they had bundled all the flowers
they dug up their elder brother, they dug him up.
They put him on the blanket.

                            •

They carried their elder brother
going o————n until they got back to their house.
When they got to their house
they laid him on a blanket
a plain one.
They laid their elder brother's body down, laid his head down.

THEY PUT THE FLOWERS ON TOP OF HIM, put the
    flowers on top and COVERED HIM WITH ANOTHER
    BLANKET.
The PAYATAMU MEN
sat down at their altar.
They sang their string of songs.
They drummed, tesese.
O———n they sang until the first one was finished.
When the second song was finished
he stirred a little.
He stirred
and when the third song was finished he moved a lot.
WHEN THE FOURTH SONG WAS FINISHED
the Payatamu man ROSE UP.

                                •

"I'm not even TIRED," so he said.
"I'm not even TIRED," he said.
THEIR ELDER BROTHER HAD COME ALIVE, but instead of
    a headdress at the back he had a hair knot on his forehead, he
    was NEPAYATAMU.
He was saying the opposite of what he MEANT.

                                •

"I'm not even tired," he said. "Hanaahhhha! our elder brother,
    you've come back to life, you are alive
but you are not the same person you were before.
But at least we can SEE YOU."
So they said, and
it was now getting LIGHT, it was getting YELLOW, it was getting
    to be MORNING.
Because he had been awakened, the day was COMING.

                                •

The Nepayatamu man
spoke: "NOW

my younger BROTHERS

•

well
I've come alive, but I'm not the same person.

•

WHAT SHALL WE DO?" he said to his younger brothers.
It was getting light
aaaaaaAAAAAAH THE SUN CAME UP.
When the Sun had come up
Nepayatamu said, "NOW, my younger BROTHERS:
they cannot do WRONG and GET AWAY WITH IT.
We must have REVENGE," so Nepayatamu SAID.
When he had spoken, he took out his flute.
Taking his flute
he blew:
such a big swallowtail butterfly
came out. When it came out it sat down.
So pretty.

•

Then Payatamu
sucked on his flute and the swallowtail went back in.

•

"NOW, we will GO
for they cannot do wrong and GET AWAY WITH IT.
NOW, our GRANDFATHERS

•

RISE UP," he said.
The BEASTS
rose up, the mountain lion

•

the bear
the badger
the shrew

the two coyotes lying by the door, all of them came out.

•

Payatamu took them
along with him
he took them o———n until
they arrived at Kyakiima, at the rock, and when they arrived there he
    took out his flute
and blew.
The swallowtail came out.
"NOW
this day
you must go where the K'uuchinina People have their home.
When they try to CATCH YOU
you will sprinkle them with your wing powder
and then they can do whatever they wish.
This is what they asked for:
they cannot do wrong and get away with it.
This day we will have revenge," so
Nepayatamu told the swallowtail. THE SWALLOWTAIL FLEW
    THERE
going up to where the women had their home, to Kyakiima.
It went there and sat on the ladder. The sunlight was coming in
and they saw its shadow: the swallowtail.
Now it came in, came in from perch to perch.
It came down the ladder, so close.
"Wait, don't touch it, we'll look at it
and use its pattern on our basket plaques," they said.

•

The SWALLOWTAIL
flew down to the KILLER HERSELF
and landed on a twig sticking out of the basket plaque she was
    making.
(high and tight) "Wait, don't touch it, I'll catch it.

When I catch it I'll kill it and we'll use its pattern, use its pattern
     on our basket plaques," she said.
And the swallowtail landed on a twig that was sticking out.
They were all around it.
It landed on the killer's own stick, on their elder sister's stick.
She tried to catch it.
It sprinkled them all with its wing powder.

                                        •

THEY WENT CRAZY.
The swallowtail
went up the ladder from perch to perch and they kept after it until
     they were all on the roof.
They left their basket plaques behind.
They kept after it, trying to catch it, hit it, it led them along toward
Nepayatamu, who was there at their field, up in the top of a
     cottonwood tree: Nepayatamu.
He was up there with his flute while they were led along by the swallowtail, and
they tried to catch it by throwing their shawls
and IT LED THEM ALONG UNTIL
they came to the middle of the field, and by now they didn't have any
     clothes on.
Just NAKED.
They kept after it and it led them ON
to where the cottonwood tree stood, and they all lay down in the shade
     to rest.
(high and tight) "Ahwa, I'm so tired."
"Me too, so tired."

                                        •

Nepayatamu
spit on them with the owl's root.
The women went to sleep.

                                        •

Now he summoned his grandfathers, "NOW, this day,
    grandfathers, enter upon my road," and
they were hiding someplace, the beasts were.

·

They came out
and had pleasure with the flesh of the women, another wrong was done, and
this went on
o———n until, when they had all gone, the women awoke.
They were NAKED.
They looked up in the cottonwood tree and saw Nepayatamu

·

sitting there with his legs dangling down.
And when
the swallowtail had come back he had sucked on his flute
and the swallowtail had gone back in.
They found him sitting up there.
"NOW GIVE US SOMETHING IN RETURN," they said. "Yes,
    I'll give you something in return," he said.

·

From the cottonwood
he took leaves.
Wetting these
he threw them down
and they became blankets.
They dressed themselves with these.
He gave each one of them something in return.

·

Nepayatamu came down, he came down: "NOW
this day
I will take you all to my house, to my own house," he said.
"Very well."
Payatamu, Nepayatamu took the lead
while all the beasts dispersed to their shrines.

•

He led the women on until they arrived there at Shuun Hill, at his
    house.
His kinswomen
got after the K'uuchinina People: "Haa— so these are the fools who
    killed our elder brother.
They're just pitiful things," they told them, they got after them.
He brought them in
Nepayatamu
brought the women in.
There were eight of them.

•

They were led in

•

and Nepayatamu's kinswomen
Payatamu's kinswomen
were shelling corn.
They were shelling corn, shelling corn
and they put the kernels on the grinding stone and made the other women
    do the grinding.
Those women
stooped over
and they only rubbed the corn, talalala, they couldn't grind it, couldn't grind it.
The Payatamu women got angry and said, "You're such big
    women
yet you can't grind it, even though
the kernels aren't hard," but they had done something to the
    kernels so that
they were hard to grind.
They got after them, moved them aside, and did the grinding
    themselves.

•

And NEPAYATAMU

got some buckskin and made moccasins for them, o——n until,
    when four days had PASSED
he had finished eight pairs of moccasins for them.
On the ^{eve} of the ^{FIFTH} day
on the fourth night
porridge was made for them
and meal cakes.

•

That night they were all WASHED, their hair was washed, their
    bodies were washed.
They were clothed
the next morning
and had their meal, they were given PLENTY to eat, PLENTY to
    drink.
Nepayatamu said, "NOW, this day
I will take you to the place where our Sun Father comes out:
because you cannot do wrong and get away with it," Nepayatamu
    told the women.

•

To his fathers, his younger brothers, he said, "NOW, my younger
    BROTHERS
my KINSWOMEN
you must disappear from this PLACE
and when the time comes at the Middle Place
when it comes at the Middle Place

•

you will be offered prayer sticks here.
And when the Clown Society becomes known at the Middle Place
it will be because of me that the Clown Society comes to be, that's
    why I
have become the way I am.
THIS DAY I will take these women to the place where the Sun
    comes out," he told them.

"VERY WELL." "Yes, that's the way it will be.
And from this place you
must disappear," their elder brother told them.
He took the K'uuchinina women out and led them toward the
    place where the Sun comes out
o——n they went

                                    •

and when they had passed Striped House
their
elder sister, the killer, got tired.
She was tired and they tried to help her
but it was no use.
It was no use, she was so tired that she kept falling down, falling
    down, she was thirsty.
"So.
Well, if IT'S NO USE, that's the way it will have to be."
And when he had spoken he sucked on his flute:
the girl went inside.
HE BLEW, and WHITE MOTHS, a whole flock of them, came
    out.

                                    •

"NOW, this is the life you will live, so that when spring is near
    you will be a sign of its coming,"
he told the girl.
She became MOTHS.

                                    •

HE TOOK THE OTHERS ALONG AND THEY GOT TIRED
    (weakly) and he kept turning them into moths and butterflies,
    on he went
o——n until their youngest sister was the only one left.
That one

                                    •

he took along BY FORCE, by force, she was very tired but he
    kept on
and it was no use, she kept falling down and he would help her up.
(return to normal voice) "YOU CAN'T MAKE IT?" "No, I can't
    make it, it's no use." "Indeed.
Well, you asked for it
for you were all very foolish."
He sucked on his flute
and the girl went inside the flute.
He blew on it
and out came a whole swarm of moths.
"NOW
this is the life you will live: whenever
winter is near
you will be a sign
that winter is coming."
So NEPAYATAMU told her.
THEN HE WAS ALONE
and he went on toward the place where the Sun Father comes out.
HE WENT ON THIS WAY until
he came to the ocean, Nepayatamu came there.
Out in the midst of the waters his father came out, the Sun.
The young man spoke:

•

"My father, my CHILD, how have you been passing the days?"
    "Happily, my child, so you've come. Now come on
OUT HERE."

•

So he told Nepayatamu, who walked into the water, going on to
    the place where
his father
was coming out.
"NOW, come to my left side and SIT DOWN.

Have you gotten what you WANTED, have you had revenge?"
"Yes, I have had my REVENGE.
I wanted to bring them here, but they weren't strong enough."
"Indeed, and THAT'S the way it SHOULD HAVE BEEN.
Now, come to me and SIT DOWN.
We shall go and look at the WORLD," and he sat down, sat down
  at his left.
The Sun went on until, around noon
they came here to ZUNI
to the Middle Place.
When they came, there was sprinkling of meal
there was saying of prayers, and some people were doing it the
  right way, while Payatamu
was taken along, at noon. When it was noon
his Sun Father said, "NOW
my father, my child
IT IS GOOD that you have come back to life this way.
WHENEVER THE CLOWN SOCIETY BEGINS AT THE
  MIDDLE PLACE, it will be made good because of you.
Now that you have come alive
we will GO
over there to your SHRINE
where I will set you down," he said.
ON THEY WENT UNTIL
they came to ASH WATER
where Nepayatamu was set down.
Nepayatamu was set down there.
That's why, when there is a Clown initiation, they have
the Clown People have
an Ash Way, that's why there's a SOCIETY of CLOWN
  PEOPLE:
when this had happened the CLOWN SOCIETY WAS
  CREATED.

This was lived LONG AGO. That's a——ll
the word was short.

NOTES

Narrated by Andrew Peynetsa on the evening of February 23, 1965, with
Walter Sanchez and myself present. The performance took forty-nine
minutes.

Kyakiima: a village that was composed of two one-story masonry house
blocks, located at the base of Corn Mountain. It was occupied during the
fifteenth, sixteenth, and early seventeenth centuries.

K'uuchinina People: eight sisters whose name is the Keresan term for yel-
low. In the system of directional colors yellow belongs to the north,
which suggests that these women may have interfered with the north-
ward movement of the sun along the horizon when they stopped
Payatamu from performing his sunrise rites. See also the notes on
Mats'aakya and on moths, below.

Shuun Hill: Shuunteky'a'ya, a high canyon terrace from which Kyakiima
can be seen. Accessible only by a steep trail, it is the site of a two-room
masonry structure used during the eighteenth century.

Payatamu: the protagonist and three other men who are junior to him;
the name is a Keresan term meaning "young man." They are brothers not
by blood but because they are members of a medicine society; the women
members are their sisters. Such societies meet to perform divinatory se-
ances and curing ceremonies.

Mats'aakya: a village contemporary with Kyakiima, composed of terraced
house blocks several stories high and located on a knoll beside the Zuni
River. It is the site of the Rock of the Sun, a shrine providing an observa-
tion point for the seasonal movement of the sun along the horizon.

"The society chief sat down facing him": a ceremonial posture, with the
legs of both parties held straight out front and their knees and feet almost
touching.

Coral's direction: an esoteric term for "south," whose color is red.

Vulture: *shu'tsina*, the turkey vulture.

The two coyotes: according to Andrew, the "true" coyote, or coyote proper, eats rabbits, lives in mountains, and has good fur; the "juniper coyote" is smaller and redder, has mangy fur, goes around in flats, is afraid of everything, and eats juniper berries, grasshoppers, and stinkbugs. The mountain lion, bear, and badger, as the hunting animals of the north, west, and south, are honored by being told to lie near the society's altar, which is on the side of the room farthest from the door. The two coyotes, who seem to be standing in for the hunter of the east (the wolf), are told to lie near the door because they have little worth.

Shrew: *ky'alhuts'i*, the hunting animal of the nadir. This term is often taken to refer to moles, but the Zuni region lacks moles entirely, whereas there are several species of shrew. Moreover, the behavior of shrews makes for a better fit with the other directional hunters. Despite their small size (about that of a mouse) they are vigorous predators, searching for food both day and night.

Tenatsali flowers: these are medicinal and come in various colors, including yellow and blue. Asked to identify tenatsali more precisely, Andrew said, "If you are a medicine man, then you know what kind of medicine that is."

Hawk: *anelhaawa*, Cooper's hawk; according to Andrew, "the fastest of all the birds." When they fly from one high perch to another they dip close to the ground, moving so swiftly they are easier to identify from their movements than from their physical characteristics.

Owl: *mewishokkwa*, an unidentified species.

Plain blankets: woven of cotton, white.

The songs: in Andrew's own medicine society (not one of the societies mentioned in this book), this story serves as a prelude and explanation for a string of songs. Andrew sang one of the songs after finishing the story, but only after motioning for the recording machine to be turned off.

Tesese: this is the sound of the pottery drum, a large jar with a skin stretched over its orifice. The jar is set on a plank laid over a resonating chamber (a pit excavated in an earthen floor).

Swallowtail butterfly: Andrew used *puulakkya*, the generic term for large butterflies, but what he had in mind was the Rocky Mountain Swallowtail, with a yellow, blue, and red wing pattern outlined in black. The wing powder of butterflies is an aphrodisiac.

Shawls: a pair of scarves, one over the other, tied near the throat and covering the shoulders and back.

"All the beasts dispersed to their shrines": that is, they returned to the places from which they had been summoned.

Corn grinding: Joseph Peynetsa commented, "A lot of ladies talk about each other. If someone grinds the corn and she can't do a good job, they consider she's not even ready for womanhood. To be efficient, a woman has to be able to do this. If not, she's *aminne*, 'good-for-nothing.'"

Foodstuffs: the porridge is *wolekwiiwe*, a paste made from blue cornmeal. The meal cakes are *he'palokkya*, made of whole wheat, something like pancakes but cooked between sheets of corn husk.

Moths: according to Andrew, the spring and fall moths referred to are small and white, the only difference between them being that the latter has a larger head. In the story he uses the generic term for moths, *nana pilikkya*, literally "grandfather (or grandson) who spills something." In effect, the sighting of the spring moths today is a reminder that the K'uuchinina women once stopped the sun from rising when it was moving to the north of its equinoctial position, while the fall moths commemorate the return of the sun to that position.

Clown Society: strictly speaking the Zuni term for this medicine society, Neweekwe, is an untranslatable proper noun, but Zunis always use "clown" when talking about this group in English, a reference to the fact that most of its public ceremonies are devoted to satire. The society's members may do or say things which are the opposite of what is logical or proper, just as Nepayatamu did when he said, "I'm not even TIRED." The Ne- in Nepayatamu is from Neweekwe.

Ash Way: the Milky Way, the trail left by Nepayatamu when he traveled across the sky. The altar of the Clown Society includes a representation of the Ash Way in the form of a painted board that reaches clear across their room, running just below the rafters.

THE SUN PRIEST
AND THE WITCH-WOMAN

NOW WE TAKE IT UP.

NOW THE ROAD BEGINS LO——NG A GO.
THERE WERE VILLAGERS AT THE MIDDLE PLACE

•

there were villagers at WIND PLACE
THERE WERE VILLAGERS at Kyakiima
and

•

at Striped Rock
there were two witches:
a witch girl and her
mother, the two of them, lived alone.
All the VILLAGERS
lived on
and, as usual, there was a PRIEST'S SON

•

whose father knew many prayers.
For this reason
the two witches had bad feelings.
They lived on this way
and whenever a ceremony came up
it was made whole through the thoughts of the Sun Priest.

That girl
SPOKE OUT:
"WHY IS IT
this priest knows so many prayers?
(tight) What should be done
about this? I think
we should shut him off.

    If we shut him off we could do whatever we WANTED
since we could have a SUN PRIEST of our own.
And perhaps by means of our prayers, well
perhaps by means of our
our PRAYERS, our SUN PRIEST would be the KEEPER
of ALL THIS EARTH, well I
think so anyway: wouldn't it be that way, wouldn't it turn out
    well?" she told her mother.

                              •

"Well, it's up to you: if you want this, you must make up your
    mind and set a date.
But
it really wouldn't be the Sun Priest alone
who would think otherwise, for he would surely have allies.
Indeed
there at Hanging Wool
the Ahayuuta
live.
He speaks to them there.
It's up to YOU: if you want this, if this is what you think
if your mind is made up, then
this EVENING
you must make it known to the others. To make it known
we will call a meeting over there
where the White Rocks sit
where some of our houses are.

When we have met
you
will make it known
to your
gathering
what you have in mind, then they will think about it: perhaps

•

they will be of the SAME MIND with yourself."
So
the witch's
mother, the girl's mother
so she told her daughter.
And so
they lived on until EVENING.
As SOON as the sun went down
a coyote gave his wets'ots'o cry
he gave his wets'ots'o cry

•

and the witches among the Zunis HEARD IT.
When they heard it: "Haa——
for what reason are they calling a meeting?"
So they said.

•

Twice there was the wets'ots'o cry.
"It must be urgent."

•

SO THE WITCHES SAID
and they went to where the White Rocks sit, the witches.
When they got there
others were going in.
They greeted one another as they went in.
They kept on going in until everyone was there.
Some time passed

and the Sun Priest

•

had a witch friend
who was a young fellow.

•

He was the one who came in late, he came in late.
Their Bow Priest said, *(tight and closed)* "Why have you come in so
    late?"
He asked the boy. "Well
(gently) I didn't hear it right away.
My mother heard it first
and she told me, so that's why I
came in last," so
the little boy said. "Indeed.
Did you stop anywhere on the way?" "No, my mother heard it
    first, I
didn't hear the meeting called, I didn't hear it, my mother heard it,
    that's why I just got here."
The little boy then sat down.

•

Their Bow Priest questioned them: "NOW
for what reason have we been called to a meeting?
Perhaps it is because of a WORD of some importance
that we have been called to a sudden meeting.
WELL NOW, SPEAK UP. WHO IS IT, and what is his reason for
    calling a meeting?" their Bow Priest asked them.

•

It was the ones from Striped Rock, the two witches
who lived alone there
who knew about this.
The girl spoke: "IT'S ME, it's because of me
that you have been called to a meeting.
TRULY

we have a SUN PRIEST.
We have our own Sun Priest
and at the Middle Place, they also have their Sun Priest.
At the Middle Place

    it is by the prayers of ^{their} Sun Priest, it is by ^{his} words
that the villagers live.
But I think that this should not be.
We too have our Sun Priest.
Why isn't our Sun Priest like the one they have at Zuni?
Why isn't he the same kind of person as theirs?
Why is it that theirs is foremost in anything sacred, why is he the
    one who
has the word?" the girl said.
Their witch, Witch Bow Priest spoke: "YES, in TRUTH
even if THAT'S what you have in MIND
and even if we
did this
together
it wouldn't turn out well for us, because of their Sun Priest:
because of HIS thoughts, the raw people
listen to his words.

•

Moreover
whenever the Sun Priest speaks of what must be done
we just follow this, we follow this
in the ceremonies
which include us.
And whenever one of us has meanness in his HEART
that's the time for starting talk
about witching someone:
then we call a meeting, when something WRONG has happened.
But what you are talking about now, what you have in mind
    would not turn out well.

What's your reason for thinking
THIS way?
What are we supposed to do?

•

If we KILLED THE SUN PRIEST
then this man here would replace him, is that what you had in
    mind, is that why you
called this meeting?"
So their Witch Bow Priest said.

•

The little boy sat there with his head down
the little boy thought about their words with his head down.

•

Then it was their
Witch Sun Priest who spoke: "YES, in TRUTH, even if that's
    what you
think about the Sun Priest
I'm NOT WILLING:
I don't know the prayers,
        how my words   heard by the raw
    or   could be   people.
This wouldn't turn out well for us.
We would be found out quickly.
Certainly
there are the Ahayuuta twins, and
they are wonderful, they are extraordinary persons.
If we made a mist$_a{}_{ke}$

then SURELY
we would be killed.
Then what would happen? After they killed us
could we still carry on?" so
their Witch Sun Priest said.

"So I don't agree, but
what   thi$_n$k
     e^{ver} ^{you}

whatever you think.
WELL NOW, SPEAK, what's this all about?" he said.
"Yes, in truth,"
the girl said,
"I know that
my feelings are not good.

●

The way you talked, the way you talked at first
if we killed him
then you would take his place," so
the girl said. "Yes, but I'm not willing to do that.
I will not do it.
ALL THE VILLAGERS
are his children.
We are his, even though we are not responsible people.
I do not have all the people as my own.
And if someone makes up his mind, if someone
is sick in his heart
in his heart
(sighing) then that's the time for us to make plans
for whatever we want to do.
But as for you, I won't do it.
However, it's up to YOU
if you are WILLING.
Whatever you have in mind
you will make up your mind to do it.
This night
you must make your plans.
You must SPEAK. If you SPEAK

to the gathering here, then everyone
who is gathered here will think about it," he told the witch girl.

                                        •

"So you AREN'T WILLING.
For THIS I have you as my MENfolk, you here.
If you aren't willing
that's why we two live by ourselves.
That's why
being mere women, we live poorly.
But I will do what I have decided to do.

                                        •

Tomorrow night

                                        •

I will go."
That's what she said, she said. "Indeed. How will you go?" they said.

                                        •

"I will go as an owl.
When I go as an owl
I will make a trap for the Sun Priest.
Whatever happens then will be up to him," the girl said. "Indeed.
It's up to YOU, if you want it.
You must   do whatever you have DE CIDED to do.
You must not waver in your thoughts.
PER HAPS, IN SOME WAY
you will be found out.
If you are KILLED
THAT WILL BE ALL, there is no one among us who would take
        pity on you, for that is not our way."
So their witch chief said.

                                        •

"Anyway, THAT'S WHY

I asked you to come. I had REALLY hoped you would all be
  willing, but TOMORROW NIGHT I will go by myself," she
  said.

•

"Very well indeed, then let's get some REST.
After a good rest
a person
is better able to kill."
That's what they said. They dispersed.
And the girl
left and went to her home at Striped Rock.
There
she spent the night.

•

The next day
she stayed there all day.
And when they had DISPERSED, the little boy
had left. When he left

•

he went along with the other witches, so he didn't stop at his
  friend's place but went straight home.

•

When he got there
to his house
his mother
was still up.
She was still up when he got there.
(high) "Ahwa, I'm so tired," he said. "Indeed, that was a long way.
It wasn't nearby," his mother said.
"For what reason
did they call a meeting?" she said.
"Well, they're planning to kill the Sun Priest:
the ones

from Striped Rock, those two.

They're the ones: because the Sun Priest

knows so many prayers

their feelings are not good.

It was for this talk of killing him

that we met.

(pained) Because I was late the Bow Priest got after me, because I was
     late."

So the little boy said. "Yes, just as I THOUGHT:

you stayed too long at your

friend's house.

That's why I told you to hurry, lest something like this should
     HAPPEN,"

she told him. "What now:

are you going to tell your friend?" *(high)* "Wait, I'll go tell him in
     the morning, for the others might see me," the little boy said.

"Then you must get up very early," she said. "Yes."

                              •

They slept through the night, and the NEXT MORNING, very
     early, the little boy got up

and went to his friend's, to the Sun Priest's.

He went over to the Sun Priest's house.

"My fathers, my mothers

how did you pass the night?" "Happily, our child, so you've
you've come, sit down," he was told, and he sat down.

                              •

When he sat down

his

Sun Priest, the one who was to be killed, questioned him: "NOW
my son, my CHILD

for what reason

were you called to a meeting?" he asked him. *(high)* "Well
they met to speak of bad things.

They met to speak of bad things:

•

that's why I'm unhappy. I became unhappy when they spoke out about
    you:
you who are the Sun Priest
of a———ll the villagers, you who know many prayers.
The raw people listen to your words of prayer.
Moreover, there at Hanging Wool Point
are 'The Two Who Keep The Roof':
that's what they said, whatever they meant, 'THE TWO WHO
    KEEP THE ROOF,'" the little boy said. "Indeed.
They meant our two fathers: whenever there is the sound of an
    enemy, they're the ones who protect us.
They're very brave," so
the Sun Priest said. "Indeed.
That's the way they talked" he said. "Indeed.
What are they going to do?
How are they going to kill me, by what means are they going to
    KILL me?"
"With an owl," he said. "Indeed.
Indeed," he said.
"Yes
with an owl.
When night comes
this evening
an owl will come."
So the little boy said.
"However
I don't know of any way to help you.
I'm not a knowledgeable person.

•

It seems I'm not a good person.
It seems I'm a person who doesn't know what's right.

(pained) I didn't know about this
until the wets'ots'o cry was given.
As you know, I was called.
So this is what I am.
I had thought I was the kind of person
who lives the way you do
but I'm
not a good person.
My mother told me to go, and when I got there late *(pained)* their
    Bow Priest got after me because I was late.
'I didn't know about it.
When
your
crier shouted out, I didn't hear it:
my mother told me,' that's what I told him. You know I was
    HERE, don't you," the little boy said. "Yes.
Indeed.

•

Well, so THAT'S
the bad thing they're thinking.
What have I done, what difficulty have I caused?" so
the Sun Priest said.
(pained) "No, nothing, it's because you know
so many prayers
that even the raw people
live by them.
Because you are the one who knows so many prayers
she has bad feelings.
That's why their
Witch Sun Priest
would take your place:
that's what she thinks, but
the one who holds that position doesn't want this, because

he doesn't know all the things you know, that's why he doesn't
    want this," the boy said. "Indeed.
Let them do whatever they want with ME.
If they would KILL me, let one of them take my place.
But there is CLANSHIP:
                            •

THIS is the institution by which I live.
Clanship does not exist for no REASON, clanship
is not an unimportant institution.
Only a member of the DOGWOOD Clan should be the Sun
    Priest."
So
the Sun Priest said, so he said.
(high) "Anyway, that's what they talked about," he said. "Indeed.
Very well indeed. WHEN
WILL IT COME?" "When the sun goes down" he said.
"Indeed.
Then are you
going to STAY HERE?" he asked him.
"No, I'll
go, if I stayed
they might find out somehow, and if something happened
if you killed her and I stayed here and they saw me
then, if they had another meeting and I went there, they would
    hold it against me. I'm going
I'm leaving," the little boy said.
"Very well indeed. Those Two you talked about:
I'm going to their house at Hanging Wool.
                            •

THAT'S WHERE I'M GOING TO SPEND THE NIGHT, LET
    THE OWL COME HERE," the Sun Priest said.
That's what the Sun Priest said.
The little boy

•

left, and because he didn't want to be found out he went around,
    went all around before he went to his house.
The Sun Priest left. When the Sun Priest left

•

he went to Hanging Wool.
When he came to Hanging Wool
where the Ahayuuta lived
the Ahayuuta twins were sitting up on their roof.

•

"My two fathers, my two children, how have you been passing the
    days?" "Happily, our father, so you've come."
So they said. "Yes, I've come to talk with you." "Indeed. Then let's
    go inside," they said.
They took him inside, the Sun Priest.
When they took him inside
their grandmother was MAKING PORRIDGE.
Their grandmother was making porridge.

•

"My mother, my child, how have you been passing the days?"
    "Happily, our father, so you've come, be seated," he was told.
They put out a seat for him and he sat down.

•

"SON," so
she said
to the elder
of the Ahayuuta brothers. "What is it?"
"Make a cigarette," so
she said
to the boy.
Her grandson made a cigarette.
He made a cigarette
and when he had finished

•

he sat down facing the Sun Priest. When he sat down facing him

•

he took Grandmother Fire by the arm
drew her forward
and lit the cigarette, lit it.
He sent mist in all directions, strengthening hearts, and blew smoke on himself.
He gave it to the Sun Priest.
The Sun Priest also sent mist in all directions, strengthening hearts, and blew
      smoke on himself.
He questioned him then

•

the Ahayuuta did:
"NOW
our FATHER
for what reason
have you entered upon our roads? Perhaps it is because of a
      WORD of some importance
that you have entered upon our ROADS. You would not do this
      for no REASON.
You would not come to talk with us for no reason, that's not your
      way
for it is through your words of prayer that we listen to YOU.
It is CERTAIN
that every DAY
you give us PRAYER MEAL
you make OFFERINGS.
The Uwanammi WATER PRIESTS
a——ll over the wide EARTH
the RAW PEOPLE
wherever they stay, they listen to your words of prayer.
So it must be for a WORD of some importance that you enter
      upon our roads.

YOU MUST MAKE THIS KNOWN TO US
so that we may think about it
as we pass the days, IS IT NOT SO?" he told his younger brother.
    "IT IS SO," he said.
Their grandmother also said, "It is so."
                                           •

"YES, in TRUTH, my fathers, my CHILDREN:
there at the MIDDLE PLACE
the ones who do not know what is right
                                           •

had a meeting last night.
When they met last night
for   some rea   son
they talked about killing me.
They thought of killing me, and TONIGHT
an owl will come, perhaps it will kill me.
So my friend
told me this morning.
That's why
I came out this way, to ask you
whether there is some way to make this turn out well," so
the Sun Priest said.
"Indeed.
It will turn out WELL, our FATHER
you must not WORRY.
You must not waver in your THOUGHTS.
They have ASKED FOR IT.
It is CERTAIN
that many of your LIFE seeds
have been DESTROYED by them.
They do not follow the RIGHT WAY."
So
the Ahayuuta

said to the Sun Priest.
"That's why
I have COME.
Perhaps you might tell me something to make it turn out well.
Perhaps
they will not kill me.

And IF THEY KILL ME, perhaps there is someone
who would take my place. This clanship I live by:
even those who don't know what is right
have their clanship. If someone were willing
he could take my place.
A————ll
our children, where the ladders descend:
like them
you who are our fathers
you have
brave hearts, all of us have brave hearts" the Sun Priest said. "Yes.
This is the way you live," the Ahayuuta twins said.

•

"But WAIT," that's what their grandmother said, the twins'
        grandmother.
"Father-child, you must wait," she said.

•

"Let me prepare you," she said, and she went into the next room.
    She went in

•

and brought out a bow. She brought out a bow and laid it down, then got a
    quiver.
"Prepare THIS for him,"
she told them, and gave
an arrow to them
to the twins.
She gave it to her grandsons and they prepared it.

They
prepared it with honey.

　　　　　　　　　　　　　　•

"NOW, you must take this along.
You must take this along
and
you mustn't get sleepy before the OWL COMES. The owl will
　　　surely land
at the top of the LADDER.

　　　　　　　　　　　　　　•

Then it will make itself known to the others
with a huhhu.

When it makes itself known with a huhhu
the others will start coming down.

They will come down there around your house

　　　　　　　　　　　　　　•

while it sounds FOUR TIMES.
It will sound the first time, the second time
and when it sounds the third time
you must put this arrow
on your bow.

THE FOURTH TIME IT SPEAKS
you will shoot it for them.
When you have shot THEIRS
LEAVE THE ARROW IN IT
and throw it down to them.
'NOW, here is your life seed, PICK IT UP.
You asked for THIS.
You may take it away,' so you will tell them.
Then they can do whatever they wish.

　　　　　　　　　　　　　　•

TOMORROW
as soon as the sun comes up
when you have brought your Sun Father out
you must not go back
to your house
but must come here.
Then we will tell you
what to do next," so
the Sun Priest
was told, that's what they told him. "Indeed. Very well." "Yes, that's the
     way it will be.
(kindly) You must not WORRY.
You must not waver in your thoughts.
There may be people who do wrong
but
you ask for daylight for everyone.
You say prayers even for the one who is not upright.
You pray for everyone.
If someone

•

is not a good person, that is unfortunate.
But IT WILL TURN OUT WELL if they want it that way.
TOMORROW, when you come back, we will know what to do,
     (pained) but don't make a MISTAKE.
You must not WORRY.
If you WOR_{RY}
this thing we've prepared for you won't work," so
the Ahayuuta grandmother said.
"If you WORRY, you won't do it right. Don't waver in your
     thoughts.
Be just the way you are right now:
if you feel this way
then you will do it right

then it will turn out well," she said.
"There is your
friend:
certainly

•

he'll be in this, for his mother has spoken to him, and certainly
   he'll be in this with you," she said.

•

"Are you
(serious) on good speaking terms with him?" "Yes. Well
yes I am, and I'm
always kind to him, as if he were my own child.
I'm always kind to him. When he was a small boy
his elders
spoke to me
about us:
they spoke to me about it, that's why we pledged our friendship.
We didn't just WASH each other to pledge friendship, it wasn't
like that.

•

I gave him a bead necklace. When I gave him a bead necklace
his elders
gave me a blanket:
THAT'S the way I pledged friendship with him, with my
my child.
I value him," he said. "Certainly
that's the way it should be," the Ahayuuta grandmother said.
(kindly) "WELL THEN, our father, have good thoughts, don't
think about this bad talk you've heard, leave it behind you.

•

YOU MUST GO HAPPILY upon the Pollen Way, you must
   think well of what you are going to do.
That way

you can do it right.
WE WILL KNOW ABOUT IT, for we will go there also.
You will not be alone," they said, the Ahayuuta twins.
"We will watch over you:
you won't be alone," they said.

•

The man
the Sun Priest was leaving. "Very well, I'm going."
"You must put this in your
quiver:
you must take along what we have prepared for you
and when
you kill the owl with it, you must leave it in when you throw the
    body down to them, and when they take it out
we'll get it back," they said. "Very well."
"Yes, that's the way it will be."
"Very well indeed, I'm going
my children
may you have a good day and evening." "Indeed, may it be the
    same with you, our father," they said.

•

The Sun Priest took his arrow
and went back to Zuni, to the Middle Place.
It was almost sunset
when he got there.
When he got there

•

he was fed. When he was fed
his wife
and his children ate with him.
His wife questioned him and he told them
what he had been told by the Ahayuuta.

•

"We'll see what happens. If I
know how, I will kill theirs.
Tomorrow
I have to go back, that's what they told me
and tonight
the Ahayuuta will come here.
From somewhere they will watch over me.
I won't be alone, that's what they told me."
"Very well indeed."
They ate
their evening meal a little early. They waited and the sun went
      down.

                                   •

Time went o————n until it was late

                                   •

then
sure enough, by the ladder
they heard it plainly, kolo
as the owl alighted.
"So, it must've come."

                                   •

Some time passed
then the owl gave its huhhu:
"Hu
huHU
hu,"
it said.
"Haa——, sure enough, it's come."
And a second time
it spoke:
again, again it gave the huhhu.
It was not to finish speaking.
"Hu hu."

When it had spoken a third time
just as he had been told, he stood by the ladder.
Sitting up there was the owl.
He put the arrow on his bow
and when it was about to give another huhhu

po
 o
  o
   o
    ok'o

    he shot it.
The owl fell.

               •

The Sun Priest hurried out
and picked it up.
It was dead.
The arrow was sticking in the owl but he didn't take it out, just as he had been
      told.
He threw it down to them, there were a lot of people below, sure
      enough:
the witches.

               •

"Here, take your
child," he told them.

               •

They dispersed.
They passed the night
and the next day, before the sun came up, he started back.
He brought out his Sun Father, then went back to the Ahayuuta.
The Ahayuuta twins
were sitting up on top when he got there.
"My two children, how did you pass the night?" "Happily, our
      father, so you've come back." "Yes, I've come back." *(high and
      hoarse)* "Then let's go inside," they said.
They went inside, and their

grandmother was MAKING PORRIDGE AGAIN.
She was making porridge
when they came in. "My mother, how did you
pass the night?" "Happily, our father, so you've come back." "Yes, I've
    come."
"It's good that you've come.
It will turn out well for you" she said.

                                        •

"NOW
our father, our child

                                        •

(serious) be seated

                                        •

for tonight
they will surely have another meeting.
As for the ones who started this talk
THIS VERY DAY
we will have a contest with them.
Perhaps they are surpassing people," so the Ahayuuta grandmother
    said
so she told him. "Indeed.
Indeed," the Sun Priest said. "Yes.
Now, my two GRANDSONS
make preparations for our father," so
the Ahayuuta grandmother told
her two grandsons.

                                        •

The twins took out their quiver, took out their quiver and
    prepared four arrows, prepared them with honey.
There was a very BROAD spearhead.
They put that
in their quiver.

                                        •

"And what about this:

                                    •

the one that
our Sun Father
gave us, should we take it along?" they asked their grandmother.
"Yes, you must take that along.
Perhaps it will make things easier," she said.
It was a TURQUOISE CLUB.
This is what the Sun, their Sun Father, had given them, and they
        had been keeping it.
THEY PUT THIS IN THEIR QUIVER ALSO. "Now let's go,"
        they said.

                                    •

They went out.
"NOW
this day, our father, our mother
we'll GO ON THE ROAD NOW.
We'll see how this day turns out," they said. "Very well, you may go,
        we'll see how this day turns out.
DON'T you make any MISTAKES," they were told.
They went across toward Striped Rock.
They went across
going on until they came to
a point, a rocky point overlooking Striped Rock
and sat down on top of it.
There, down below, smoke was coming out of their house.
Smoke was coming out.

                                    •

"Is that their house?" "Yes, that's the house where they live.
Wa———y over there is their cornfield," he said. "Indeed."
(aside) It was where a small arroyo came out, that's where they had their field.

                                    •

Soon, the woman came out and went to her cornfield. After a
while, her mother came out and went there also.
"Now let's go," they said.
They went down
went on down until they were close
to their house. Meanwhile the women were going about in their cornfield, they
were hoeing.

·

It was the elder of the Ahayuuta brothers who said, "Wait now.
How should we do this? Should we
destroy their house first?" he said.
His younger brother said, "Don't.
Let's alarm them, so that
they'll go inside.
As soon as they go inside
then we'll kill them," he said.
"All right," he said.
His younger brother
sat down
(aside) beneath a tree.
When he sat down: "NOW, this day
our father, who lives with us
the mountain lion:
now enter upon my road," the Ahayuuta said, the Ahayuuta said.

·

After a while
the mountain lion came.
He came to where they were waiting. The women were still at their
cornfield
going about hoeing.
The mountain lion came up and said, "My fathers, my children, how
have you been?" "Happy, our
father-child, so you've come now."

"Yes.

NOW, for what reason have you summoned ME?
Perhaps it is because of a WORD of some importance that you
  have summoned me," he told them.
"YES, in TRUTH

     •

our GRANDFATHER, our FATHER, our CHILD
it concerns our father here, the Sun Priest: a———ll you raw people
listen to his words of prayer and live by them.
He offers you hard things
he offers you prayer meal.
Because of this, there was talk of KILLING him.
Last night

     •

he was supposed to have been killed by an owl
and so
he came to our house
to ask what he should do.
This day
we will KILL the women who live here, this is the house of the
  ones who started the talk of killing him.
Over there they are going about in their field.
I was going to call out in imitation of you
(low and gravelly) but perhaps I wouldn't have done it well:
that's why I summoned you.
When you make your sound
and they hear you
THEY'LL RUN
THEY'LL GO INSIDE
then we'll kill them, THAT'S WHAT
we have in mind, that's why we've come here," he said. "Indeed.
It should turn out well, certainly.
We listen to the prayers of our father here, and live by them."

"Indeed. So this is what has happened.
Because of the thoughts of these two
it has happened.
THAT'S why we'll kill them.
This NIGHT
we'll go to White Rocks, for the others will certainly have a
    meeting," so

                                    •

the Ahayuuta said. *(low)* "Indeed. Very well indeed, then I'll alarm
    them." *(high)* "Go ahead and alarm them, and we'll see what
    they do.
Now, our father, we'll
set you up here," they said, and they took their turquoise club and
    SET IT UP.
When they set it up
they looked at it.
(tight) "This won't do for me.
It's too close
too close for me. Why don't you set it up a little further back?
That'll be better for me.
I'll be last in line, I won't step beyond the club," so
the mountain lion said.
(high and hoarse) "Yes, yes, WAIT, LET'S
set it up there."
(aside) And they moved further back and set up their turquoise
    club.
Some distance behind them the mountain lion got down on all
    fours.
(low and gravelly) He gave his tuwoo, tuwoo.
They heard it, THEY CAME RUNNING!!
They CAME RUNNING and went inside their house.

                                    •

The Ahayuuta twins went and stood there

beside their door.

The Sun Priest

the one who was to have been killed stood in their doorway *(aside)*
    and the two Ahayuuta got behind him.

The mountain lion

got behind them.

They stood there before the house.

          •

"So you've COME now, so you've COME now," she said. "Yes."

"Indeed.

so you've come.

For what reason have you COME?

What do you mean by COMING HERE?" SO THE WITCH
    GIRL'S

mother said. "Indeed.

Well, ON THE NIGHT you called a meeting

you wanted to kill me, that's why

THIS _{DAY}

          •

it will be our turn to kill YOU.

Because

I stand first among you, you wanted to have your

Witch Sun Priest

take my place, you thought of doing wrong.

You made up your mind.

I asked help

from my two fathers here.

THIS _{DAY}

since you asked for it

we will end your daylight.

TO^{NIGHT THE O}THERS WILL MEET

AND we will kill all of them there.
WHEN ALL OF YOU ARE FINISHED
THEN we will have ONE WAY of thinking as we live.
We will not have bad feelings toward one another.
IT'S TRUE that you have your GARDEN SEEDS
and where all the ladders descend there is good flesh
BUT you have been very foolish.
SO I have made up my MIND.
Even though you are no good
I HAVE ASKED DAYLIGHT FOR YOU *(tight)* but it seems you
    want SOMETHING MORE.
THAT'S WHY, on this day
you will pass away.
Over there
when the others meet, we will kill them ALL," the Sun Priest said
to the witches.
They didn't want it.
"YES, we will kill you.

·

LOOK AT YOUR SUN FATHER FOR THE LAST TIME," the
    Sun Priest said.

·

They put their
arrows
the ones that had been prepared, on their bows and the twins shot
    them
they shot them.
WHEN THEY SHOT THEM they both died.
The twins spoke to their turquoise club: "NOW
our father-child
you will strike them a second time, for they aren't really dead yet,"
    they said.
They released their turquoise club, so

and this time

he struck their hearts.

Then they were dead.

"So, we've DONE IT. NOW, our GRANDFATHER, our father-
    CHILD

you must destroy their house," they told the mountain lion.

The mountain lion went up, went up on the roof

and started digging. As he dug

he threw down the rafters and completely ruined their house.

When ALL THE RAFTERS had fallen in:

"Let's go now."

But first, the Ahayuuta said

to the mountain lion: "NOW, our grandfather, our child

well

that's why we needed you, now you may go back to your
    SHRINE.

When NIGHT comes

we will be without you:

we

will KILL THEM."

So

they told the mountain lion. "Very well indeed.

GO RIGHT AHEAD and do it, but I will say THIS to YOU:

•

you

have done wrong.

You must make prayer sticks.

All your children, where the ladders descend:

if they are to be valued

you must make these prayer sticks.

•

There

at Corn Mountain

at the SPRING there
you must plant these prayer sticks
so that
where all the ladders descend, your children
our fathers
will be safe.
For you will have destroyed many lives.

            •

That's why you must make prayer sticks.
You must SET A DATE.
At NIGHT
and during the DAY
you must think of this.
On the FOURTH night
in one house
in your house
you must make preparations.
When you have made prepara .
                  tions

THEN
we
will make it known
to your daylight children.
Of A———LL your village children, the POOR PEOPLE will be
    the only ones left.

           •

By means of OUR thoughts
A———LL of us will watch over you from the shrines where we
    live, all around.
ALL OF US   down there
        will go
to your house.
When this GOOD NIGHT comes
then we will make

a medicine society for you.

YOUR THOUGHTS WILL BE ROOTED IN THIS as you live.

Wherever there is someone who DOESN'T KNOW WHAT IS
RIGHT

someone who thinks in another way

then by means of OUR medicine, by means of OUR thoughts

you will see

that wrongdoer.

THAT'S

what the GAME will be."

THAT'S WHAT

the mountain lion told the Sun Priest.

"Very well." "Yes, that's the way it will be.

YOU MUST MAKE PREPARATIONS and wait.

WHEN THE TIME COMES

we will go there," so

the mountain lion said. "Very well." "Yes, that's the way it will
be."

"Very well, then you must go."

"Well, I'll be GOING, my fathers, my children, may you have a
good day and evening."

"May you also have a good day."

Then the Ahayuuta twins

took the Sun Priest to their house.

When they got to Hanging Wool

when they got to Hanging Wool

their grandmother

was waiting when they got there.

When they entered: "My grandmother, how have you been?" "Happy,
so you've come back."

"Our mother, our child, how have you been?" "Happy, so you've
come, be seated," she said.

When they sat down

(with pleasure) THEIR GRANDMOTHER SET OUT A MEAL.
She fed them, their grandmother fed them. They ate
and ate
and when they were full: "Thanks." "Eat plenty," she said.

•

When the meal had been cleared away
she sat down facing him, the Ahayuuta grandmother did.
She sat down facing the Sun Priest. "NOW, this day

•

you have set forth
upon your Pollen Way.
Did you do what you INTENDED to do?" "Yes, we've killed
    both of them. Our
grandfather, the mountain lion, destroyed their house.
THIS NIGHT
we will go
to the others
and KILL THEM too.
After we have killed them
TOMORROW I will work on the prayer sticks:
that's what our grandfather
the mountain lion
told us, is it not so?" "It is so, that's what he said," the Ahayuuta twins
    said.

•

"SO THEN
you will do this, and it will turn out well.
OTHERWISE it would NOT turn out WELL.
That's what we told you at the START.

•

You

•

must get the WORD around

to ALL the raw people.
WHEN YOU HAVE GOTTEN THE WORD
             TO THEM
you will offer them prayer meal
offer them hard things.
When they come to your house
this will be the GOOD NIGHT.
EVERYONE IN THE VIL
             LAGE MUST BATHE,
      you must tell them that.
EVEN   DON'T   GO   YOUR
      IF THEY   WANT TO   TO   HOUSE
they must bathe.

THEN THE   RAW   PEOPLE, WITH THEIR UN   KNOWABLE
      PO
         WERS
      will pluck out whatever is inside them.
That's the way it will be.
         AFTER
HERE
this is the way our daylight children will live.
And these Ahayuuta twins, who live as Bow Priests:
they will DEPART from here.
These Bow Priest twins will bring the Saniyakya Society to light.
Also the Society of Bow Priests will become known.
BECAUSE OF THEIR THOUGHTS
you will live with brave hearts."
So the Ahayuuta grandmother
told the Sun Priest
so she told him.
"Very well." "Yes, that's the way it will be.
You must have good thoughts."
"VERY WELL INDEED, now I must GO, my FATHERS, my
      MOTHER, my CHILDREN

may you have a good day and evening." "By all means may it be
the same with you."

•

He left, and when he left the little Ahayuuta
followed him: "WAIT, father," he said.
"What is it?" he said.
(high) "When
the SUN GOES DOWN, you will leave your HOUSE

•

and we will START OUT
and get there first
and I will give the *(gravelly)* WETS'OTS'O CALL," SO THE
    LITTLE AHAYUUTA SAID.
(high and hoarse) "Because the one who had been calling them
    together is already dead
I will be the one to give the wets'ots'o,
        per ^haps I'll know h_ow,"
    that's what the younger brother Ahayuuta said.
(smiling) "VERY WELL." "Yes, that's the way it will be.
Now you may go," he said.
The Sun Priest returned to his home.
He stayed there until the sun went down.
After they had eaten
the Sun Priest went out, he went out and went on his way.
THERE was the WETS'OTS'O, the COYOTE.
It was the little Ahayuuta
giving the wets'ots'o.

•

The Sun Priest went on, went on until
he had passed the witches' houses.
On a small hill
the Ahayuuta
were waiting. "Come on over, here we are," they said.

They waited there
and the witches began ARRIVING, SURE ENOUGH.
They were arriving
and entering.
They waited outside for some time
until there was no one else.
But his friend DIDN'T COME
his friend didn't come.

•

IT GREW VERY LATE, but his friend didn't come.
"Your friend hasn't come," the Ahayuuta said. "No, he hasn't come yet."
"I wonder why he hasn't come, or maybe he's on his way."
"Well no, his mother must've told him not to come," the elder brother Ahayuuta
    said.
"He must've been told not to come."
(high and hoarse) "Perhaps he'll be the only one left, and maybe
he'll go the right way.
With his garden seeds, perhaps all our children, where the ladders
    descend
will go the right way.
Let him be spared," the Ahayuuta said.
"NOW LET'S GO," they said.

•

"You must enter first, and when you enter
we will stand behind you. Here is our
turquoise club:
you must set it up in front of you.
And this spearhead:
you will set it up also.

•

You will speak to them
about the contest.
When you have spoken

and they have answered you: 'You should be first, because you
    wanted to kill me.
You should be first.

                                    •

You must try to kill me first. Then, if you don't kill me, perhaps
    I'll kill you,'" so
the Sun Priest
was to say:
that's what they told him to do.
THEY ENTERED. When they entered

                                    •

the Sun Priest
came down
to the foot of the ladder:
"My fathers, my CHILDREN
how are you this evening?" he said.
"Happy, our father, so you've come
SIT DOWN.
We had just gathered when you came in," SO THEY TOLD HIM.

                                    •

The Ahayuuta twins stood behind him and nobody saw them.
They stood behind his back.
The Sun Priest spoke: "NOW
my children
FOR WHAT REASON
did you want to KILL me?
THIS NIGHT we will have a CONTEST.
YOUR medicine is strong
but even though I am just a POOR person
I am WILLING."
So he told them.
"Indeed. Well then
you should be FIRST," so their

Witch Bow Priest said. "Oh no
I will not be first.

•

YOU WILL BE FIRST BECAUSE YOU ARE THE WONDER
    WORKERS.

•

IF I DON'T DIE
then I might
do something to you, even though I am a POOR person.
Do whatever you wish to ME.
THEN you will be HAPPY," the Sun Priest told them.

•

Their witch chief said, "VERY WELL INDEED, we will go
    FIRST if you are WILLING."
The Ahayuuta said, *(whisper)* "Now hurry:
set up your turquoise club
set up your spearhead," so
the Ahayuuta twins told him, from behind his back.
Now he set them up, set up the turquoise club

•

set up the spearhead.
"Ready?" he asked them.
"Now," they said.
The ones in the first row released their
weapons, k'u-cha-cha-cha-cha-cha————
and where he stood
cactus needles and other things fell down.
The SECOND row, the THIRD, the FOURTH row then released
    theirs.

•

•

•

"IS THAT ALL?" he said. "OUR WEAPONS are all gone," they
said. "Indeed.
Very well."
"Now it's your turn."

•

He picked up his turquoise club: "NOW, this night, my father, my child
you must kill all of them, you must not spare anyone.
Let all of them be killed," he told it.

•

The Ahayuuta told it, *(high)* "If anyone is left, well, make sure no one is left," he
said.
The Sun Priest spoke to them again.

•

HE RELEASED HIS TURQUOISE CLUB, and it went around
the first time
the second, the third, IT WENT AROUND THE FOURTH
TIME
and the turquoise club was then taken
by the Ahayuuta.

•

"You must pick up the spearhead and go around carefully. You
must circle all around until you have come back to your
starting point."

•

So the Ahayuuta said. There was blood

•

there was blood all around NOW, blood.
"You must be wary as you go around," they told him, the twins told
him.
He went on and on and on among the corpses, but he didn't see
anyone left.
"They're all gone now."
"Well, now our worries are ended.

• 206 •

That's all there is to the contest, our FATHER.
You must go happily upon the Pollen Way, and just as
our grandfather said
you must make prayer sticks tomorrow," they said. "Very well."
The Ahayuuta twins said, "We're GOING, may you have a good
     night." "Very well, may it be the same
with you, may you have a good night," he told the twins.
They LEFT, then he went to his house.
THE NEXT DAY he cut PRAYER STICKS, the PRIEST.
The Sun Priest cut sticks.

                              •

When they were finished

                              •

he planted the sticks
at Circling Water
at the spring.
HE SET A DATE.
Each night, then
he said prayers
alone.
When the eve of the ceremony came
the Sun Priest summoned his Bow Priest, he summoned his Bow Priest.
The Bow Priest came to his house.

                              •

"NOW, for what reason have you summoned me? Perhaps it is
     because of a WORD of some importance," he said. "YES, in
     TRUTH
my father, my CHILD
you are our village CHIEF.
You live by the dry bow," he said. "YES, in truth, that's the way I
     LIVE."
So he said.
"THIS NIGHT

you will make it known to your children that without exception
they will bathe tomorrow, without exception they must bathe
   their bodies
EVEN if they don't come to ^{my} house, ^even if they stay in their
   own houses.
Our fathers
the BEAST PRIESTS
will come.
They will look ALL AROUND AMONG US.
BECAUSE OF ^{THOSE} WHO DON'T KNOW WHAT'S
   RIGHT, WE MAY BE ^{SICK}
and they will remove this from us. BECAUSE OF THIS
because the medicine societies will become known
you will tell your children
that I have set a DATE.
This is the THIRD day. TOMORROW NIGHT
they will come."
So he said. "You will speak of this
when you make the announcement to your children," he said.
"Very well."
"Yes, that's the way it will be."

•

HE LEFT and
shouted it out
telling them to bathe.
The next night
the beasts would come, that's what he said as he announced it.
He shouted it out.
IN ^{KEEPING} WITH THE ^{WORDS} OF THE
   ANNOUNCEMENT EVERYONE IN THE VIL_{LAGE}

BATHED, EVEN THOSE WHO DIDN'T GO TO ^{HIS}
HOUSE but _{stayed home.}
They lived on, and WHEN THE SUN WENT DOWN

•

the beasts CAME.
They had their medicine water.
They came
and entered the Sun Priest's house.
The mountain lion was first, then the bear
badger
wolf
eagle
shrew:
they came in single file.

•

After a time
their Bow Priest came in:
the white bear.

•

"My fathers, my children, how are you this evening?" "Happy, our
fathers, so you've come now, BE SEATED," they said, and
their

•

ROOM was BARE.
They sat down. When they sat down, they set up their
altar, and
a meal painting

•

they made a meal painting
they set up their ears of corn, set out their medicine water
when they sat down.

•

They sang their string of songs.

They sang their string of songs o————n

and when their songs were almost finished

      •

their

chief got up, got up while they were still singing and went around, went

  around, and when he had gone around the fourth time

      •

then his younger brothers got up and walked around, walked

  around, laying bare what was inside the villagers. And they

asked for a bowl, they were given a bowl, and that's where they

  PUT THINGS.

A lot of

sickness was put in there.

When it was getting light, when day was coming: "Perhaps this will DO.

This is about all we can do, for we must not stay until the sun

  comes up:

that would not be good," they said.

THOSE people were the REAL raw people.

This is the way the medicine societies were to be:

THAT'S WHAT HAD HAPPENED.

And HIS FRIEND was spared: just as

the Ahayuuta twins had said, his mother had TOLD HIM not to

  go:

that's why his friend was left out.

IT IS BY HIS GARDEN SEEDS, today it is by these garden seeds

that we LIVE.

THIS WAS LIVED LONG AGO. *(aside)* That's a————ll

the word was short.

NOTES

Narrated by Andrew Peynetsa on the evening of March 10, 1965, with his wife, several other members of his family, Walter Sanchez, and myself present. The performance took fifty-seven minutes. For Andrew, this was the season's final session for telling tales *(telapnaawe)*. He explained that on March 13, "I'll cut my prayer sticks for the snakes." On the 14th he would go into session with his medicine society, "praying for the snakes to come out." From then until fall, he could only narrate "things that really happened. Otherwise, a snake will smile at you. He'll bite you." Zuni ceremonies are often scheduled for the weekend nearest what would otherwise be the proper date, in order to accommodate people who have jobs or attend school. In this case March 17, with a full moon, would have been the ideal date, but the 14th was a Sunday. The 1965 snake season, lasting seven moons, was ceremonially ended on Sunday, October 10, which happily coincided with a full moon.

"As usual, there was a PRIEST'S SON": two nights before this, Andrew had told two stories (not published here) in which the protagonist was a priest's son.

Sun Priest: Pekwinne, the highest-ranking of all Zuni priests, keeper of the calendar; he greeted the Sun Father every morning with offerings and prayers. According to Andrew, "He was supposed to keep out of arguments. He wasn't supposed to kill anything, or even step on an ant." The office is now vacant, and its duties have been assumed by the second-ranking priest.

Ahayuuta: twin boys, sons of the Sun, protectors of the Zuni people. "The Two Who Keep The Roof," an esoteric name for them, refers to the fact that the surface of the earth forms the roof of four lower worlds. According to Joseph Peynetsa, "The Ahayuuta have long hair and they're dirty; they sort of look like sheepherders." In the "long ago" they lived with their maternal grandmother.

Witches: motivated by jealousy or grudges, they cause illness and death, principally by magically shooting foreign objects into the bodies of their victims. In former times, at least, they were organized into a clandestine medicine society and had a Bow Priest and Sun Priest of their own. Any member could call a meeting by giving the coyote call.

Owl: this is *muhukwi*, the great horned owl, whose call is accurately rendered in the scene where it lands on the roof of the Sun Priest's house.

Clanship: the Zunis are divided into a dozen clans; membership is inherited through the mother.

The cigarette: wild tobacco, rolled in a cornhusk. The full ritual phrase for lighting a cigarette is, "He took his grandmother by the arm and made her sit down in the doorway," but in the present instance Andrew switches to ordinary language after "by the arm." I supplied "Fire" in making the translation so that Grandmother Fire would not be confused with the Ahayuuta grandmother. The "mist" sent in all directions "strengthens the hearts" of the raw people.

"All our children, where the ladders descend": this refers to the villagers (daylight people), as does "life seeds."

Honeyed arrows: these are effective against witches; ordinary arrows are not.

"Pollen Way": life.

Offerings: "hard things" and "prayer meal" both refer primarily to a mixture of cornmeal with crushed turquoise, shell, and coral.

The killing of the witches: they are difficult to kill, and that is why the girl and her mother were struck twice; the girl, in fact, had already been "killed" once before, when she came as an owl.

"You have done wrong": the mountain lion tells the Sun Priest this because it is wrong to take human life, even a witch's life. Joseph explained, "To save himself and his village children, the Sun Priest had to plant feathers, so that perhaps their lives would be spared. It doesn't mean forgiveness—in the white man's way it would say he prays for forgiveness—he did it so that his children would be *aatehya*, [valued], free from evil thoughts, the evil."

"The POOR PEOPLE will be the only ones left": that is, people who lack the powers of witches.

Saniyakya Society: also called the Coyote Society; a medicine society for hunters.

Society of Bow Priests: this formerly consisted of all Zunis who had killed an enemy; the Bow Priest proper, mentioned in this and other stories, was a member.

Beast priests: the chief patrons of several Zuni medicine societies whose place of origin is in the east (see "When Newness Was Made," Part II) and whose songs are in Keresan. In the story the beasts themselves act as a society, coming to a Zuni house in person and setting up an altar (an enclosure of painted slats with a wooden mobile suspended above it), making a painting on the floor (with cornmeal), and setting out a bowl of medicine water. The first six beasts come from the six directions, in the sequence north, west, south, east, zenith, and nadir. But the shrew, in sixth place, is merely a burrowing animal, whereas the seventh animal, the white bear, comes from "STRAIGHT DOWN," according to Andrew. In Keresan cosmology, white is the color of the fourth and lowest underworld.

"Good Night": at the winter solstice, a ceremony in which medicine societies cure, without fee, any villagers who come to the houses where they meet. Among the society members are shamans who are able to see and remove the sickness even in people who do not present themselves in person. On the first Good Night, in the story, "the REAL raw people" came to do the curing; today their human representatives do it.

"It is by these garden seeds that we LIVE": this refers to yellow corn, which was brought from the underworld (see "When Newness Was Made," Part I) by the first witch. If all the witches had been killed, including the Sun Priest's friend, it would have meant the death of yellow corn.

PELT KID AND
HIS GRANDMOTHER

NOW WE TAKE IT UP. THERE WERE VILLAGERS AT THE
    MIDDLE PLACE
and
PELT KID LIVED WITH HIS GRANDMOTHER. *(tries to
    suppress laughter)*

•

They were living together this way, and at the Middle Place
the villagers
came down to get water
at their
well
and that Pelt Kid was very stupid, he just didn't know anything.
One night when they were still up
he told his grandmother, "Tomorrow, I
would like to gather wood."
So he told his grandmother. "Well, you may go
for we're almost out of wood," she said.
"Then we should
get some rest," he said, and
they slept through the night, and the next day his grandmother
got up, then
she made some corn cakes and they ate. When they had eaten he

put his roll of thongs on his back and
went down, went on down toward the south.
Before he left, his grandmother
had told him:
"Grandson, when you
gather wood, when the tree
falls
you must run away from it," his grandmother had told him.
"Well then
I'll try to do that," he had said.
He went on until
he came to where a dried-up tree stood, and he started to cut it
    down.
He laid his thongs aside and started cutting.
Finally the TREE STARTED FALLING and he RAN AWAY,
    ALL THE WAY BACK TO HIS GRANDMOTHER.
"Dear me! grandson, why did you come back so soon?" his
    grandmother said.

•

"Well, didn't you
tell me that when I cut the tree and the tree fell, I SHOULD RUN
    AWAY? AND I LEFT ALL MY THONGS THERE."
    (almost laughs)

•

So he said.
"YOU BIG FOOL, YOU SHOULD'VE RUN ONLY A
    SHORT DISTANCE FROM THE TREE, THEN YOU
SHOULD'VE RETURNED to chop it up and make a bundle
and you should've brought that home on your back, that's what I
    meant, you shouldn't have run all the way home."
"Why did you have to give me INSTRUCTIONS?
But anyway

let's eat, then I'll go back to make a bundle of wood and then come
    back here," he said.
When they had eaten: "Well, I'm going."
Then the boy went on his way until
he came to where he had cut the tree, then he made a bundle of
    wood. When he had finished the bundle he cut some juniper
    leaves.
He put these
on his back where the load was going to rest, then put the bundle
    there

•

and started on his way, going short distances and then resting. He
    went on his way until he got back to his house.
He loosed his bundle and
went down inside
then the two of them ate.
"Now you have learned something, I have taught you.
So now you'll be going after wood, and when you've cut the tree
    and it falls, you must watch out. You must run only a short
    distance, you
mustn't run all the way home, that's not what I told you." "Well,
    at first
I thought I was supposed to come all the way back here,
that's why I ran back. Next time, I
won't do that."
So the boy said. Then they slept through the night. They slept
    through the night, and the next day, he
took his bow and
over at Rockpile Mountain he went around
pulling cottontails out of their burrows. He went around until he
    had killed four cottontails, then brought them home.

When he got back, he and his grandmother slept through the
      night. They slept through the night, and the next day he went
      down to his
field and went about hoeing. When it was about this time *(points
      almost straight up)*
about noon, he went back up to eat. "I want to go
to the Middle Place."
"Please come back soon," she said
for it was already afternoon. "You must
be careful of yourself."
So she told him.
"W-Why
why did you say that?" he said. "Well
you must be on the alert, for
without doubt, you
will be noticed by the GIRLS," she said, for HIS VOICE WAS
      VERY HOARSE.
His voice was very hoarse, and he went to the well
he came to the well.
Sure enough
the girls were coming down to get their water and going back up.
"Are you coming down to get water?" he said, with his really
      hoarse voice.
"Yes.

•

Why don't we
go up to my house?
My, but you're cute 'n silly," so
the girl who came down first
told him. "Well now, I can't
go with you, for I must
go home.
When I get there

I'll ask my grandmother, and perhaps

•

if I ask her whether I can go with you, she'll consent, and then I'll
go with you, *(pained)* I'm so bashful I can't just
go right into a person's house," he said, making himself silly.
Then another girl came: "Who is this cute fellow here?" "Well
I don't know, he was here when I came down and he spoke to me.
My, but his voice is CUTE," she said.
"WHAT'S THE MATTER WITH MY VOICE?" the boy said.
   "Well, your voice is really cute. Let's go.
Why don't we go on up?" The one who came second said, "I'LL
   TAKE HIM WITH ME," AND THEY WERE ARGUING
   OVER THE BOY, the two of them were arguing.
(tight) "But I can't go with either of you, for I must go back to my
   grandmother, then
I'll ask my grandmother.
When she tells me what to do I'll go with one of you," so
the boy said. "Well, HE'S MINE, for whoever finds something
   first
will be the one to take it," the first girl said. "Well now
why don't you both go back up, for I'm going home."
And then
the boy went on until
he got back to his grandmother, and when they had eaten he questioned his
   grandmother:
"When I left for the village, you told me to
be careful of myself, and
when I got there I
drank and then I was just standing there
when a girl came down to get water.
She wanted me to go with her, and
(pained) IS THERE SOMETHING WRONG WITH MY
   VOICE?" he said.

"Well, poor thing, you don't speak well, for your voice is hoarse."
    "So THAT'S why she was admiring me
and wanting to take me home with her.
But I didn't consent, and then another girl came
and the first one said:
'I was the first one to find him, and whoever finds something first
    will be the one to take it.'
And I told them
'Wait, wait, I must go home, then I'll
ask my grandmother
and when she tells me what to do, then I'll go with one of you.'
That's what I said, and so
I didn't go with either of them, that's why I've
come back," he said.
"Well

                                    •

well, I will tell you this:
if a girl asks you to go
to her house
and if you go with her
then you must
(slowly) keep your bow guard near your eyes while you eat," his
    grandmother told him.
"But I'll wait:
I won't go tomorrow, instead I'll
go hunting
for cottontails, since our food is getting low." "Well, it's up to you," she
    said
and then they
went to sleep. The next day
he got up and took his bow and

                                    •

went to his usual cottontail-hunting place, going around until he
    had killed four cottontails, then he took them home. It was
    evening when he got there
and they ate and then slept through the night.
The next day he got up and
went down to his field, going about hoeing.
Around noon he came back up. When they had eaten he said, "I might
    go
well, I might go to the village," he said. "It's up to you.
But if some
girl should want you to go with her
then don't waver in your thoughts
for it happens that a boy
(slowly) will come to have in-laws somewhere," she said.
(tight) "WHAT DO YOU MEAN BY THAT?" "Well, if you
    think of marrying a girl
and you go to live somewhere else
you must still think of me now and then:
you mustn't
forget all about me." "Well, I won't forget," he said.
And so
he left, going to his
usual place, and sat up there. Sure enough they were coming down
coming down to get water, and one of them
filled her dipper with water and splashed him, *(almost spraying)*
    KERSHPLASHHHHHH, and he went around shivering.
"I really think you're cute, why don't we go up?" she said.
"All right, let's
go on up," and while they were there the sun went down, and
the girl took the lead with the boy following her, the two of them went up.

●

When she took him
inside her house: "My

fathers, how have you
been passing the days?" "Happily, sit down, so you've come," they
said.
Then they
put out a seat for him

•

and the boy sat down. The girl fixed a meal and they sat down to eat.
When they sat down to eat, well then
he remembered
he remembered: "Oh, my grandmother, you gave me some instructions."
He took off his bow guard and LOOKED THROUGH IT
WHILE HE ATE.
HE WAS SITTING THERE LOOKING THROUGH HIS BOW
GUARD, and the householders were laughing. *(tight)* "Why
are you doing that?" they said
and they were laughing.
Then their father spoke to him: *(clearing throat)* "Son, why are you
eating that way?" "Well, because MY GRANDMOTHER
TOLD ME
that I should eat this way, that when I ate with my in-laws
I should keep my bow guard near my eyes, that's what she told me
and that's why I'm eating this way," he said. "Indeed. So that's
what you were told," they said
and THEY COULDN'T STOP LAUGHING. When the boy was
finished:
"I'm going out to pee," he said, and he WENT OUTSIDE TO
PEE and
went all the way back to his grandmother.
He ran away.
He entered
ta la^aa_a_{a.}

(tight) "Dear me! grandson, why have you come?" she said.

•

(excited) "Well, YOU GAVE ME BAD INSTRUCTIONS, for you
    told me to keep my bow guard near my eyes while I ate. I
    took my bow guard off and I
LOOKED THROUGH IT WHILE I ATE, *(pained)* and they
    really couldn't stop laughing, and I was so embarrassed I came
    home," he said. *(clicks tongue)*
"Dear me! you big fool.
That's not what I told you, YOU'RE ONLY SUPPOSED TO
    SHADE YOUR EYES WITH YOUR BOW GUARD
    WHILE YOU EAT, YOU'RE NOT SUPPOSED TO TAKE
    IT OFF AND LOOK THROUGH IT."
So his grandmother told him. "But I went ahead and TOOK OFF
    MY BOW GUARD AND LOOKED THROUGH IT
SO I COULDN'T SEE STRAIGHT TO REACH THE FOOD,
    and that's why *(almost laughs)*

•

that's why they couldn't stop laughing, and I was so embarrassed I
    said I wanted to pee, to pee, and when I WENT OUT TO
    PEE I came back here."
"Dear me! grandson, you weren't supposed to do that, but to keep
    your bow guard near your eyes while you ate:
that's the way the SAYING goes."
So his grandmother told him. "You must go back." "Why should
    I? I made a fool of myself," he said.

•

THEN HE SPENT THE NIGHT
WITH HIS GRANDMOTHER, and the next day he didn't go to
    the village.
Those girls
the ones who had wanted to take him home

came down to get water and waited for him, thinking he might
    come again, but he didn't come, and he still hadn't come
    when four days had passed, and
then
he spoke to his grandmother: "Why don't I
go back to the village?"
So he said. "Why not, it's
up to you, but don't

                                •

(sighing) do anything
that would embarrass you," she said. "No, I won't," he said.

                                •

And then
he took his
little animal skin, which
he used as a kilt, and tied it around his waist. When he had tied it
    around, he WENT BACK to the village, and when
he got there, he sat at his usual sitting place, then one of them
    came down and talked to him.
Finally the sun went down
and she took him up with her.
She took him up with her, and when
they entered her house, he greeted them: "My fathers, how have you been
    passing the days?" "Happily, our child, so you've come," they
    said. "Well, she brought me, that's why I came," he said, with
    his hoarse voice.
And then
the one who had brought him fixed a meal.
Then their father spoke:

                                •

"Put away
our child's animal," so

he said

so he said, and the boy

then remembered

his animal skin.

(low and tight) "Ee——, they can't do that, it's my kilt, and if they roll it up what'll
    I do for a kilt?

I have to go out to pee," he said, and THE BOY WENT OUT
    AND HEADED FOR HIS GRANDMOTHER.

He ran away.

And so

he entered,

       la_a
     ta ^aa_a.

"Dear me! grandson, you big fool, what have you done now?"

"Well, when this girl took me home with her

their father said:

'Put away

our child's animal,' and I WANTED THIS ANIMAL SKIN OF
    MINE so I came back," so

he said to his grandmother.

"Dear me! you big fool, that's not what he meant, he was talking
    about SOME MEAT TO ROAST," so *(almost laughs)*

                         •

so his grandmother told him.

"You should've told me that before." "GO BACK." "Well I'm too
    embarrassed to go back, it's better for me to stay," he said

and he spent the night

with his grandmother, and some days passed, and he didn't go
    back.

And when

four days had passed, he went back again, and when

he got to the well, the first one

who had talked to him

came to where he was sitting and said, "Why did you
say you were going out to pee and then
go away? We waited for you but you never came back in," she
    said. "Because, when I
looked through my bow guard while I ate you laughed, and I was so
    embarrassed I left," he said.
"So that's why you left. But please don't go away again.
Let's go on up." "All right
let's go," he said
and then
the girl got her water and took him to the place he had gone the
    first time, and they went in and ate. They ate
and there was another room where the girl slept.
After a time: "Well

                                        •

let's get some rest, for it's been a long day," their father said. The
    boy was taken into the next room, and then
the girl made the bed and they both lay down. When the girl
had fallen asleep, he started feeling her, and then he felt where her breasts were,
    her breasts.
He touched them, such hard round lumps
that's what he felt.
(tight) "Ee——, you're swelling up, and if you die while I'm sleeping with
    you I'll be killed for it."
AND THEN THE BOY WENT OUT AND RAN AWAY.
He ran all the way back to his grandmother, and his grandmother
    scolded him. He told her
how he had felt the girl's body.
"Dear me! you big fool, that's what we're like," his grandmother
    said, and SHE SHOWED HIM HER BREASTS.
"WHY DIDN'T YOU TELL ME THAT BEFORE I WENT?"
(laughing) so the boy said.

They slept through the night, and a few days later he went back.

    Again he was taken along

he was taken inside, and

when they had eaten, the two of them

lay down.

He felt her again.

But wait, before he had left home his grandmother had given him

    instructions:

"Son

when you get married

you must look for the hills," she had said.

•

And so he had gone to get married and they were lying down, and when

his wife had gone to sleep:

(tight and slow) "Oh, drat! you told me

to look for the hills, and if it's steamy there I should stick my pecker in, now I

    remember what you told me."

It was late at night when the boy walked out on his wife, and then

he went up to the Badger Hills and felt around there, but there

    wasn't any STEAMY place, he went around that way until:

"OH _{NO,} I'm _{going} back,

    you've given me the wrong instructions."

It was beginning to get light by the time he got back to his

    grandmother's house.

As they went to bed his grandmother questioned him:

•

"For what reason did you come back?" "Well, you told me

to look for the hills, and I went over to the Badger Hills and went

    around all night looking for those hills

and you told me that where it was steamy I should stick my pecker

    in, *(tight)* but I've been all over the hills and none of the cracks

    in the rocks there are steamy, so I came back."

• 229 •

So

he told his grandmother.

"That's NOT what I MEANT:

HERE are the hills we have," she said, his grandmother told him.

  "Well, I don't want to get married."

So the boy said, and they lived on.

He went down to his field to hoe

and somehow

one girl

found this out and went to where he was HOEING. When she
  came to where he was hoeing:

●

"So you've come," he said. "Yes, I've come."

So, so she said. "All right, let's

go inside," he said

and he took her

into his house.

●

"My grandmother, how have you been passing the days?"

  "Happily, so you've come." "Yes, I've

come," she said.

"Yes, he was down there

at his field and I spoke to him

and he brought me up here, so we came in," she said.

Then they fed her and afterwards questioned her. When they
  questioned her: "Well

I want to marry this child of yours, that's why I thought of
  coming here

that's why I've come

for we've

already

been together one night

when I brought him up, but for some reason he went away.

He went outside and never came back, and I
was told to come here, so I came," she said.

•

"Well, he's such a
fool, so
while you were sleeping he
felt your breasts, and when he touched them
your breasts
felt like hard swellings and he thought you might die while he was
    sleeping with you, that's why he left, but I've given him a
    talking to. Well, why don't you
go back together?"
so she said.
"All right, let's go," the boy said, then she took the boy out with her
and so
the two of them
entered upon the roads of their elders, and again she brought him in.
After she brought the boy in they were lying down again, and he touched
    her
cunt, and
it was cracked: *(tight)* "Ee——, someone must've hit you with an axe,
    you're badly wounded.
I was told not to go back, but I must go, this shouldn't be."
So the boy said, and he WENT OUT and went back to his
    grandmother.
His grandmother wasn't asleep yet when he got there:
"Dear me! grandson, what's your reason for scurrying back here?"
    "Well, when
my wife
was sleeping I felt her
and SOMEONE MUST'VE HIT HER WITH AN AXE, and
    there's SUCH a crack.

WHEN I FOUND OUT I was afraid she'd die while I was
    sleeping with her, so I came back." "Dear me! grandson, that's
    what we're LIKE," his grandmother said, and his grandmother
    (laughs)
showed him her cunt. "Oh well, I didn't want to get married
    anyway," he said. "Why didn't you tell me this before?"
    "Because it shouldn't be this way, for we value our bodies.
    You're such a fool, and because you're such a fool I had to
    show you mine," his grandmother told him. *(laughs)*
They lived on this way, and because the boy was such a fool he
    never got married. This was lived long ago. That's a—ll the
    word was short. *(laughs)*

NOTES

Narrated by Walter Sanchez on the evening of March 23, 1965, with Andrew Peynetsa, Andrew's wife, son, two small granddaughters, and myself present. Only Walter's laughter has been noted in the translation. The performance took twenty-one minutes. Walter told no more tales after this date, shifting to other kinds of narratives. For Andrew the tale-telling season had already ended (see the notes to the previous story), but Walter, not being a member of a medicine society, had less reason to be strict.

Pelt Kid: in Zuni this is Kempewi Ts'ana, literally "Pelt Little-One"; the translation "Pelt Kid" was suggested by Andrew.

Thongs: these were for tying the wood into a bundle.

"Pulling cottontails out": this is done with a barbed stick (see "The Girl and the Little Ahayuuta" for a detailed description). Pelt Kid carried his bow in case he might get a shot at a rabbit, just as a rabbit hunter today might carry both a gun and a stick; according to Joseph Peynetsa, one gets more rabbits with a stick than with a gun.

Pelt Kid's hoarse voice: Walter speaks in a hoarse voice all the time, so he was unable to use hoarseness to distinguish the quotations of Pelt Kid from the body of the story. Andrew, on the other hand, was able to imitate the hoarseness of the younger brother Ahayuuta in "The Sun Priest and the Witch Woman."

The well: a large, open, walk-in well. Joseph Peynetsa commented, "When I was a kid there wasn't a well like that anymore, but there were maybe three places around the village where they had faucets, where the girls went to get water with buckets. Boys would meet their girl friends there. Now, with water in the houses, they have activities like basketball games and movies where kids go and meet their boy or girl friends."

"Keep your bow guard near your eyes while you eat": Joseph explained, "When you get married you're supposed to be bashful and eat like this," and he shaded his eyes with his left wrist, where a bow guard would be worn. It would be impolite not to act bashful. The play on meaning in the original Zuni is somewhat different from the one in my translation:

Pelt Kid is told to *tuna pikwayi* his bow guard, which means either to "look past" or to "look through," and he mistakenly makes the latter interpretation.

"A boy will come to have in-laws somewhere": Zuni newlyweds normally take up residence with the family of the wife. Today, as in the story, the act of getting married consists of little more than a man's moving in with his wife's family.

"I'm going out to pee": such a statement is perfectly proper in mixed company and might be made by a person of either sex.

"Talaaaaa": the sound of a person descending a ladder at great speed.

"Put away our child's animal": the word for "animal" here is *wemme*, which means either a fur-bearing animal or its pelt. The man was referring to the butchered carcass of an animal which had been brought in from the hunt by one of his children.

"Pecker": Pelt Kid uses *shuminne*, a quaint archaism, rather than *tu'linne*, which is the ordinary word for penis.

"The two of them entered upon the roads of their elders": that is, they entered the lives of her parents.

THE SHUMEEKULI

Well then
there were villagers at HAWIKKU
there were villagers at GYPSUM PLACE

•

there were villagers at WIND PLACE, these were the villages
and a rain priest
there at Gypsum Place
spoke of having a Yaaya, a Yaaya dance.
When the word went out, people from all the villages

•

started gathering.
The date had been set and
they lived on.

•

For four nights
they practiced the Yaaya.
The Yaaya practice went on, and
they were gathering:
for four nights they kept gathering.
O———n they went, until
the day came.
And the HELIX PEOPLE

WENT INTO SESSION, and on the eve of the ceremony their
    Shumeekuli dancers came.

                                        •

The Shumeekuli came

                                        •

and the next day was to be the day

                                        •

for dancing the Yaaya.
Then it was the morning of the dance.
On the morning of the dance
the villagers gathered
and then
they were
getting up to dance.
O———n they went, until, at noon, they stopped to eat, and when they had eaten
    they got up again.
They got up in the afternoon

                                        •

and when they had done about
two sets, there were four rings of dancers.
Then the HELIX PEOPLE BROUGHT IN THEIR
SHUMEEKULI
and when these were brought in, the Horned Ones were also
    brought in.
They kept on dancing this way UNTIL THEIR
White Shumeekuli came, he was brought in when
there were four rings of dancers
and all the villagers had gathered:
there was a BIG CROWD, a big crowd, and
the dance kept on.
Their White Shumeekuli
kept going around the tree. He danced around it, and for some reason
he went crazy.

•

The people HELD ON TIGHT, but somehow he broke through
   their rings and ran away.

                                •

He ran and ran
and they ran after him.

                                •

They ran after him, but
they couldn't catch him and still they kept after him shouting as they went.
He was far ahead, the White Shumeekuli was far ahead of them.
They kept on going until

                                •

they came near SHUMINNKYA.
Someone was herding out there
he was herding, his sheep were spread out there when they came shouting.
"There   Shu   way,   out
     goes our White   meekuli, running a   ' whoever is
          there please   help   us.
CATCH HIM FOR US," they were shouting as they kept after
   him.
(low and tense) "Oh yes, there's a Yaaya dance today, something must've
   happened."
So the herder said, and the shouting was getting close.
After a time, their Shumeekuli
came into view.
He was still running.
The herder stood under a tree where he was going to pass
and waited for him, then
going straight on
the Shumeekuli headed for
the place where the herder stood.

                                •

Sure enough, just as

he came up
past the TREE
the herder caught him for them.
There he caught him:
the White Shumeekuli
who had run away from the Yaaya dance.
The others came to get him
and took him back.

                              •

They brought him back, and when they
tried to unmask him
the mask
was stuck
to his face.
He was changing over.

                              •

When they unmasked the young man, some of his
flesh peeled off.

                              •

Then, the one who had come as the White Shumeekuli
lived only four days before he died.

                              •

They LIVED ON
until, at ZUNI

                              •

when the Middle Place had become known

                              •

the date was again set for the Yaaya, and when the date had been
    set they gathered for four nights.
They gathered for practice, that's the way
they lived
and when the day of the Yaaya arrived
the villagers came together on the morning of the dance.

*

Again the YAAYA
dance began
and again the Shumeekuli dancers were brought in.
They were brought in and they danced properly, but then
there came one who costumed himself as the White Shumeekuli,
     and he went around
until it happened AGAIN:
he went crazy.
He struggled then, but
they held onto him.
It happens whenever somebody impersonates that one:
because of the flesh that got inside that mask in former times
when someone comes into the Yaaya dance as the White
     Shumeekuli
something will inevitably happen to his mind. This is what
happened, and because this happened
the White Shumeekuli came to be feared.
That's all.

NOTES

Narrated by Andrew Peynetsa on March 23, 1965, immediately after
Walter Sanchez told "Pelt Kid and His Grandmother." That the present
story is not a tale *(telapnanne)* is signaled by its lack of that genre's formal
opening and closing lines. The main episode takes place after the founding
of the village of Hawikku (the event that ends "When Newness Was
Made," Part I) and before the Middle Place has been found (in Part II).

Hawikku: a village that was composed of large house blocks several sto-
ries high, located on a ridge overlooking the flood plain of the Zuni
River. The main period of occupation runs from about 1400 until 1680,

but there may be much earlier remains at deeper levels. When Coronado arrived in 1540, Hawikku was the first Zuni village he saw.

Gypsum Place: Kechipaawa, a village that was composed of terraced house blocks surrounding two plazas, located on a mesa overlooking the irrigated farmlands of the contemporary Zuni hamlet of Ojo Caliente. Occupation began somewhat later than for the main period at Hawikku and ended at about the same time.

Yaaya: a dance whose name is Keresan and refers to the medicine society officials who participate. A Douglas fir is felled and set in the middle of the plaza, where unmasked men and women dance around it in concentric rings.

Helix People: Shumaakwe, a medicine society which specializes in curing convulsions by means of helical seashells. Only its members may impersonate the Shumeekuli and the Horned Ones (see below).

Shumeekuli: dancers who wear flat face masks rather than the head-covering helmet masks worn by the impersonators of most kachinas; the faces are painted with terraced cloud and falling rain motifs. There are six kinds of Shumeekuli: yellow, blue, red, white, multicolored, and black. They dance inside the concentric rings of Yaaya dancers. Formerly there were Shumeekuli dancers at the Keresan village of Zia and the Tewa village of Hano. Their place of origin, according to Zuni tradition, was the Sandia Mountains.

Horned Ones: these have helmet masks; the "horn" is a long feather, fastened at the top of the mask and sweeping forward out over the face. They dance outside the Yaaya rings.

"For some reason he went crazy": it is understood that he violated the sexual continence required of those who have made a commitment to participate in a masked dance, or that he resented or harbored doubts about his participation. Later wearers of his mask went crazy because they were, in effect, impersonating him.

WHEN NEWNESS WAS MADE

PART I

Well then
this
is when NEWNESS WAS MADE.
When newness was made
when the earth was still soft
the first people came out
the ones who had been living in the first room beneath.
When they came out they made their villages
they made their houses a———ll around the land.
They were living this way
but it was the Sun's thinking
that this
was not right
not the way to live.
They did not offer him prayer sticks, prayer meal.
"Well, perhaps if the ones who live in the second room come out,
　　it will be good."

•

so THEN
when the ones who lived in the second room came out
THEIR LIGHTNING SMELL
killed the ones who had already come out.

All of them died
and the second people lived o————n for some years
but they did not think of anything, it was not right.
Those who lived in the third room beneath were summoned.
When they came out
when the third ones came out their lightning smell killed all the
     second ones.
Their ruins are all around the land
as you can see.
Around the mountains where there is no water today, you could
     get water just by pulling up the grass
because the earth was soft.
This is the way they lived, when newness was made.
The ^{Sun} _{was} thinking
that they did not think of anything.
The ones who were living in the fourth room
were needed

                •

but
the Sun was thinking

                •

he was thinking
that he did not know what would happen now.

              •

The clouds, the clouds were swelling.
The clouds were getting better aaaaaaAAAAAAH THE RAIN
     CAME
fine drops came, it rai————ned, it rained and rained
it rained all night.
Where there were waterfalls
the water made foam.
Well, you know how water can make foam
certainly

it can make foam

•

certainly
that water
made suds.
It was there
where the suds were made
that the two Bow Priests
sprouted.
There the two Ahayuuta
received life.
Their father brought them to life.
They came out of the suds.
When they came out: "Aha———
so we've SPROUTED." "Yes yes."
Then they stepped forward a little and stood there.

•

"Well
what are we going to do
what will our ROAD be?"
"Well I don't know."

•

At noon
when it was about noon
their Sun Father came down
near where they stood
and stepping forward a little
he came to them where they stood.
"How, father, how have you been passing the days?" "Happily, my
    CHILDREN.
Have you sprouted now?" he asked them. "Yes we've sprouted."
    "Indeed."
"What's your reason for having us sprout?

Is it because something is going to happen?
Or is it because of
a WORD of some importance, something that's going to be said:
is that why you
brought us to life?"
So the Ahayuuta asked the Sun. "YES, in TRUTH
my CHILDREN
all these, our daylight, our people
have emerged, have come. When I summoned the ones in the first
　　　room
they came out and stood in my daylight.
I thought of them but they never offered me prayer meal.
They never offered me prayer sticks.
Because of this I summoned the ones in the second room beneath.
The first ones out
made their houses all around, made villages.

THE ^{SE}COND ONES OUT, BECAUSE OF THEIR
　　　LIGHT_{NING} SMELL
DID AWAY WITH THE FIRST ONES.
The second ones made villages when they came out.
And because I thought,
'The way they are living is not what I had in mind,'
I summoned the ones who lived
in the third room.
When the third ones came out their lightning smell killed the
　　　second ones.

THE ONES IN THE ^{FOURTH} ROOM ARE STILL ^{DOWN}

　　　THERE
and because I know I will need them
I have GIVEN YOU LIFE.
You will GO INSIDE.

You will bring them out, and PERHAPS THEN
as I have in mind
they will offer me prayer meal."
That's what the Sun
told his two children. "So.
So, is this why you brought us to life?" "Yes, this is why I brought
    you to life."
"Very well inDEED.
We will TRY.
This place where they may or may not live is FAR
there in the room full of SOOT
the ones who live in the fourth room," so the Ahayuuta SAID.
When they had said .
                   it:
"Well we're GOING
our FATHER.
Have good THOUGHTS.
Whatever happens when we enter upon their roads, IT WILL BE,"
    they said.
"By all means may you also have good THOUGHTS.
CERTAINLY YOU WILL BRING THEM OUT WITH YOU,"
    their father said. "Very well."
THE TWINS WENT ON
until they came to the Place of Emergence.
A hole was open there.
"Well, perhaps HERE."

                            •

THEY ENTERED.
When they entered, entered the first room
it was full of the color of dawn.
The second
room they entered
was full of yellow.

IN THE ^{THIRD} ROOM THEY ENTERED

    they could hardly make anything out.

THERE IN THE ^{FOURTH} ROOM

when they entered

IT WAS FULL OF DARKNESS, NOTHING COULD BE
    SEEN

nothing could be made out.

THEY GOT THEIR FOOTING

when they came to the bottom.

               •

Then they went some distance

toward the west and came upon two

               •

who perhaps LIVED there, VILLAGERS

someone was close by, a DEER

someone was going around hunting, following a DEER, and they
    met him.

He came to where they were standing:

they didn't see him until he came to where they were standing.

"Haa——, so you've come," he said. "Yes."

(weakly) "What are you doing going around here?" he asked the
    two Ahayuuta.

"I'm following a deer, have you seen him?"

(tight) "Well it's full of darkness here, how could we see a deer? We
    can't see anything.

WHERE DO YOU LIVE?" they asked him.

(weakly) "This way

toward the west:

that's where we live." "Indeed.

THAT'S WHERE WE'RE GOING," the two Ahayuuta said.

    (weakly) "Indeed. Well, I'll take you along."

"ALL RIGHT, BUT WE CAN'T SEE. How can we find the
    way?" *(weakly)* "Even so, we can find the way quite well."
"All right, but we still can't see. Wait
let us do something," and they made CEDAR-BARK TORCHES.
When they had made cedar-bark torches they
made them blossom
lit them
AND THE ONE WHO HAD BEEN IN THE DARK COULD
    HARDLY SEE
"Tísshomahhá
put those things out, I CAN'T SEE," he said.
"IF YOU WOULD JUST FOLLOW ME, we could go."
They put out their cedar-bark torches.
He took them toward the west, they went on, went on
until they arrived at a village.
"THIS is where we LIVE."

                              •

"So this is where you LIVE.
Are there
perhaps
people who live, are there people who live by the sacred things, do
    they have
a house here?
Isn't there

                              •

that sort of
household around here somewhere?" they said. *(weakly)* "Well
    perhaps I
might know why it is that you came.
Well, LET'S GO," he said, and THEY WENT TOWARD THE
    PLAZA and entered it.

                              •

The priest's

the Sun Priest's house was the one they approached.
They went up and entered where the Sun Priest
lived, that must have been the way it was.
They entered his dwelling.
"My fathers, my children, how have you been passing the days?"
"Happily, our children, so you've come.
Be seated," they said. IT WAS FULL OF DARKNESS, THEY
      WERE ALL SPITTING ON ONE ANOTHER: BECAUSE
      IT WAS FULL OF DARKNESS
THEY COULD NOT SEE
WHERE ANYONE WAS.

                  ●

THEN
the one whose house this was questioned them: "NOW
for what reason have you entered upon our ROADS?
Who might you
be?" he asked them.
"WELL, I

                 ●

I AM MA'ASEWI," the elder brother said.
"And I am Uyuyuwi."
"Indeed.
Why are you named this way?"
"Our Sun Father
brought us to life.
Because he sent us in
we have come.
Because we must take you with us out into the daylight
BECAUSE OF THESE WORDS, because of these instructions,
     we have entered upon your ROADS."
SO
the two Ahayuuta said.
"Indeed.

•

But even if that's what you have in mind
how will it be done?
THIS PLACE WHERE YOU SPROUTED:
DO YOU HAVE THE MEANS FOR GETTING OUT THERE
    successfully?
What is known about this?"
SO HE
the Sun Priest
said to them.

•

"WELL
well, no," the Ahayuuta said.
"But that's why we have entered upon your roads."
That's what the Ahayuuta said. "Indeed.
But if we did this
it wouldn't be right if we went out by ourselves.
Now, THERE toward the NORTH
is our father the North Priest.
Now, why don't you summon HIM?
Perhaps he will be the one who
will know
how to get OUT.
For certainly these words have been SPOKEN.
It cannot be OTHERWISE.
And whatever you have DECIDED
SO IT WILL BE," SO
the Sun Priest said, the Sun Priest. "Very well indeed. I'LL GO,"
    that's what the elder brother Ahayuuta said.
He went toward the north.
He went on
until he reached the North Ocean.
A house stood there.

It stood there.
"Well perhaps
the one who lives here is home,"
he said, and he went up to where the house stood and entered.
The North Priest was there.

·

"My ^{FA}THERRR

how have you been passing the days?" "Happily, my CHILD
so you've come, be seated," he told him.
"Yes, I've
come." "Indeed.
SIT DOWN," he told him, and he sat down.
The North Priest questioned him: "NOW
my father, child
for what reason
have you entered upon my ROAD?
You would not enter upon my road for no reason.
Perhaps it is because of a WORD of some importance
that you enter upon my road.
You must make this known to me
so that I may think about it
as I pass the days," the North Priest said.
Then the elder brother Ahayuuta said, "YES, in TRUTH
my FATHER, my CHILD

·

because our Sun FATHER
has instructed us to take YOU
out into his daylight
into his daylight
we came to the village there.
Because they did not know
how to get out
YOU had to be summoned

and that is why
I have come to speak with you," he said. "Indeed.

•

Indeed. Since you have in truth spoken the word, it cannot be
    OTHERWISE.
Well, WAIT A MOMENT," the North Priest said.
HE ASSEMBLED HIS SACRED THINGS.
He assembled his wild seeds, all his sacred things.
"WELL I'M READY," he said. "I'm ready now, so let's
be on our way."
He took his sacred things, took his wild seeds, garden seeds.
Then
the Ahayuuta
took the North Priest with him.
They went on until
they came to where the younger brother was.
"My fathers, my children, how have you been passing the days?" the Ahayuuta
    said.
"Happily, so you've come now."
When the North Priest entered:
"My CHILDREN
my fathers, my mothers
how have you been passing the days?" "Happily, our father, sit down," they told
    him.
When he sat down he put down his sacred things.
When he had put down his sacred things
he questioned them, the North Priest did: "NOW
my FATHERS
my CHILDREN
for what reason
have you summoned ME?
Perhaps it is because there is something important to say that you
    have summoned me.

You must make this known to me
so that I may think about it as I pass the days."
So he said. "YES, in TRUTH, our two fathers HERE
have entered upon our ROADS.
They have spoken of taking us out into their Sun Father's daylight
but they do not know how.
Perhaps you might know something, since your thoughts are
        rooted in your sacred things," so
the Sun Priest said.
"YES, in TRUTH
my CHILDREN
even if that's what you THINK about me
I do not know how to get OUT.
Perhaps my younger brother there, the Evening PRIEST:
perhaps he would know how to do THIS.
You should summon him," so

                                        •

the North Priest said.
The younger brother Ahayuuta said:
"I'LL GO," the younger brother Ahayuuta said.
He stood up.

                                        •

When he stood up: "My fathers, my children, I will go on the
        ROAD.
It might be during

                                        •

the night or during the day when I enter upon your roads again."
"Very well then.
May you go happily."
The younger brother Ahayuuta went out and

                                        •

went toward the west, going along westward until he came to the ocean.
A house stood there.

"Well perhaps this
is where you live,"
he said, and went up
and went inside
where the Evening Priest was.
When he went inside:
"My father, my child, how have you
been passing the days?" "Happily, my CHILD
so you've come, sit down, be seated." He sat down, sat down.
The Evening Priest asked him, questioned him: "NOW
my CHILD, for what reason have you entered upon my ROAD?
You would not enter upon my road for no REASON.
Perhaps it is because of a WORD of some importance
that you enter upon my road." "YES, in TRUTH
our Sun FATHER
brought us to LIFE.
When he brought us to life
he spoke of our taking these villagers
the ones who live here
out into the Sun Father's daylight:
that's why he made our lives whole. We went inside
and came to the village
but they
did not know how to get out, and so
your elder brother
the North Priest was summoned
and because he did not know
and BECAUSE YOU WERE THE NEXT TO BE SPOKEN OF
I have come
to summon you," the little Ahayuuta said. "Indeed.
Since you have in truth spoken the WORD
it cannot be OTHERWISE.
Well, WAIT A MOMENT," he said

and going into the next room
he readied
his sacred things, his wild seeds, garden seeds
he readied them.
"NOW
let's be on our way."
They went out and went on.
They came to where the gathering was.
When they came to where the gathering was

•

they entered. "My fathers, my children, how have you been?"
    "Happy."
"My CHILDREN
my fathers, my elder BROTHERS
how have you been passing the days?" "Happily, my younger
    brother, sit down," the North Priest said.
"Happily, be seated," they were told.
The Evening Priest sat down.
When he had put down his sacred things
put down his wild seeds, garden seeds
he questioned them:
"NOW
my CHILDREN
for what reason have you summoned ME?
Perhaps it is because of a WORD of some importance
that you have summoned me.
You must make this known to me
so that I may think about it
as I pass the days," he said.
"YES, in TRUTH, our two fathers HERE
have entered upon our ROADS.
Because their Sun Father
has spoken to them of taking us out into the daylight

they have entered upon our roads
but because we did not know how to get out
your elder brother here, the North Priest
was summoned, but he did not know
and because YOU WERE THE NEXT TO BE SPOKEN OF
you were summoned," so

                           •

the Sun Priest said. "Indeed.
But I do not know about THIS.
Perhaps our younger brother THERE
the Coral PRIEST
perhaps he would KNOW.
Well then, you should summon him," so
he said.
"Well, I'LL GO," the elder brother Ahayuuta said.
He went toward the coral.
He came to the Coral Ocean.
A house stood there.
"Perhaps
this is where you live,"

                           •

and he went up
and entered.
The Coral
Priest was there.
"My father, my child, how have you been passing the days?"
    "Happily, my FATHER
so you've come, sit down," he said.
HE SAT DOWN, the Ahayuuta sat down.
The Coral Priest questioned him: "NOW
my CHILD
for what reason
have you entered upon my ROAD?

Perhaps it is because of a WORD of some importance that
you have entered upon my road. You would not do this for no
    reason," so
the Coral Priest said. "YES, in TRUTH
because our Sun FATHER
who brought us to LIFE
spoke the word
of bringing YOU out
we came inside
to the village there, but they did not know
how to get out.
Your elder brothers
the North Priest
the Evening Priest
were both summoned
but because they did not know how to get out
THEY ASKED FOR YOU NEXT
and so I am summoning you," the Ahayuuta said. "Indeed.
Since you have in truth spoken the WORD
it cannot be OTHERWISE.
Well, WAIT A MOMENT"
he said, and he went into the next room
to assemble
his sacred things, he assembled his wild seeds, garden seeds.
When he was ready:
"Well, I'M READY.

                            •

Now let's be on our way."
THE AHAYUUTA WENT THIS WAY *(gestures northward)*
the elder brother did, and
brought the Coral Priest with him.
They came to where the gathering was
and went inside: "My fathers, my children, how have you been?" "Happy

be seated," they said.

The Coral Priest said, "My fathers, my CHILDREN

how have you been passing the days?" "Happily, our CHILD

be seated," they told him. He put down his sacred things, put

    down his wild seeds, garden seeds.

He questioned them: "NOW

for what reason have you SUMMONED me?" he said.

"YES, in TRUTH

our two FATHERS

have come.

Their father

the Sun

who brought them to life

spoke the word of taking us out

and ^{so they en} tered up ^{on our} roads.

But your elder brothers did not have the knowledge

of how to get out

and because they did not know, YOU WERE THE NEXT

to be spoken of, and so you were the one

we summoned," he said. "Indeed.

How ^{ever}

I do not know about this.

But it cannot be otherwise, since you have in truth spoken the

    WORD.

Well, our younger BROTHER

the Morning Priest should be SUMMONED, for he might

    KNOW about this."

So

the Coral Priest said.

"Well, I'll GO."

The younger brother Ahayuuta

standing up

approached

the east

going along until

he came to the edge

                                              •

of the water, where a house stood. "Well

well perhaps that's it."

He went up to it.

When he got there

he went through the door

and the Morning Priest was there.

"My father, my child, how have you been passing the days?"

    "Happily, my FATHER

so you've COME.

Sit down," he told him.

The Ahayuuta sat down.

                                         •

Then

the Morning Priest questioned him: "NOW, my father, my

    CHILD

for what reason have you entered upon my ROAD?

Perhaps it is because of a WORD of some importance that

you have entered upon my road, for you would not do this for no

    reason," so

the Morning Priest said to the Ahayuuta. "YES

in TRUTH

my father, my CHILD

our Sun FATHER

who brought us to life

spoke of taking THESE VILLAGERS out

all of you

and so he sent us in.

When we came to the village they did not know

how to get out.
A———ll your elder bro
                    thers
from all around
have been brought together
but because they did not know
your elder brother, the Coral Priest
NEXT SPOKE OF YOU, and so
I have come
to summon you," he said. "Indeed.
Since you have in TRUTH spoken the WORD
it cannot be OTHERWISE.
Well, WAIT A MOMENT," and
going into the next room, he gathered his sacred things, his wild
        seeds, garden seeds.
When he was ready:
"Well, I'M READY." "Very well indeed."
Going out
and going on
they came to the village. When they came to the village

                        •

they went inside.

                            •

There was a crowd of people.
When the Ahayuuta entered:
"My fathers, how have you been?" "Happy."
When the Morning Priest entered:
"My fathers, my CHILDREN, my elder BROTHERS
how have you been passing the days?" "Happily, our younger
        brother.
So you've come, be seated," they said.
He put down his sacred things, put down his wild seeds, garden
        seeds.
He sat down.

•

"NOW
what is your reason
for summoning ME?
You must make this known to ME.
Perhaps it is because there is a word of some IMPORTANCE
that you have SUMMONED me," so
the Morning Priest said.
"YES, in TRUTH
our two fathers HERE
whose father the SUN
brought them to life
came in to us
because he spoke the word of taking us out.
They came here to our village
but because no one knew how to get out
your elder brothers here

•

have been summoned, and even though they DID NOT KNOW
        how to get out
perhaps you might know
how to get out:
that's why we have summoned you," he said.
"Indeed.
But even if that's what you have in mind, I do not know about
        THIS.
I, least of ALL.
What about our two fathers HERE?
Perhaps they know how to do this after all," so
the Morning Priest said.
The two Ahayuuta said, "Well
well I DON'T KNOW.
But I will try something.

My FATHERS
my CHILDREN
PREPARE YOURSELVES," they told them.

So they told them.

THE ^{ONES} WHO LIVED BY THE ^{SA}CRED THINGS PUT

THEIR ^{SA}CRED THINGS ON THEIR BACKS, THEIR

WILD SEEDS

ALL THE ^{VIL}LAGERS WERE TOLD
    ALL THE VILLAGERS
TOLD ONE ANOTHER.

The twins took them along
and went toward the east, toward where the two of them had
    come from
and the villagers
went with them.

•

O————n they went until they were ^{al}most where the ^{twins}
    had come down in^{.side:}
"YOU MAY REST HERE," they told them.

They put down their sacred things.

"WAIT HERE _{WHILE WE GO} ON,"
    they said.

•

They went to the place where they had come down.
"What are we going to do?" "Well perhaps we should
MAKE THE YELLOW PRAYER STICKS," so
the elder brother Ahayuuta said.

•

"Well, we might

approach the north," the elder brother Ahayuuta said.

"Very well."

THERE THEY COMPLETED THE YELLOW PRAYER
    STICKS.

WHEN THEY WERE FI_{NISHED}

THERE AT THE PLACE WHERE THEY WERE GOING TO
    GET OUT

they stood up the prayer sticks.

WHEN THEY HAD STOOD UP THE PRAYER _{STICKS}

a fir tree

•

GREW there.

IT ^{GREW UNTIL IT REACHED THE NEXT} PLACE

THE ^{THIRD} ROOM

AND STOOD

sticking out there a little.

"Perhaps this will do."

•

"Very well indeed, perhaps this will do, perhaps it's sticking out a
    little," he said.

"Now let's go back."

Then the two Ahayuuta

after making things ready

went back to where the others were.

"My fathers, my children, how have you been?"

"Happy, our fathers, so you've COME.

Has a WAY been FOUND now?" they asked them.

"The WAY has been FOUND NOW, prepare yourselves NOW.

Let's get on the road," they told them.

They put their sacred things on their backs, their garden seeds

wild seeds.

•

"ARE YOU READY NOW?" "YES, WE'RE READY."
"Well, let's be on our way." They went on, went on until
when they came to where the twins had stood up the prayer sticks
a fir tree stood THERE.
It stood there:
"NOW, my CHILDREN
my fathers, my children
YOU MUST CLIMB UP THE BRANCHES UNTIL YOU GET
     OUT."
So the twins told them. "Indeed.
Very well, this is the way it will be."
The younger brother Ahayuuta

•

went up the fir tree, he was the first to go out, and sure enough it stuck out a little
     into the third
room.
HE GOT OUT FIRST
and sat down.
They all climbed UP.
       aaah
aaᵃᵃ
they stepped from branch to branch, GOING UP until they had
     all come out.
When everyone was out the elder brother Ahayuuta was the last one.
"Are they all out now?" "Yes, they're all out."
They rested nearby.
"Now we can wait here awhile," they said.

•

In the third room the twins
stood up.
"Now what will be done?"
"We will bring the BLUE prayer sticks to life. We

must approach evening's direction," he said. "Very well indeed."

·

They approached evening's direction and FINISHED the blue prayer
    sticks.
When they had fi   blue
         nished the   prayer sticks
and stood them up

·

an aspen

·

grew there.
The aspen grew
until
it reached
the second room
and stood there.
As it stood

·

they thought, "Well, it must be sticking out a little." "Yes, perhaps this will do."
"Yes, let's go."
THEY WENT ON UNTIL
they came to where the others were.
"My fathers, my children, how have you been?" "Happy, our
    FATHERS.
Now
has a way been found?"
"The WAY has been FOUND NOW, prepare yourselves NOW,"
    they told them.
They put their sacred things
on their backs.
The twins took them along until
they came to where it stood.
The aspen stood there.
"NOW, our children, you must do as before:

you must climb up the branches until you get out."
So they said.
"Very well indeed."

•

They climbed up until they had ALL come out.
They let them rest nearby.
"Now what will be done?" "Well, we'll
make the red prayer sticks" they said.
They approached coral's direction.
They finished the red prayer sticks, and when they were finished they set them up
   on the ground.

•

A COTTONWOOD

•

stood UP.
A narrow-leafed cottonwood grew.
There in the next room
IT STOOD STICKING OUT, IT STOOD OUT INTO A
   PLACE FULL OF THE COLOR OF DAWN
full of yellow.

•

They went back to where the others were.
"My fathers, my children, how have you been?" "Happy, our
   FATHERS.
Has a WAY been FOUND now?"
"The WAY has been FOUND NOW, prepare yourselves NOW,"
   they told them.
They put their sacred things on their backs, put their wild seeds,
   garden seeds on their backs.
The twins took them along until

•

they came to where the cottonwood stood. "NOW, in order to get out,
   climb the branches until you are there."

Again they climbed out, aaaaAAAAH until they were ALL out.
"Are they all out now?" "Yes, they're all out."
It was full of the color of dawn
a yellow room.
They let them rest nearby.
The twins said, "NOW
what will be done?"
"Well, we must make the white prayer sticks.
We must approach the morning," so
the elder brother Ahayuuta said.
They finished the WHITE PRAYER STICKS.
WHEN THEY FINISHED THEY SET THEM UP ON THE
    GROUND.
A CANE PLANT
GREW there.
The cane plant grew UNTIL IT STOOD STICKING OUT
INTO THE SUN FATHER'S DAYLIGHT.
It stood there
branching.

•

"Perhaps this will do, for this will be the fourth time we go out,"
    the elder brother Ahayuuta said.
"Yes, perhaps
this will do."
Then they went back to where the others were.

•

"NOW, my fathers, my children, how have you been?" "Happy,
    our FATHERS.
Now
has a WAY been FOUND?"
"The WAY has been FOUND NOW, prepare yourselves NOW,"
    they told them.

"VERY WELL." Again they put their sacred things on their backs,
    their wild seeds, garden seeds
they put them on their backs.
The twins took them along
until they came to where the cane plant stood.
IT WAS STANDING LIKE AN ARROW.
"NOW YOU MUST STEP FROM BRANCH TO BRANCH
    AGAIN
UNTIL WE COME OUT, OUT INTO OUR SUN FATHER'S
    DAYLIGHT.
    EVEN THOUGH IT WILL BE HA_{RD}
YOU MUST DO YOUR BEST
to look at your father
for you will hardly be able to SEE.
There in the room full of soot, when we entered upon your roads,
    we could hardly SEE.
This is the way it will be with you, CERTAINLY."
SO THEY TOLD THEM.
They climbed UP.
SURE ENOUGH, THE MOMENT THEY CAME OUT they
    dropped to the ground.
They could not bear it.
Their eyes saw nothing.
Even so, o———n they all came out.
"Are they all out now?" "Yes, they're all out."

                                    •

"Tísshomahhá, my CHILDREN
YOU MUST DO YOUR BEST TO OPEN YOUR EYES." "Yes,
    but it's hard."
That's the way they were, o————n

RESTING WHILE THEIR EYES GREW A LITTLE
   STRONGER

until their eyes were STRONG ENOUGH
to see.
They were all looking at their Sun Father.

•

"Tísshomahhá, our FATHERS
WHAT EXTRAORDINARY PERSONS YOU ARE," they told
   the twins. "Indeed?
Extraordinary persons we are NOT.
It is because of the thoughts of our Sun Father that we KNOW
   THESE THINGS.
BECAUSE OF HIS THOUGHTS WE MUST ALL GO ALONG
   NOW
for some distance
and then we will rest."
So they told them.
"Prepare yourselves."
They put their sacred things on their backs. The twins then
took them o————n
going on for some distance
until they arrived somewhere, having gone a long way.

•

The Sun went down.
"NOW
we will stay here four days," he said. THEY WERE GOING TO
   STAY FOUR YEARS.
FOR FOUR YEARS THEY LIVED
where they had stopped.

•

The first year came

the second, the third
AND IN THE ^{FOURTH} YEAR
THERE WAS A RUMBLING WHERE THEY HAD
    EMERGED.
There was a rumbling.
The ones who had the sacred things said, "AHAaaa
there is someone ELSE *(dogs bark outside)*
for there is his SOUND.
You two should go and find OUT.
It must be an extraordinary person
to make this rumbling," so
the ones who had the sacred things said to the twins.
The twins went to the Place of Emergence.
WHEN THEY CAME TO THE PLACE OF EMERGENCE
THERE he SAT.
A SORCERER.
Someone UNCLEAN.
Someone DANGEROUS.
A WITCH.

                                        •

"So——it's YOU.
What is your reason for coming OUT?
Having you in this won't be good," so
the Ahayuuta said. "Indeed
but that's just the way it IS.

                                        •

I am a person with garden seeds," he said. THEY WERE GOING
    TO KILL HIM.
They were going to kill him, but he didn't want it.
"Very well, it's up to YOU.
FIRST YOU MUST KILL THIS, THEN YOU CAN KILL ME,"
    he said, and he showed them
his EAR OF YELLOW CORN.

"THESE are my garden SEEDS.
Yes, the others have come OUT
but their only seeds
are the ones they came out with.
THIS KIND OF CORN SEED is not among them.
THEIR FLESH
will not be good:
THAT IS WHY
I HAVE COME OUT.
But if you are going to kill me, YOU MUST KILL THIS
THEN YOU CAN KILL ME."
So the sorcerer told them.
They thought about it.
When they had thought about it
they did not KILL him.
They DID NOT KILL him:
"Well, let's be on our WAY.
When we get there, we will see what happens."
They took the witch with them.
When they came to where the others were
the people looked at him, an unclean person, a dangerous person.
THEN THEY WERE NOT HAPPY, the people.

•

(sighing) "Tísshomahhá
HAVING HIM IN THIS WON'T BE GOOD," THEY SAID.
"INDEED, but I live by these garden SEEDS.
These yellow ones
are my garden seeds.
Even with all the other wild   gar
                          seeds,   den seeds
the garden seeds by which you
grow
even so
the women's flesh will not be good.

• 274 •

THIS EAR OF CORN
will make their flesh heavy.

•

That's why
I have COME OUT," he said.
"Indeed.
But you must live a better LIFE.
The kind of person you are now: you must not be such a person,"
     they TOLD him. When they had told him
they lived on
until the fourth day
and the sorcerer spoke:

•

"NOW
you must give me one of your LITTLE ONES.
(rasping) I will WITCH him," he said, the WITCH.
The witch.
The ones who had the sacred things were not happy.

•

The House Chief
had a child.
"GO AHEAD, try this one," he said, and he GAVE UP HIS
     LITTLE ONE.
When he had given up his little one, this child
was witched.
Having been hurt
the little boy died.

•

His elders
held him.
ON THE FOURTH DAY
he might return:
preparations were made

so that this might be.
Preparations were made

•

and when he had been gone
four days

•

the House Chief said to the two Bow Priests, "You must go to the Place of
    Emergence.
Our child
whose road was ended:
you must find out why it is that this had to be."
So he said. They were LONELY for him, LONELY for their little
    one.
The two Bow Priests
went back, it was the second time they had gone back.
WHEN THEY CAME TO THE PLACE OF EMERGENCE,
    THE LITTLE BOY WAS PLAYING THERE, PLAYING
    BY HIMSELF.
When they entered upon his road: "Tísshomahhá, our
CHILD
so you are living here, not far from us," they said. "Yes
this
is how I LIVE.
When you return you must tell my elders
that they MUST NOT CRY
for when the time COMES
then I will enter upon their roads," the little boy said. "Indeed."
"That is why
this happened to me.
They should not cry," he told them. "Very well."
They took the word back
to where the others were and told them. "Indeed.
Then that's the way it will be hereafter."

• 276 •

WHEN THIS HAD BEEN SAID, the two Bow Priests
spoke to THE ONES WHO HAD THE SACRED THINGS:
    "NOW
our fathers, our CHILDREN
PREPARE yourselves NOW, we've been here FOUR DAYS"
they said.
THEY HAD STAYED FOUR YEARS.

                •

THEY STARTED OUT FROM THERE
AND WENT ON
until they came to MOSS LAKE.
When they came
to this lake
they were still only MOSS PEOPLE.
They had tails of moss.
Their hands were webbed.
Their feet were webbed.

                •

When they came there to Moss Lake
when the twins had brought them there:
"NOW, my CHILDREN
for a time you must settle HERE.
THE WAY YOU ARE MADE is not
suitable, it will not do," the twins told them.
They sat down there.
When they had sat down
THE TWINS WASHED THEM. WHEN THEY WASHED
    THEM
THEIR MOSS CAME OFF.
WHEN THEY HAD WASHED ALL OF THEM
they UNDID the webs of their hands.
They used their spearhead to undo the webs. They CUT OFF the
    tails.

It seems we had testicles on our foreheads.
THEY CUT ALL THESE OFF.
THEY MADE US THE KIND OF PEOPLE WE ARE NOW,
    they
completed us.
THERE   MOSS
    AT
LAKE, WE WERE WASHED. Our ELDERS, when NEWNESS
    WAS MADE
were WASHED there, and that is why it is NAMED MOSS
    LAKE.
THEY MOVED ON
             FROM THERE.
    MOVING ON, THEY WENT ALONG
FOR SOME YEARS
until they came to THE PLACE WHERE THE PEOPLE WERE
    DIVIDED.
COMING TO THE PLACE WHERE THE PEOPLE WERE
    DIVIDED, they stayed there.
They were staying there
and because THE WITCH WAS AMONG THEM
NOT ALL OF THEM
wanted to come this way.

•

The Ahayuuta said to them, "NOW
my fathers, my children
now we must

•

TEST YOU," they told them. "Indeed."
The twins sat down nearby
and they made
the CROW EGG and
the PARROT EGG.
They carried these back to where the others were.

"NOW, my FATHERS, my CHILDREN
perhaps you will be WISE:
you must choose
BETWEEN THESE TWO."
So
they told them.
ON THIS SIDE
in the direction where the Middle of the world would be
was the CROW EGG, BEAUTIFUL
SPOTTED with BLUE.
THE PARROT EGG WAS NOT BEAUTIFUL.

                 •

There
those who were to go in coral's direction
chose the parrot egg

                 •

and those who were to come this way chose the crow egg.

                 •

THERE, BECAUSE THE WITCH WAS AMONG THEM
the people were DIVIDED.
When the people were DIVIDED
those who came this way brought their crow egg
not knowing
that this would be the CROW.
They went o————n until they came to Kachina Village.
WHEN THEY CAME TO KACHINA VILLAGE

                 •

when they came to the place where Kachina Village would be
the Ahayuuta
coming to the waters there, said:
"NOW
my children, you must cross here."
So they told them.

They crossed
with their children on their backs.
THEIR ^{CHIL}DREN

TURNED INTO ^{WA}TER SNAKES, ^{TUR}TLES
AND ^{BIT} THEIR ^{EL}DERS, ^{HALF} THE ^{CHILDREN} WERE
DROPPED

AND IT WAS NOT GOOD.
"WAIT
WAIT WAIT, BEFORE EVERYONE HAS GONE IN, YOU
YOU MUST NOT DROP YOUR CHILDREN WHEN THEY
    BITE YOU, PERHAPS IT WILL WORK OUT THIS
    WAY."
Half the people had already gone in
and when the Ahayuuta said this

•

the others held their children firmly on their backs.
They bit and scratched, but they did not let them go and
    REACHED THE OTHER SIDE.
SOME OF THE CHILDREN WERE LEFT BEHIND THERE.
Leaving some behind
THEY SETTLED NEARBY.

•

On Old People's Mountain
Molanhakto emerged.
When he emerged:
"MOLANHAKTO and SIIWILU SIYEETS'A
MUST GO ON AHEAD OF US."
The Ahayuuta spoke
instructing the people that these two would go on ahead.

A ^{SHORT DIS}TANCE FROM KACHINA VILLAGE

MOUN_{TAIN}
THESE TWO

•

SAT DOWN.
They sat down:

•

Siiwilu Siyeets'a

•

and her
elder brother Siiwilu Siwa.
As the YOUNGER SISTER
SAT THERE
sat there with her dress pulled up
her brother
became excited by his sister.
There he touched his younger sister.
It ended.
THIS BECAME THEIR SHRINE:
THOSE ^{KO}YEMSHI, IN THEIR ^{ROW}
WERE BORN THERE
AND KA^{CHINA VIL}LAGE BE^{GAN} THERE.
HALF OUR CHIL_{DREN WERE} ^{LOST} THERE
STAYED THERE, and so
it was named Kachina Village.
When THIS had HAPPENED
the Ahayuuta brought the people ON, THEY WENT ON
until they came to Hawikku.
WHEN THEY ^{CAME TO HA}WIKKU
THEY BUILT A VILLAGE.

• 281 •

WHEN THEY BUILT A VIL_{LAGE THERE}
when they built their FIRST village

•

JUST _{AS THE} SUN _{HAD} WANTED IT
they offered him PRAYER MEAL
^{PRAYER STICKS:}
they offered him
THIS is the way it was when NEWNESS WAS MADE
^{THAT'S WHY}
and
we live by the prayer sticks.
THEY ^{MADE} THEIR ^{VIL}LAGE THERE

•

AND THE VILLAGE GREW.
SUN PRIESTS WERE MADE.
THE ^{SA}CRED THINGS
were all put in place.
THIS _{IS WHAT} ^{HAP}PENED
and a village was built at Hawikku.

•

It happened long ago. That's all.

NOTES

Narrated by Andrew Peynetsa on the evening of March 26, 1965, with his wife, son, Walter Sanchez, and myself present. The performance took fifty-two minutes.

The four rooms beneath are entire worlds under this one, numbered, like the stories in Zuni buildings, from the top down.

Lightning smell: *k'oli,* the smell of ozone, present just after a lightning strike, or when two pieces of electric quartz are rubbed together, or when an electric current arcs across a gap.

Ruins: the Zuni area has hundreds of ruins of Pueblo Indian (Anasazi) villages. Some are attributed by the Zunis to their own ancestors and others are not; it is the latter to which the narrator refers.

"You could get water just by pulling up the grass": that is, the hole made by pulling up the grass would become a spring.

"The water made foam": the muddy freshets which follow rain in the Zuni area are sudsy below waterfalls because of alkaline soils.

Priests of the directions: these are rain priests (see the notes to "The Boy and the Deer"). In the rank order north, west, south, east, they are the human representatives of the rain-bringing Uwanammi who live on the shores of the four oceans.

Sacred things: various powerful objects possessed by a priest, among them a "sacred bundle" (mentioned in "The Hopis and the Famine") and collections of seeds. When these objects are present in a public ceremony, they are covered with blankets.

Seeds: the garden seeds *(tooshoowe)* referred to include, according to Andrew, corn, beans, squash, chili, wheat, peaches, pumpkins, melons, and onions; they do not include cabbage, grapes, alfalfa, or rye, "because they came in recent times." The wild seeds *(kyawawulaawe)* were the seeds of all the native wild plants of the Zuni area.

"Your thoughts are rooted in your sacred things": Joseph Peynetsa explained this phrase as follows: "Just as orphans are dependent on their grandmother, so a priest is dependent on his sacred things."

Trees: the "fir" was a Douglas fir, and the "aspen" a quaking aspen; I am unsure of the identity of the third tree, which is *lhanil k'oha* in Zuni. In the case of the cane plant "branches" refers to the leaves, all of which are attached to a central stem. Andrew later gave an alternate version of the sequence of four plants: ponderosa pine, Douglas fir, aspen, and cane.

"There was a rumbling": this was *tununu,* which is the sound of an earthquake or landslide rather than the sound of thunder.

Place of Emergence: in a location not quite of this world, somewhere downstream from and far to the west of Kachina Village.

Dogs bark outside: at this precise point the dogs outside Andrew's house started barking (as if someone were coming) and continued for several lines. It happened late at night, making this part of the story even more terrifying than it would have been.

House Chief: an alternate term for the Priest of the North.

The death of the boy: this was the beginning of human death and of the afterlife. The boy came to life again after four days, but he was no longer a daylight person and could not rejoin his parents. By saying, "When the time comes I will enter upon your roads," he meant that he would rejoin them when they died.

Moss Lake: somewhere between the Place of Emergence and Kachina Village. Of this episode Joseph remarked, "It sounds like evolution."

Place Where the People Were Divided: somewhere between Moss Lake and Kachina Village. One of Andrew's sons later remarked on the irony of the choice of the crow egg, saying, "Zunis always do like something pretty," which is to say something *tso'ya,* "multicolored" or "variegated."

Kachina Village: the children who were lost there became the first inhabitants of this place, and ever since then daylight people who die as children have become water snakes and turtles, just as they did. The boy who died before this time went back to the place of emergence, which is what now happens to adult daylight people who have died four times.

Molanhakto (or Siiwilu Siwa) and Siiwilu Siyeets'a: their children, the Koyemshi, were born with mental and physical defects; they are clown kachinas (not the same as the Neweekwe clowns of "The Women and the Man"). Because their impersonators wear soft brown masks with lumpy facial features, they are called "Mudheads" in English.

Old People's Mountain and Kachina Village Mountain: hills with caves in them, a short distance from Kachina Village.

"They built their first village": that is, Hawikku was the first village with buildings of masonry. According to Andrew, the people planted yellow corn for the first time there. He broke the story at this point "because it's an easy place to remember."

NICK

Well
then
some time ago, it was the usual thing
with the Zuni people
that there were WITCHES in their TOWN
and when one of them was CAUGHT
he was STRUNG UP, they STRUNG him up themselves.
So this was the way they lived
and someone, it was Suchiina,
she was caught somewhere.
When she was CAUGHT, then the BOW PRIESTS STRUNG
    HER UP.
They STRUNG HER UP
that's how
Suchiina got strung up,
at that time donkeys wandered around town
she was calling the donkeys. When she called the donkeys
she went "chk-chk,"
the donkeys gathered around her
(tense voice) she stood on one of them
on the back of a donkey, on its back
resting her weight.

(normal voice) So the BOW PRIESTS, when this came to LIGHT

•

they drove her donkey away;
(gravely) and while she was up there she cried.
They beat her head with their clubs while she was up there
(normal) so this is the way they were living
when
TUMAHKA
was caught someplace in the same way.
When he was caught
he was STRUNG UP. Once he'd been strung up
that man stayed up
until he was LET DOWN.
Suchiina was let down first, then she was questioned:
(evenly and close-mouthed) "When someone has handsome children

•

this is something
(gravely) that just shouldn't be," she said, probably
that's the way it probably HAPPENED
when she was CAUGHT.
She TOLD about herself, when someone has handsome children
witches don't feel good about it.
That's why witches, if you're living well
if you're just living well
witches will *(smooth, almost whispering)* test your strength.
(gravely again) This is the way they were living

•

(normal) when this TUMAHKA was caught
STRUNG up
and let down, then it was his turn to talk about what he'd done,
he was strung up there
then RELEASED.

Because he knew the WAYS of the AMERICANS quite well
he made marks on paper
calling the soldiers to come from Bear Water.

                                        •

Time went ON
until it reached the MIDPOINT. When the medicine societies
        went into seclusion at the Midpoint
the SOLDIERS came, they passed through here
and it was down there
where the Shalakos race, that's where the soldiers camped.
At that time there were no houses, no stores in that place
and that's where the soldiers set up their tents.
THUNderers, BIG ones
were SET UP facing the TOWN.

                                        •

The chief of the soldiers

                                        •

                                        •

(sighing) now
went looking for
someone, the chief of the town.
Kwantooniyu, he's the one
who was singled out.
SOMEone, a
relative of his, it was WEEWA
a mere transvestite
but it seems he was STRONG
had a fight
with the chief of the soldiers.
They fought BECAUSE OF WHAT THIS
TUMAHKA had DONE, because he'd made MARKS on PAPER
        the SOLDIERS had COME

but it CAME to be KNOWN just how THAT MAN had been
   living
that it WASN'T JUST
out of a LACK of GOODNESS
or just because of CRUELTY that he came to be STRUNG UP,
   no such words
were behind all this.
The TRUTH became KNOWN,
that he was STRUNG UP for being a WITCH, THAT'S what
the chief of the soldiers TOLD the other SOLDIERS:
the matter of the Zuni people was settled.
And the SOCIETY of HELIX People
had FIXED the SPRINGS.
They notified the people.

                              •

When EVERYONE had HAULED WATER, ALL the SPRINGS
   were fixed. Once they were fixed
when the HORSES drank, MULES drank, they were DYING.
THERE at ZUNI
by the time things were settled and the Zuni people were calm, the
   SOLDIERS wanted to BREAK CAMP,
a lot of the mules they had brought were just stretched out.
The SPRINGS had been fixed, RIGHT around here ALL the
   springs had been fixed.
As the SOLDIERS CAME BY HERE THEIR MULES drank,
   DYING as they CAME
and it seems they came through here again when they

                              •

went back to where they were stationed.
And the BOW PRIESTS were captured. When they were captured,
   they were TAKEN away to LUUNA.

The bow priests were locked up at Luuna. When they were locked up, they lived on that way
(gravely) they ended up stretched out.
(normal) Because of TUMAHKA'S way of thinking.
Well, one MIGHT have THOUGHT he was just LIVING a PEACEABLE life, GIVEN the way the AMERICANS got word of it:
living a peaceable life
and JUST for MINDING his OWN BUSINESS he got STRUNG UP, he was getting himself killed, strung up there
so he got angry and sent paper with marks on it.
The TRUTH was BROUGHT to LIGHT:
it wasn't that way,
it was because he was not living a peaceable life that he was captured, then there was talk.
And that man
called the soldiers out of spite, in order to get the whole town stretched out.
(gravely) The bow priests were locked up.
(normal) They had STRUNG THAT MAN up, so they were LOCKED up.
Ever since they were LOCKED UP AT LUUNA
our bow priests have been in decline.

•

And THIS was when the MIDPOINT had come. The MEDICINE societies were in SECLUSION. Well, what happened wasn't happy.
A LIFE was being threatened, and so

•

•

the SOLDIERS came.

The townspeople weren't happy, given that the whole town might
    end up stretched out. Since the medicine societies were in
    seclusion
FOOD was brought to the MEMBERS, but no one was thinking
"Yes, I'll eat," given that the whole town might end up stretched out.
They were not happy,
THIS is the way it WAS
when the medicine societies were in seclusion.
In the society we belong to now
our
late father
was a small boy then
and when FOOD was brought NO ONE ATE.
(in a child's voice) "Let me eat now
so I'll be good and full when I die."
(normal) That's what
our
late father said:
being a small boy, one doesn't know very much.
SUCH were the words he SPOKE
while he sat there EATING. The members of the society were not
    happy.
Because of TUMAHKA'S way of THINKING
the witches were saved.
The WAY things are going NOW
if a witch is caught, he doesn't get STRUNG UP
because of the AMERICAN way of thinking.
(sharply) THINGS WERE GOING PERFECTLY WELL when
    THIS happened
when he just had to expose his people. The TRUTH of the
    MATTER came to LIGHT.
He wasn't strung up for no REASON.
He got STRUNG UP because he was CAUGHT as a WITCH

and because the TRUE WORD became KNOWN
they were released, released:
the Zuni people were not mowed DOWN.
That's all.

NOTES

Narrated by Andrew Peynetsa on March 26, 1965. Earlier in the same evening he had told Part I of "When Newness was Made," breaking that story shortly after an episode that deals with a decision to spare the life of the first of all witches. He saved Part II, which has nothing to do with witches, for another evening. In effect, the present story is a flash-forward beyond Part II, picking up the theme of witchcraft a generation before Andrew was born. Despite the story's recency, he argued that it could be considered a part of "When Newness Was Made." He noted that when the soldiers came to Zuni along the edge of the river valley that leads from Nutria down to the town of Zuni itself, their horses and wagons made deep tracks, meaning that the earth was still soft at that time and not hard as it is now. Moreover, he said, "There's a spot near Nutria where the soldiers camped. They fed hay to their horses and there were tumbleweed seeds in it. Now only tumbleweeds grow on that spot and they've spread all over." In effect, then, this is the origin story for tumbleweeds. More importantly, it tells of the abrogation of Zuni sovereignty by the U.S. Army, which climaxed with a six-month occupation of the village in 1897-98. The Bow Priesthood, a society of warriors that had long been the center of military and police power at Zuni, went into a permanent decline.

"He was strung up": witches were not hanged by the neck, but with their arms pulled back over a wooden rail and tied behind them; their legs were left dangling. This was done in public, outside the seventeenth-century Spanish mission church at Zuni.

Tumahka: this man, whose English name was Nick, later became the head of the secular Zuni government (which had been established during

Spanish rule) and served as an informant for various ethnographers, including Elsie Clews Parsons, Alfred Kroeber, Ruth Benedict, and Ruth Bunzel.

Americans: the Zuni term is *melika*, from Spanish *americano*. It is often translated as "white," but Zunis reserve *k'ohanna*, their term for the color white, for albinos. The category covered by *melika* excludes *mumaakwe* (Mormons) but covers all other Anglo-Americans, of whom African Americans are considered a subcategory.

Bear Water: this is Anshe Ky'an'a, the Zuni name for Fort Wingate, located a short distance east of Gallup.

Midpoint: *itiwan'a*, referring to the solstices (in this case the winter one), which divide the year into two equal parts. The same term, which can also be translated as "Middle Place," serves as one of the names for the town of Zuni.

"They passed through here": a reference to the farming hamlet of Upper Nutria, where the story was being told. It lies on an old wagon road that connected Fort Wingate with Zuni.

"Where the Shalakos race": an open area on the south bank of the Zuni River, opposite the central part of town. The ten-foot kachinas known as *Sha'lako* race here at the close of their ceremony, shortly before the winter solstice.

Thunderers: a literal translation of *towo''anaawe*, the term for guns; "big ones" are cannons.

Helix People: Shumaakwe, a medicine society that also figures in "The Shumeekuli." It once included an order called Ts'u' Lhana or "Big Shell," devoted to the subtler arts of warfare–in the present case, the "fixing" (poisoning) of springs.

Luuna: the Zuni name for the town of Los Lunas, south of Albuquerque, formerly the site of a federal prison.

When we finished our work on this story, Joseph Peynetsa commented, "Why *did* those soldiers come to Zuni? It was none of their business."

WHEN NEWNESS WAS MADE

PART II

Well then

when newness was made they came to Hawikku and built a village
      there.

They built a village at Hawikku and lived on there.

                              •

They built their houses there. As they built their houses

the village grew, it grew.

They didn't know that the Middle Place was over here, so they
      built their village at Hawikku.

There were many people, so they constructed large buildings in
      that village. They lived on there for some years

lived on, lived on

                              •

until

some of them

went over to Gypsum Place and built houses there.

They built a village at Gypsum Place

and lived on there.

They went on living

and those

who had gone over to Gypsum Place lived there, but

not everyone settled there, only a few, and they were the ones who
    thought of
the YAAYA
Dance: because they were wise
they created the Yaaya Dance, and it was from their Yaaya Dance
    that the White Shumeekuli ran away.
When ^{this} had happened and
several YEARS had PASSED
they came
to WIND PLACE.
They came to Wind Place and built houses there.
As you can see, there were many houses
where they lived
and some way
somehow they brought in the stones, somehow they brought in
    the rafters
and laid them across.
They lived on
building their houses.

They lived ^{on} there
until
when some years had passed
those
two Bow Priests
the two Ahayuuta
THOSE _{TWO}
thought:
"WHAT will be DONE about
these
our
daylight fathers, our children?

Where could they really SETTLE DOWN, pass their days
where should their VILLAGE be?
Now think about it."
So he told his younger brother.
His younger brother said:
"Well I DON'T KNOW.
Well
there is a———ll the wide earth

•

and the MIDDLE PLACE might be just anywhere."
That's what they were talking about
when they thought of that water strider.
After thinking of him

•

they went there
to the Priest Kiva. Arriving at the House Chief's, at the House
    Chief's house, they spoke of this matter
and the rain priests had a meeting.
The rain priests had a meeting.

•

The Sun Priest
spoke to them:
"Well, our two fathers here
it seems
have been ᵗʰⁱⁿking about the loᶜᵃtion of the ᴹⁱᵈdle Place
and by means of their thoughts we will find out
the location of this place.
Because of these two
because of their thoughts
this will be.
Not even by our combined effort
could we know
such a thing.

It is our two fathers here
who have the knowledge.

•

How else could this be DONE?
Now then, THINK about it."

•

When the rain priests
thought about it, they DIDN'T KNOW.
"Well, JUST AS YOU HAVE SAID
whatever these two have in mind will have to be.
IF THEY REALLY KNOW OF A DEFINITE PLACE FOR US
        TO LIVE
THEN CLEARLY we should live there," so
the rain priests said.
"Very well indeed.
I'm GOING," the twins said.
They came this way until they CAME TO ZUNI.
When they came here to the present village, they summoned the
        water strider.

•

ONCE IT WAS SUM_{MONED}
it entered upon their roads.
There they spoke to it: "NOW
this very day
we have summoned you here.

•

You
must bend over here.
YOU MUST STRETCH OUT YOUR ARMS AND LEGS.
BY THE POSI_{TION}
OF YOUR HEART

the Middle Place will then become known."
So they said. "Indeed.
Is this your reason for summoning me?"
"Yes, this is why we have summoned you.
Now then, stretch yourself OUT.
By the position of your heart

IT WILL BE KNOWN
WHERE THE MIDDLE PLACE IS," so
the Ahayuuta told it.
"Very well."
Bending over toward the east
it stretched out, stretched out all its legs.
When they were ALL OUT FLAT,
     WHEN THE AR MS

LE GS
stretched
A——LL A ROUND TO THE O CEANS
its heart
rested

at the site named the MID DLE PLACE.

•

They stood there:
"Very well, here is the middle
here is the middle of the EARTH,"
they said, and WENT BACK.
When the two Ahayuuta had found it

•

they went back to Wind Place, they arrived at the Priest Kiva,
     where the rain priests were meeting, and then they
entered:

"My fathers, my children, how have you
been?" "Happy
our fathers, so you've come, sit down," they told them.
The twins sat down.
"NOW, you have gone on the road.
When you
left you spoke of finding the Middle Place.
Has it been FOUND now?"
"IT HAS BEEN FOUND, the one who
is our child
the water strider
HAS STRETCHED OUT ITS LEGS
and the site of the Middle Place has been found.
THERE
ON THE FOURTH DAY
you must go there.

●

WHEN YOU HAVE GONE THERE YOU WILL BUILD
HOU SES
you will settle a village there.
WHEN YOU HAVE SET TLED A VIL LAGE THERE
when all of you have settled in that village
then we will see what happens next."
So the twins told them. "Very well.
This is the way it will be."

●

THERE THE AHAYUUTA TOLD THEM ABOUT THIS
and the people
told one another.
The location of the Middle Place had been found.

ON THE FOURTH DAY THEY WENT THERE to build their
    houses, they went on, went on
for some years
until the houses were finished.
When the houses were finished
THAT   HEART   EARTH
    WHICH IS THE   OF THE
    whatever it is
was thought of
by the twins.

                •

THERE
where
the House Chief stays, there it IS, the HEART of the earth
whatever it is
perhaps a stone.
    (*audience member*) Yes, a stone.
                •

THAT'S   WHERE

IT ^{I}S.
EVERYTHING
A——LL OVER THE WIDE EARTH
well
EVERYTHING DEPENDED ON THIS AND ON THE
    MIDDLE PLACE FOR FERTILITY.
FOR THEIR PART
the RAIN PRIESTS
would sit down to ask for rain.
WHEN IT RAINED   ZUNI IT WOULD RAIN A——LL
            AT
    OVER THE EARTH.
WHEN THEY

first started living this way
ALL the village people, at Santo Domingo
at HOPI
ALL THE VILLAGERS WOULD ANXIOUSLY AWAIT THE
    TIME
WHEN OUR RAIN PRIESTS WENT INTO SECLUSION AT
    ZUNI, THE SUMMERTIME
but now
the way things are going
moisture is scarce.

•

THIS IS THE WAY IT HAPPENED
that the MIDDLE PLACE was FOUND. The MIDDLE PLACE
    was FOUND

•

AND

•

the SANIYAKYA SOCIETY
had its beginning.
JUST AS
THE ^{SA}CRED THINGS HAD ^{THEIR} BEGINNING
WHEN ^{THEY}
EMERGED
so also
the Coyote Society
the Saniyakya Society began.
THEY BE^{GAN} THERE AND CAME A^{LONG}
until they entered Kachina Village.
THERE they recited prayers.
WHEN THEY ^{ENTERED KACHINA VIL}_{LAGE}
    they recited prayers, and today

they do the same.
THEY E^{MERGED} THERE. WHEN THE ^{SA}NIYAKYA
    SOCIETY E^{MERGED}
the YUCCA WREATH had its beginning.
THEY WENT ALONG
until they came to the Prairie-Dog Hills.
WHEN THEY CAME TO THE PRAIRIE-DOG HILLS
they had a contest with the SACRED THINGS.

WHEN THEY HAD A ^{CON}TEST WITH THE ^{SA}CRED

    THINGS
the sacred things
brought their heavy rain.

•

The heavy rain came, but it was NOT
like the fine rain which soaks the earth, it did not soak the earth.
THE ^{SA}NIYAKYA SO^{CI}ETY
then
sang their string of songs.
WHEN THEY ^{SANG} THEIR ^{STRING} OF ^{PRIEST}LY SONGS
THE FINE RAIN CAME, FOUR DAYS and four nights were
    filled with fine rain.
THERE
the Saniyakya Society
was singled out
as the most extraordinary, most wonderful group
when newness was made.

•

THEY BE^{GAN} THERE
and the Prairie-Dog Hills became the site of their shrine.

THAT'S WHY, AS THINGS GO TO^{DAY}
when the solstice comes
prayer sticks are made
for the Saniyakya Society:
that is their payment.
When THIS had happened
when the sacred things
had their beginning
and the Saniyakya Society had begun
it was THEN that the
Life-Fulfilling Societies
had their beginning.

THE ^{LIFE-}FULFILLING
SOCIETIES BE^{GAN}
there in the fourth room:
some of the people were still living in the fourth room beneath.
When the Life-Fulfilling Societies
WHEN ^{THEY}
WERE ^{SUMMONED}
they emerged.
_EMERGING
they came out and stood in their Sun Father's daylight.

•

THEY SAW THE FOUR POLLEN WAYS.
"Which one will be our road?" they said.
"We'll take the MIDDLE road
we'll go
THIS WAY, toward the east.
At Shipaapuli'ma
we will settle down together."

Ku'asaya
Iyatiiku
the White House People
Poshayaank'i:
they put
their LIFE-SEEDS in place.
Their
bow priests
set up shrines all around them.
The mountain lion
bear
badger
wolf
eagle
shrew
set up shrines all around them.

•

These
set up shrines.
The Life-Fulfilling Societies
sprouted their strings of songs.
WHEN THE STRINGS OF SONGS HAD SPROUTED

•

they came to the Middle Place. When they came
to the Middle Place

•

they were put in the room
of the priests.
When they had been put in place
then
the beasts of prey
made their strings of songs.

THERE WERE THOSE WHO SAT ^{NEA}REST, AND THE
SE_{COND,} THIRD, FOURTH, _{THE} FIFTH ONES, THE
SIXTH _{ONES SAT ALL A}ROUND
as the strings of songs sprouted.
WHEN A STRING _{OF} SONGS _{WAS} SUNG
THOSE _{WHO SAT} NEAREST
learned the entire string.
THE ^{SE}COND ONES COULDN'T ^{GET} IT ALL,
   and so
that's the way it still is with the societies
as they live on.
THAT'S WHAT HAP_{PENED:}
the Life-Fulfilling Societies sprouted.
They had their beginning.
When THIS had been straightened out
ANOTHER society
then
had its beginning:
the Clown Society.

•

FAR OFF AT ASH _{WATER}
at the spring
of the Clowns
the Clowns had their beginning.
^{CAME ALONG}
THEY
until they came to the Middle Place.

•

At that time

we were irresponsible.
It seems that we didn't love
our mothers
all the kinds of corn.
Our elders, our grandfathers, our grandmothers, the people who
    lived before us
DID NOT LOVE THEM, and so
the Corn Mothers ABANDONED them.

THE ^{CORN MOTHERS} _ABANDONED THEM

    and went toward the coral.

THERE _{IN THE} ^{CO}_{RAL} OCEAN

out in the water
a goose
nestled the ears of corn
and NO WAY
to bring them back was known.
THERE WAS NO SEED CORN.
They were living
WITHOUT SEED CORN.
They were full of anxiety.

•

Even the rain priests
though they were wise
did not know HOW TO GO ON LIVING.
THE CLOWNS were summoned.

•

When the Clowns were summoned
Nepayatamu
came to the Priest Kiva.

•

He entered the Priest Kiva: "My fathers, my children, how
have you been?" "Happy, our child

sit down," they told him, and he sat down. When he sat down

•

the Sun Priest questioned him: "NOW, our father, CHILD
we have summoned you HERE.
PER^{HAPS,} AS WE HAVE IN ^{MIND}
you might
find our Corn Mothers.

•

Our Corn Mothers aren't here, they've GONE somewhere.
Because we were irresponsible, we lost the sight of our mothers.
Since
you are an extraordinary person
perhaps
you might find them.
You might bring them back to us."
So they told Nepayatamu. "Indeed.

•

But even if that's what you have in mind
I don't know WHERE they WENT.

•

How-EVER
IT'S UP TO YOU," he told them.
"IF YOU ^{WISH}
then I
will look for them."

•

Then Nepayatamu told them:
"THERE WILL BE FASTING.
IF YOU WANT _{IT}
IF YOU ARE WIL_{LING}
to go into fasting

then I will look for them."
So he told them.
The rain priests
began thinking.
They began thinking.
They talked.

•

Their House Chief said, "Well then
this is the way it will be:
WE ARE WILLING, for truly
we were irresponsible and lost our mothers, and so
we will go into fasting, we are WILLING to fast."
"IF YOU ARE WILLING TO FAST, IT MUST BE
my own sort of fast.
IF YOU FAST IN THIS WAY
THEN I WILL GO," he told them.
"Yes, we are WILLING."
"ARE YOU VERY CERTAIN you are willing?"
"We are willing." "Very well indeed.
THIS VERY DAY
you will go into fasting.
THIS VERY DAY
I will go toward the coral," he said, NEPAYATAMU.
He told the rain priests. "Very well."

•

"Well then, I'm GOING, my FATHERS.
May you be happy as you pass the DAYS.
IF WE ARE FORTUNATE

•

it might be on the fourth
or perhaps the eighth day
when I bring them back to you. MAYbe.
PerHAPS.

CERTAINLY YOU WANT THIS," he told them.
"Yes, we want it."
Then Nepayatamu went out and went toward the Coral Ocean.

•

On he went
spending three nights on the way
and after the FOURTH night he came to the Coral Ocean.
Out in the water
lay the goose.
She was nestling the ears of corn.
THERE WAS NO WAY
to get across.

•

He began thinking
pacing up and down.
He was pacing up and down beside the waves.

•

A duck came to him.
"What are you doing?" the duck said. *(sadly)* "Well
our mothers

•

have abandoned
the Middle Place
and I'm looking for them." "Indeed.
(tight and nasal) AND YOU'VE COME HERE, but even so
what do you
plan to do?" the duck said.

•

"Well, our fathers at the Middle Place
the rain priests
were WILLING when I spoke of FASTING
and so I've come."
So

he told the duck. "Indeed.
Very well indeed
then LET'S GO ON OUT THERE," the duck said. The duck

                         •

the duck
sat down in the water.
Nepayatamu sat
on the duck's back
and they flew out there
until they came to where the goose lay.
"My mother, my CHILD
how have you been passing the days?" Nepayatamu said. "Happily,
    our FATHER.
So you've come," she said. "We've come."
"Indeed.
FOR WHAT REASON
have you entered upon our roads?
Perhaps it is because of a WORD of some importance
that you have entered upon our roads, for you would not do this
    for no reason," so
the goose
told Nepayatamu. "YES, in TRUTH
my mother, my CHILD
there at the Middle Place our fathers, the RAIN PRIESTS
have lost the sight
of their MOTHERS
all the kinds of corn.
Because they have ABANDONED us
I am looking for them." "Indeed.
BUT DO THEY REALLY LOVE THEM?" she asked
    NEPAYATAMU.

                         •

"Yes

it must be that they really love them.
WHAT THEN?"
Nepayatamu said.
"I am nestling them.
Right here I'm nestling them
but if you
have set a day for them
THEN ^{THEY}
will certainly have
that day.
Through THEIR FLESH

•

the women
among our daylight children
will have good flesh.
Their flesh will smell of corn."
Those
were the words of the goose.
"But if THIS is what you want
perhaps you will be very CAREFUL.

•

YOU ARE IN NEED
so you may GO AHEAD and take them JUST AS THEY ARE
and THAT will be IT.
But IF YOU HAVE DIFFICULTY on the way
then that's the way it will have to be."
Those were the words
she spoke to Nepayatamu. "NOW
our father, CHILD
you may hold them in your arms," she told him.

•

He gathered up
ALL THE KINDS OF CORN

with his arms
locked together

•

and then Nepayatamu was FORBIDDEN to SPEAK.
"Now you must not speak
until

THE ^{CORN} MOTHERS HAVE ^{EN}TERED THE ^{PRIEST}

KIVA

•

and have been put down together in their place.
As for the prayer sticks that have been made

THE ^{PRAYER} STICKS WILL ^{GO}

•

there
where the ones named MOLAAWE
are supposed to stay.
The prayer sticks will enter there.

THE ^{PRAYER} STICKS

will be put down together in their place.

•

YOU will be the one who thinks
of entering with them.

HERE^{AF}TER

this
is the ritual you will follow.
THIS IS THE WAY YOU WILL LIVE
and these are your instructions."

•

THE FASTING was held very sacred in the time
of our elders

when we were beginning to grow up.
When it was time for the MOLAAWE to come
no one made any NOISE.
No one ATE anything.
Because of this
there would be no pests, that's why
in former times
the people regarded their
religion
as precious.
BE^{CAUSE THIS HAPPENED THE}_N
when the Molaawe enter today
the same procedure is followed:
Nepayatamu
does not speak
when he enters
and the rain priests are completely quiet inside, well you
have seen this yourself, at the kiva.
                                        •

When this happened, BECAUSE THIS HAPPENED THE
        CORN MOTHERS CAME BACK, and so today we still see
our Corn Mothers.
That, well that's all.

NOTES

Narrated by Andrew Peynetsa on the evening of March 29, 1965, with his wife, son, Walter Sanchez, and myself present. The audience comment came from his wife. The performance took twenty-six minutes.

The water strider: this insect is able to skim over the top of water; its four longest legs form an equilateral cross, and in the story each of them reaches to an ocean.

The Middle Place: noting from maps that Zuni is not equidistant from the Arctic Ocean, the Pacific, the Gulf of Mexico, and the Atlantic, Zunis still feel that their village must be at the center of something, and they sometimes have informal discussions as to what that something might be. Joseph Peynetsa ventured this: "Maybe the Zunis needed a center so they wouldn't be like the Navajos and so they would all stick together."

"The Heart of the Earth": this is never seen by the Zuni public, but it is said to be a stone. The welfare of the entire earth is tied up in it.

The "seclusion" of the rain priests: during the rainy season all the rain priests, one after another, go on a retreat to pray to the Uwanammi (see also the notes to "The Boy and the Deer"). "Moisture is scarce" today, it is said, because rain priests make mistakes.

Yucca wreath: the members of the Saniyakya Society were wearing wreaths around their heads when they emerged; no other society uses such wreaths.

Heavy rain, fine rain: the former, with large, splattering drops, tends to run off without soaking the earth; the latter, with small drops, may last for hours and slowly soak in.

Life-Fulfilling Societies: these are the Zuni medicine societies that stage the "Good Night" ceremony. They are modeled after the original Life-Fulfilling Society whose members are the White House People, including Ku'asaya, Iyatiiku, and Poshayaank'i (all Keresan names). Of Ku'asaya and Iyatiiku Andrew said, "Maybe they're animals, I don't know. They're just named in the story." Of Poshayaank'i he said, "Almost like a human, but he looks like fire," and he added that he burned the timber wherever he passed on his way east.

Shipaapuli'ma: this is in the east, but like the Place of Emergence in the west (see Part I of "When Newness Was Made"), it is not quite of this world. Andrew conceived the two places as occupying opposite ends of a straight east-west axis. He described Shipaapuli'ma as being clear on the other side of the Sandia Mountains, which rise east of the Rio Grande.

"There were those who sat nearest": the Life-Fulfilling Societies are ranked according to the completeness of their knowledge.

"We didn't love our mothers": that is, corn was wasted.

Corn Mothers: Joseph commented, "There must be something about those plants. In *Dear Abby* someone wrote in that they thought a lady was crazy because she talked to her plants. Then a lady wrote that plants grow better when you talk to them. The Zunis talk to their corn. When I read that I thought, 'Well, the Zunis aren't the only ones who talk to their plants.' Then a man wrote in, sarcastic: 'What about the plants you don't want? Should you cuss them and then they'll go away?' But I don't think that would work. The Zunis go in the field, early in the morning, and sprinkle cornmeal and say, 'You, our children,' and tell them to hurry."

Duck: *eya*, a mallard.

Goose: *owa*, the Canada goose.

The Fasting: a period at the winter solstice when it is forbidden to do business, eat greasy foods, take trash or ashes out of the house, or have fire outdoors (thus the street lights are turned off and some people do not operate their automobiles). The full Fasting lasts ten days, but some people shorten its observance to eight or even four days. The "Good Night" falls on the fourth night of the Fasting.

The Molaawe: impersonators of the Corn Mothers. They come six days before the Fasting and six days after the famous Sha'lako ceremony. The name could be interpreted as referring to squash or melon patches.

A STORY WAS MADE

NOW THE ROAD BEGINS LO—NG A GO.

•

It seems

•

the children
when the hunting season opened
it seems their fathers left them and went out hunting in different
    directions
while these two *(indicates his two grandsons)*
let their sheep out, they let their sheep out and
the two of them
went out herding.
And their fathers had gone out elsewhere.
They went around, all day they went around.
And their grandfather
was working in the fields until late afternoon and
he came up and
their grandmother told him
"Our grandsons
killed a deer." "Where?"
"Over there someplace around back."
"I see.

What happened?" "ONE of them came after a KNIFE.
He got the knife and I
told him to castrate it, maybe they castrated it."
"I see."
"Oh dear, my poor grandsons
maybe you'll do it right."
So their grandmother had told them.
And now their grandfather had come and, "It looks like I'll have to
     go and get it,"
he said, and he
went to his wagon
and got it READY.
He headed out and went around to Tree Crescent, he got there and
that's where the sheep were spread out, he got there. "Where?
     Where is it?"
"At the far side of that clearing, by a grove of trees, that's where."

•

"Why don't you get in and we'll go."
Those two boys
just left their sheep. Both of them were all covered with blood.
Their grandfather took them along, they went on over there.
"Where?" "Right over there by that grove of trees."
They went over to the trees. "Right over there.
On the north side."
They got to the far end of the trees, to a clearing, "HOW did this
     HAPPEN?"
"Oh— there were three of them.
One of them
was crippled, and there was a doe, and her
we just let her be.
When they came up
the other two stopped
with this one in front:

pow!
I dropped him.
I dropped him
but then I didn't have a knife.
So, 'Well
well now,'"
he said to the other boy, "Listen:
you go get a knife and I'll look after the sheep."
So then this
other boy
went to get the knife
he went to their grandmother's.
He went to their grandmother's and
ran all the way.
"Oh dear, grandson
why is it you're
running like this?"
"Well we've killed a deer," he said. "WHERE?" she said. "Over
    there.
It's a great big buck." "Oh dear, my grandsons, so you've
ended someone's ROAD.
Perhaps
one of your fathers might end someone's road too."
So their grandmother said.
"When your grandfather comes I'll tell him."
Sure enough, when their grandfather came she told him, so now all
    of them were going along together, together
the two boys with their grandfather, and when they got to where
    the deer was, it was so big.
"What are we going to DO?"
"LISTEN:
why don't we put him in the wagon antlers first
then we'll all lift up on the other end."

So then

they put him in the wagon antlers first and they all got together and lifted him up
and finally they managed to get him in. "Now that he's in, let's go back."
"Where are the lungs and the heart?"
"Well, lying over there."
"Hey—— they're big ones, a lot of fat around the lungs."
"Yes indeed there's a lot of fat, but it got sand on it, let's go."
Then their grandfather turned around and they came along

•

came along until they got to where the road was too rough for the wagon
and the BOLTS got LOOSE on the tongue.
Then the two boys
got left behind there and their grandfather went on
and when he looked back his
wagon was way back there.
"Why didn't you SPEAK UP when that happened?"
They laughed and
he backed up, their grandfather fixed it for them.
They came along, came along until

•

they
got to their yard. "How're we going to get it down?"
There were two old ladies, their grandmother and
and
Sayku's mother. "With those two women, we can probably get it down."
They laid a plank from the wagon to the door and pulled it down.
They put it down inside.
Now the sun was about to go down
it was halfway behind the horizon when their fathers came home.
When their fathers came home their deer was lying inside.
It had thirteen points.
"Oh— who killed it?"
"Well these two killed it."

"Thanks be."
After a while
others came in.
Everyone breathed life from their deer and went back outside.
They went outside, went outside, and their
grandfather
said a prayer, he said a prayer and they all came back in
to sprinkle cornmeal, and in this way they completed it.
Then the father of the boy who killed the deer said, "NOW
this was a day
when something terrible happened to me." "What?"
"Well now
I thought there was a bear in the canyon, that's what I thought.
It was growling, 'Where could it be?'"
This was the father of the little boy who killed the deer.
"Where was it?" "Well right there by that gap in the canyon."
"Where? Where was it?" "It was right there by that gap, he was
    growling.
I thought it was a BEAR, so I went up very quietly.
I went up very quietly and when I got CLOSE to it
right up close
it kept on growling.
So I got my gun in a good position.
'Well, when I see him I'll blast him.'"
When he looked over the hill
he wasn't GROWLing, he was SNORing, ASLEEP.
It was a HUNTER.
"Aw—— it sounded just like a bear."
Then he went on down there.
"HOW COME you're sleeping so hard, you're growling like a
    bear," he told him.
This was the father
of the little boy who killed the deer

that's who was talking.

"Well I just lay down here and I must've slept for a long time, I
    was so tired."

So he said. "I see.

But that shouldn't happen."

So he told him.

"Anyway let's go now, the sun's going down."

Both of them went on down.

When their father got home he told them about it.

"How could this happen? A person out hunting isn't supposed to
    go to sleep,"

he told their grandfather.

•

"Well then

•

well then, what can I DO about it?"

"Why not make up a story?"

"Why not?" he asked the boys' grandmother.

"It's up to you." "Let's go ahead and make one up.

We'll tell it as if it happened long ago."

So their grandfather talked about what had happened.

A STORY was MADE.

He talked about what had happened

and when it was all straightened out

it was about the father whose boy had killed a deer, and that

hunter who had gone to sleep

and was snoring and wasn't a bear growling, it wasn't a bear but a
    sleeping hunter.

This happened long ago, that's all—— the word was short.

NOTES

Narrated by Andrew Peynetsa on the evening of June 17, 1972. He began by saying, *Sonti inoote,* "Now the road begins long ago," which is the second half of the standard opening for a *telapnanne* or "tale." At the end he used both parts of the closing, first saying, *Le'n inoote teyatikya,* "This happened long ago," and then, *Lee semkonikya,* "That's all, the word is short." It was the middle of the season when tales should not be told, but afterwards he explained himself by saying, "That's a true story, even though I pretended it was a *telapnanne.*" The events had taken place the previous November, and he was speaking in the same house, in the Zuni farming hamlet of Upper Nutria, as the one where the deer is brought in the story. The grandparents in the story are Andrew and his wife Kathryn, the two boys are their grandsons, and the father of the boy who killed the deer is their eldest son. All except that son were present for the telling, along with one of his younger brothers, Barbara Tedlock, and myself.

The sheep: ordinarily these do not exist in the "long ago" world of tales. In a religious setting Andrew would have been required to use a Zuni circumlocution if he needed to refer to them, but here he used the term *kyaneelu,* from Spanish *carnero.* Among all his tales, this is the only one containing a word of European origin.

The wagon: like sheep, wagons are ordinarily excluded from tales, but Andrew did keep this detail archaic to the extent of not mentioning that he pulled the wagon with a tractor. If this incident had happened seven years earlier, when the other stories in this book were told, he would have been using a team of two horses.

Tree Crescent: a place on the far side of the hill that borders Upper Nutria on the southeast.

Sayku's mother: for all except this person, a neighbor, Andrew avoids using proper names when referring to the actors in his story. He thus stays close to the pattern followed for nearly all the human characters in tales, and even for this woman he takes the indirect route of naming her with reference to her son. Further, he chooses her son's Zuni name rather than the English name he would have been given when he first went to school.

The canyon in the story is on the headwaters of the Rio Nutria, a short distance northeast of Upper Nutria. Afterwards Andrew explained that the canyon walls amplified the snoring. The son who was present for the telling then remarked, "It looks like it's two canyons, but it's only one," thus adding to the other paradoxes in the story. Meanwhile the two grandsons went to get the deer's antlers, which were on the roof (that is where antlers are kept); they wanted us to count the points, which numbered thirteen. When they went out to put the antlers back, they stayed on the roof longer than expected and then came running inside, telling everyone, "Come outside and you'll see something amazing." It turned out to be a display of northern lights, very rare at this latitude (35°) and never before witnessed by any of the Zunis present. On the way back into the house Andrew offered a comment, nasalizing his vowels and changing his *g* to a *ch* in order to imitate a Navajo accent: "It's strange."

Bibliography

Listed in the first section below are previously published sources for texts and translations of Zuni narratives, speeches, and songs. The next two sections are devoted to texts and translations that are based on sound recordings and take account of the dramatic features of oral performances, first for Amerindian languages and then for other languages in various parts of the world. Next come scripts based on performances in English. In the final section are sources that do not appear in the other lists but are cited in this book or were consulted in the process of producing it.

Zuni texts and translations

Benedict, Ruth. 1935. *Zuni Mythology.* 2 vols. Columbia University Contributions to Anthropology 21. New York: Columbia University Press.

Boas, Franz. 1922. "Tales of Spanish Provenience from Zuni." *Journal of American Folklore* 35:62-98.

Bunzel, Ruth. 1932a. "Zuñi Origin Myths." *Annual Report of the Bureau of American Ethnology* 47:545-609.

———. 1932b. "Zuñi Ritual Poetry." *Annual Report of the Bureau of American Ethnology* 47:611-835.

———. 1932c. "Zuñi Katcinas: An Analytical Study." *Annual Report of the Bureau of American Ethnology* 47:837-1086.

———. 1933. *Zuni Texts.* Publications of the American Ethnological Society 15. New York: G. E. Stechert.

Cushing, Frank Hamilton. 1883. "Zuni Fetiches." *Annual Report of the Bureau of American Ethnology* 2:9-43.

———. 1896. "Outlines of Zuni Creation Myths." *Annual Report of the Bureau of American Ethnology* 13:321-447.

———. 1901. *Zuñi Folk Tales.* New York: G. P. Putnam's Sons.

Handy, Edward L. 1918. "Zuni Tales." *Journal of American Folklore* 31:451-71.

Herzog, George. 1936. "A Comparison of Pueblo and Pima Musical Styles." *Journal of American Folklore* 49:283-417.

Kate, H. F. C. ten. 1917. "A Zuni Folk-Tale." *Journal of American Folklore* 30:496-99.

Parsons, Elsie Clews. 1917. "Notes on Zuni." *Memoirs of the American Anthropological Association* 4:151-327.

———. 1918. "Pueblo-Indian Folk-Tales, Probably of Spanish Provenience." *Journal of American Folklore* 31:216-55.

———. 1923. "The Origin Myth of Zuni." *Journal of American Folklore* 36:135-62.

———. 1924. "The Scalp Ceremonial of Zuni." *Memoirs of the American Anthropological Association* 31:1-42.

———. 1930. "Zuni Tales." *Journal of American Folklore* 43:1-58.

Parsons, Elsie Clews, and Franz Boas. 1920. "Spanish Tales from Laguna and Zuni, New Mexico." *Journal of American Folklore* 33:47-72.

Smith, Watson, and John M. Roberts. 1954. *Zuni Law: A Field of Values.* Papers of the Peabody Museum of American Archaeology and Ethnology 43(1).

Stevenson, Matilda Coxe. 1904. "The Zuñi Indians: Their Mythology, Esoteric Fraternities, and Ceremonies." *Annual Report of the Bureau of American Ethnology* 23:3-634.

Tedlock, Barbara. 1980. "Songs of the Zuni Kachina Society: Composition, Rehearsal, and Performance." In *Southwestern Indian Ritual Drama,* edited by Charlotte J. Frisbie, pp. 7-35. Albuquerque: University of New Mexico Press.

———. 1992. *The Beautiful and the Dangerous: Encounters with the Zuni Indians.* New York: Viking.

Tedlock, Dennis. 1970. "Finding the Middle of the Earth." *Alcheringa* o. s. 1:67-80.

———. 1971a. "On the Translation of Style in Oral Narrative." *Journal of American Folklore* 84:114-33.

———. 1971b. "When the Old Timers Went Deer Hunting." *Alcheringa* o. s. 3:76-81.

———. 1972. *Finding the Center: Narrative Poetry of the Zuni Indians.* From performances in the Zuni by Andrew Peynetsa and Walter Sanchez. New York: The Dial Press.

———. 1973. "The Story of How a Story Was Made." *Alcheringa* o. s. 5:120-25 and insert disk recording.

———. 1978. "Coyote and Junco." In *Coyote Stories,* edited by William Bright. *International Journal of American Linguistics, Native American Texts Series,* monograph 1:171-77.

———. 1983. *The Spoken Word and the Work of Interpretation.* University of Pennsylvania Publications in Communication and Conduct. Philadelphia: University of Pennsylvania Press.

———. 1988. "The Witches Were Saved: A Zuni Origin Story." *Journal of*

American Folklore 101:312-20.

———. 1994. "Stories of Kachinas and the Dance of Life and Death." In *Kachinas in the Pueblo World,* edited by Polly Schaafsma, pp. 161-74. Albuquerque: University of New Mexico Press.

Wyaco, Virgil. 1998. *A Zuni Life: A Pueblo Indian in Two Worlds.* Transcribed and edited by J. A. Jones. Albuquerque: University of New Mexico Press.

Young, M. Jane. 1988. *Signs from the Ancestors: Zuni Cultural Symbolism and Perceptions of Rock Art.* Albuquerque: University of New Mexico Press.

Zuni People, The. 1972. *The Zunis: Self-Portrayals.* Albuquerque: University of New Mexico Press.

Scripted translations from other Amerindian languages

Bell, Kurt. 1986. "The First Whales." Transcribed and translated by Elsie Mather and Phyllis Morrow. *Alaska Quarterly Review* 4, nos. 3-4:59-74. (Yup'ik Eskimo)

Bierwert, Crisca. 1996. *Lushootseed Texts: An Introduction to Puget Salish Narrative Aesthetics.* Seattle: University of Washington Press.

Binalí Biye', Tódíchi'íi'nii (Timothy Benally Sr.). 1994. "Ma'ii Jooldloshí Hane': Stories about Coyote: The One Who Trots." In *Coming to Light: Contemporary Translations of the Native Literatures of North America,* edited by Brian Swann, pp. 601-5. New York: Random House. (Navajo)

Burns, Allan F. 1983. *An Epoch of Miracles: Oral Literature of the Yucatec Maya.* Austin: University of Texas Press.

Cruikshank, Julie, and Angela Sidney. 1994. "How the World Began." In *Coming to Light: Contemporary Translations of the Native Literatures of North America,* edited by Brian Swann, pp. 138-50. New York: Random House. (Tagish/Tlingit)

Dalton, Jessie. 1986. "Speech for the Removal of Grief." Transcribed and translated by Nora Dauenhauer. *Alaska Quarterly Review* 4, nos. 3-4:116-28. (Tlingit)

Dauenhauer, Nora Marks, and Richard Dauenhauer. 1987. *Haa Shuká, Our Ancestors: Tlingit Oral Narratives.* Seattle: University of Washington Press.

———. 1990. *Haa Tuwunáagu Yís, for Healing Our Spirit: Tlingit Oratory.* Seattle: University of Washington Press.

Evan, Anthony, and Jane McGary. 1994. "'Raven' and 'Fog Woman'." In *Coming to Light: Contemporary Translations of the Native Literatures of North America,* edited by Brian Swann, pp. 92-109. New York: Random House. (Dena'ina)

Evers, Larry, and Felipe S. Molina. 1987. *Yaqui Deer Songs / Maso Bwikam:*

A *Native American Poetry*. Tucson: University of Arizona Press.

Farnell, Brenda M. 1995. *Do You See What I Mean? Plains Indian Sign Talk and the Embodiment of Action*. Austin: University of Texas Press. (Nakota)

———. 1995. *Wiyuta: Assiniboine Storytelling with Signs*. Compact disk and manual. Austin: University of Texas Press. (Nakota)

Guss, David M. 1989. *To Weave and Sing: Art, Symbol, and Narrative in the South American Rain Forest*. Berkeley: University of California Press. (Yekuana)

Hammond, Austin. 1986. "Speech for the Removal of Grief." Transcribed and translated by Nora Dauenhauer. *Alaska Quarterly Review* 4, nos. 3-4:129-31. (Tlingit)

Harry, Anna Nelson. 1986. "Lament for Eyak." Transcribed and translated by Michael Krauss. *Alaska Quarterly Review* 4, nos. 3-4:23-25. (Eyak)

Henry of Huslia, Chief. 1979. *The Stories That Chief Henry Told*. Transcribed and translated by Eliza Jones, edited by Ron Scollon. Fairbanks: Alaska Native Language Center. (Central Koyukon)

Hill, Jane H. 1995. "The Voices of Don Gabriel: Responsibility and Self in a Modern Mexicano Narrative." In *The Dialogic Emergence of Culture*, edited by Dennis Tedlock and Bruce Mannheim, pp. 97-147. Urbana: University of Illinois Press. (Nahuatl)

Howard-Malverde, Rosaleen. 1989. "Storytelling Strategies in Quechua Narrative Performance." *Journal of Latin American Lore* 15:3-71.

James, Susie. 1973. *Sít; Ḵaa Ḵáx̱ Kana.aá: Glacier Bay History*. Transcribed by Nora Florendo. Sitka: Tlingit Readers.

Kadashan, David. 1986. "Speech for the Removal of Grief." Transcribed and translated by Nora Dauenhauer. *Alaska Quarterly Review* 4, nos. 3-4:109-15. (Tlingit)

Kaplan, Lawrence D. 1988. *Ugiuvangmiut Quliapyuit: King Island Tales*. Translated by Margaret Seegana and Gertrude Analoak from performances by Frank Ellanna, Aloysius Pikonganna, Mary Muktoyuk, Magdaline Omiak, Catherine Kasgnoc, Annie Pullock, and Clara Sirloak. Fairbanks: Alaska Native Language Center and University of Alaska Press. (Inupiaq Eskimo)

Knab, Tim. 1980. "Three Tales from the Sierra de Puebla." *Alcheringa* n. s. 4, no. 2:2-36. (Nahuatl)

Marks, Willie. 1986. "Raven, Seagull, and the Crane." Transcribed and translated by Nora Dauenhauer. *Alaska Quarterly Review* 4, nos. 3-4:89-90. (Tlingit)

Morrow, Phyllis, and Elsie Mather. 1994. "Two Tellings of the Story of Uterneq: 'The Woman Who Returned from the Dead.'" In *Coming to Light: Contemporary Translations of the Native Literatures of North America*, edited by Brian Swann, pp. 37-56. New York: Random

House. (Yup'ik Eskimo)

Nyman, Elizabeth, and Jeff Leer. 1993. *Gágiwduł.àt: Brought Forth to Reconfirm. The Legacy of a Taku River Tlingit Clan*. Whitehorse and Fairbanks: Yukon Native Language Center and Alaska Native Language Center.

Orr, Eliza Cingarkaq, and Ben Orr. 1995. *Qanemcikarluni Tekitnarqelartuq: One Must Arrive with a Story to Tell. Traditional Narratives by the Elders of Tununak, Alaska*. Fairbanks: Lower Kuskokwim School District and Alaska Native Language Center. (Yup'ik Eskimo)

Paul, Gaither. 1980. *Stories for my Grandchildren*. Transcribed and edited by Ron Scollon. Fairbanks: Alaska Native Language Center. (Tanacross)

Sammons, Kay. 1992. "Translating Poetic Features in the Sierra Popoluca Story of Homshuk." In *On the Translation of Native American Literatures*, edited by Brian Swann, pp. 368-86. Washington: Smithsonian Institution Press.

Scollon, Ron, and Suzanne B. K. Scollon. 1979. *Linguistic Convergence: An Ethnography of Speaking at Fort Chipewyan, Alberta*. New York: Academic Press, pp. 45-51. (Chipewyan)

Sherzer, Joel. 1987. "Poetic Structuring of Kuna Discourse: The Line." In *Native American Discourse: Poetics and Rhetoric*, edited by Joel Sherzer and Anthony C. Woodbury, pp. 124-37. New York: Cambridge University Press.

———. 1990. *Verbal Art in San Blas: Kuna Culture through its Discourse*. New York: Cambridge University Press.

Tedlock, Dennis. 1983. *The Spoken Word and the Work of Interpretation*. Philadelphia: University of Pennsylvania Press. (Quiché Maya)

———. 1987. "Hearing a Voice in an Ancient Text: Quiché Maya Poetics in Performance." In *Native American Discourse: Poetics and Rhetoric*, edited by Joel Sherzer and Anthony C. Woodbury, pp. 140-75. New York: Cambridge University Press.

———. 1993. *Breath on the Mirror: Mythic Voices and Visions of the Living Maya*. San Francisco: Harper. Reprint edition (1997), Albuquerque: University of New Mexico Press. (Quiché Maya)

———. 1998. "Toward a Poetics of Polyphony and Translatability." In *Close Listening: Poetry and the Performed Word*, edited by Charles Bernstein, pp. 178-99. New York: Oxford University Press. (Quiché, Chol, and Yucatec Maya).

Toelken, Barre. 1994. "Coyote, Skunk, and the Prairie Dogs." In *Coming to Light: Contemporary Translations of the Native Literatures of North America*, edited by Brian Swann, pp. 590-600. New York: Random House. (Navajo)

Toelken, Barre, and Tacheeni Scott. 1981. "Poetic Retranslation and the

'Pretty Languages' of Yellowman." In *Traditional Literatures of the American Indian: Texts and Interpretations*, edited by Karl Kroeber, pp. 65-116. Lincoln: University of Nebraska Press. (Navajo)

Urban, Greg. 1986. "The Semiotic Functions of Macro-Parallelism in the Shokleng Origin Myth." In *Native South American Discourse*, edited by Joel Sherzer and Greg Urban, pp. 15-57. Berlin: Mouton.

Wiget, Andrew. 1987. "Telling the Tale: A Performance Analysis of a Hopi Coyote Story." In *Recovering the Word: Essays on Native American Literature*, edited by Brian Swann and Arnold Krupat, pp. 297-336. Berkeley: University of California Press.

Woodbury, Anthony C. 1984. *Cev'armuit Qanemciit Qulirait-Llu: Eskimo Narratives and Tales from Chevak, Alaska*. Fairbanks: Alaska Native Language Center.

Woodbury, Anthony C., and Leo Moses. 1994. "Mary Kokrak: Five Brothers and Their Younger Sister." In *Coming to Light: Contemporary Translations of the Native Literatures of North America*, edited by Brian Swann, pp. 15-36. New York: Random House. (Yup'ik Eskimo)

Worm, Mary. 1986. "The Crow and the Mink." Transcribed and translated by Elsie Mather and Phyllis Morrow. *Alaska Quarterly Review* 4, nos. 3-4:46-58. (Yup'ik Eskimo)

Zuboff, Robert. 1973. *Kudatan Kahídee: The Salmon Box*. Transcribed by Henry Davis, Gabriel George, and Crystal McKay. Sitka: Tlingit Readers.

——. 1973. *Táax'aa: Mosquito*. Transcribed by Dick Dauenhauer. Sitka: Tlingit Readers.

Scripted translations from other languages

Conquergood, Dwight. 1989. *I Am a Shaman: A Life Story with Ethnographic Commentary*. Southeast Asian Refugee Studies. Occasional Papers 8. Center for Urban and Regional Affairs. Minneapolis: University of Minnesota. (Hmong)

Fabian, Johannes. 1990. *Power and Performance: Ethnographic Explorations through Proverbial Wisdom and Theater in Shaba, Zaire*. Madison: University of Wisconsin Press. (Swahili)

Facey, Ellen E. 1988. *Nguna Voices: Text and Culture from Central Vanuatu*. Calgary: University of Calgary Press. (Ngunese)

Mills, Margaret. 1983. "An Afghan Folktale." *The Harvard Advocate* 117, no. 3a:58-66. (Persian)

——. 1991. *Rhetoric and Politics in Afghan Traditional Storytelling*. Philadelphia: University of Pennsylvania Press. (Persian)

Mueke, Stephen, Alan Rumsey, and Banjo Wirrunmarra. 1985. "Pigeon the Outlaw: History as Texts." *Aboriginal History* 9:81-100. (Ungarinyin, an Australian language)

Okpewho, Isidore. 1998. *Once upon a Kingdom: Myth, Hegemony, and*

Identity. Bloomington: Indiana University Press. (Igbo)

Price, Richard, and Sally Price. 1991. *Two Evenings in Saramaka.* Chicago: University of Chicago Press. (Saramaka, spoken by Suriname Maroons)

Seitel, Peter. 1980. *See So That We May See: Performances and Interpretations of Traditional Tales from Tanzania.* Bloomington: Indiana University Press. (Haya)

Scripts based on performances in English

Antin, David. 1972. "Talking at Pomona." *Alcheringa/Ethnopoetics* o. s. 4:42-44.

——. 1976. *Talking at the Boundaries.* New York: New Directions.

Bauman, Richard. 1986. *Story, Performance, and Event: Contextual Studies of Oral Narrative.* Cambridge: Cambridge University Press, pp. 95-96. (Anglo-American)

Crowley, Daniel. 1973. "The Singing Pepper Tree." Told by Luzilla Jones. *Alcheringa* o. s. 5:107-9. (Afro-American)

Fine, Elizabeth C. 1984. *The Folklore Text: from Performance to Print.* Bloomington: Indiana University Press, pp. 180-200. (Afro-American)

Gold, Peter. 1972. "From 'Easter Sunrise Sermon.'" Performed by the Rev. W. T. Goodwin. *Alcheringa* o. s. 4:1-14. (Afro-American)

Norton, Laura. 1986. "The Boy Who Found the Lost." Transcribed by Richard Dauenhauer. *Alaska Quarterly Review* 4, nos. 3-4:79-88. (Native American)

Rios, Ted. 1980. "The Egg." Recorded by Kathleen Sands. *Sun Tracks* 6:151-54. (Native American)

Silko, Leslie Marmon. 1981. *Storyteller.* New York: Seaver. (Native American)

Tedlock, Dennis. 1975. "Learning to Listen: Oral History as Poetry." *boundary 2* 3:707-26.

——. 1976. "Toward the Restoration of the Word in the Modern World." *Alcheringa* n. s. 2, no. 2:120-32.

——. 1991. "The Speaker of Tales Has More Than One String to Play On." In *Anthropological Poetics*, edited by Ivan Brady, pp. 309-40. Savage, Maryland: Rowman and Littlefield.

Titon, Jeff. 1976. "Son House: Two Narratives," *Alcheringa* n. s. 2, no. 1:2-9. (Afro-American)

——. 1988. *Powerhouse for God: Speech, Chant, and Song in an Appalachian Baptist Church.* Austin: University of Texas Press.

Titon, Jeff, and Ken George. 1977. "Dressed in the Armor of God." Performed by the Rev. John Sherfey. *Alcheringa* n. s. 3, no. 2:10-31. (Anglo-American)

——. 1978. "Testimonies." Performed by Rachel Franklin, Edith Cubbage, and the Rev. John Sherfey. *Alcheringa* n. s. 4, no. 1:69-83. (Afro- and Anglo-American)

Other sources

Bakhtin, M.M. 1981. *The Dialogic Imagination.* Translated by Caryl Emerson and Michael Holquist. Austin: University of Texas Press.

Bunzel, Ruth L. 1929. *The Pueblo Potter: A Study of Creative Imagination in Primitive Art.* Columbia University Contributions to Anthropology 8. New York: Columbia University Press.

Ferguson, T.J. 1996. *Historic Zuni Architecture and Society: An Archaeological Application of Space Syntax.* Anthropological Papers of the University of Arizona 60.

Ferguson, T.J., and E. Richard Hart. 1985. *A Zuni Atlas.* Norman: University of Oklahoma Press.

Hymes, Dell. 1962. "The Ethnography of Speaking." In *Anthropology and Human Behavior,* edited by Thomas Gladwin and William C. Sturtevant, pp. 13-53. Washington, DC: Anthropological Society of Washington.

———. 1965. "Some North Pacific Coast Poems: A Problem in Anthropological Philology." *American Anthropologist* 67:316-41.

———. 1975. "Breakthrough Into Performance." In *Folklore: Performance and Communication,* edited by Dan Ben-Amos and Kenneth Goldstein, pp. 11-74. The Hague: Mouton.

———. 1980. "Particle, Pause, and Pattern in Native American Verse." *American Indian Culture and Research Journal* 4:7-51.

Kintigh, Keith W. 1985. *Settlement, Subsistence, and Society in Late Zuni Prehistory.* Anthropological Papers of the University of Arizona 44. Tucson: University of Arizona Press.

Mera, H.P. 1938. *The "Rain Bird": A Study in Pueblo Design.* Memoirs of the Laboratory of Anthropology 2. Santa Fe.

Murray, David. 1991. *Forked Tongues: Speech, Writing and Representation in North American Indian Texts.* Bloomington: Indiana University Press.

Newman, Stanley. 1958. *Zuni Dictionary.* Indiana University Research Center in Anthropology, Folklore, and Linguistics Publication 6. Bloomington.

———. 1965. *Zuni Grammar.* University of New Mexico Publications in Anthropology 14. Albuquerque.

Olson, Charles. 1966. *Selected Writings.* Edited by Robert Creeley. New York: New Directions.

Rothenberg, Jerome. 1968. "Intro and Selections from *Technicians of the Sacred.*" *Stony Brook* 1-2:206-22.

———. 1969. "Ethnopoetics" (an anthology). *Stony Brook* 3-4:288-327.

Smith, Watson, Richard B. Woodbury, and Nathalie F. S. Woodbury. 1966. *The Excavation of Hawikuh by Frederick Webb Hodge: Report of the Hendricks-Hodge Expedition 1917-1923.* Contributions from the Museum of the American Indian Heye Foundation 20. New York: Museum of the American Indian.

Tedlock, Dennis. 1979. "Zuni Religion and World View." In *Handbook of North American Indians,* v. 9, Southwest, edited by Alfonso Ortiz, pp. 499-508. Washington: Smithsonian Institution.

Woodbury, Anthony C. 1987. "Rhetorical Structure in a Central Alaskan Yupik Eskimo Traditional Narrative." In *Native American Discourse: Poetics and Rhetoric,* edited by Joel Sherzer and Anthony C. Woodbury, pp. 176-239. New York: Cambridge University Press.

Printed in the United States
75885LV00003B/82-99